PALGRAVE STUDIES IN THEATRE AND PERFORMANCE HISTORY is a series devoted to the best of theatre/performance scholarship currently available, accessible, and free of jargon. It strives to include a wide range of topics, from the more traditional to those performance forms that in recent years have helped broaden the understanding of what theatre as a category might include (from variety forms as diverse as the circus and burlesque to street buskers, stage magic, and musical theatre, among many others). Although historical, critical, or analytical studies are of special interest, more theoretical projects, if not the dominant thrust of a study, but utilized as important underpinning or as a historiographical or analytical method of exploration, are also of interest. Textual studies of drama or other types of less traditional performance texts are also germane to the series if placed in their cultural, historical, social, or political and economic context. There is no geographical focus for this series and works of excellence of a diverse and international nature, including comparative studies, are sought.

The editor of the series is Don B. Wilmeth (EMERITUS, Brown University), Ph.D., University of Illinois, who brings to the series over a dozen years as editor of a book series on American theatre and drama, in addition to his own extensive experience as an editor of books and journals. He is the author of several award-winning books and has received numerous career achievement awards, including one for sustained excellence in editing from the Association for Theatre in Higher Education.

Also in the series:

Undressed for Success by Brenda Foley
Theatre, Performance, and the Historical Avant-garde by Günter Berghaus
Theatre, Politics, and Markets in Fin-de-Siècle Paris by Sally Charnow
Ghosts of Theatre and Cinema in the Brain by Mark Pizzato
Moscow Theatres for Young People by Manon van de Water
Absence and Memory in Colonial American Theatre by Odai Johnson
Vaudeville Wars: How the Keith-Albee and Orpheum Circuits Controlled the
  Big-Time and Its Performers by Arthur Frank Wertheim
Performance and Femininity in Eighteenth-Century German Women's Writing by
  Wendy Arons
Operatic China: Staging Chinese Identity across the Pacific by Daphne P. Lei
Transatlantic Stage Stars in Vaudeville and Variety: Celebrity Turns by Leigh Woods
Interrogating America through Theatre and Performance edited by
  William W. Demastes and Iris Smith Fischer
Plays in American Periodicals, 1890–1918 by Susan Harris Smith
Representation and Identity from Versailles to the Present: The Performing Subject
  by Alan Sikes
Directors and the New Musical Drama: British and American Musical Theatre in
  the 1980s and 90s by Miranda Lundskaer-Nielsen
Beyond the Golden Door: Jewish-American Drama and Jewish-American Experience
  by Julius Novick

Staging the People

Community and Identity in the Federal Theatre Project

Elizabeth A. Osborne

First published in 2011 by
PALGRAVE MACMILLAN®
in the United States—a division of St. Martin's Press LLC,
175 Fifth Avenue, New York, NY 10010.

Where this book is distributed in the UK, Europe and the rest of the world,
this is by Palgrave Macmillan, a division of Macmillan Publishers Limited,
registered in England, company number 785998, of Houndmills,
Basingstoke, Hampshire RG21 6XS.

Palgrave Macmillan is the global academic imprint of the above companies
and has companies and representatives throughout the world.

Palgrave® and Macmillan® are registered trademarks in the United States,
the United Kingdom, Europe and other countries.

ISBN: 978–0–230–11331–2

Library of Congress Cataloging-in-Publication Data

Osborne, Elizabeth A., 1977–
    Staging the people : community and identity in the Federal Theatre
Project / Elizabeth A. Osborne.
        p. cm.—(Palgrave studies in theatre and performance history)
        ISBN 978–0–230–11331–2 (hardback)
        1. Federal Theatre Project (U.S.)—History. 2. Theater and society—
United States—History—20th century. 3. National characteristics,
American—History—20th century. I. Title.
PN2270.F43O83 2011
792.0973—dc22   2010047890

A catalogue record of the book is available from the British Library.

Design by Newgen Imaging Systems (P) Ltd., Chennai, India.

First edition: June 2011

10 9 8 7 6 5 4 3 2 1

Printed in the United States of America.

To my parents Jack and Mary Ann,
my son Connor,
and all who were a part of the Federal Theatre Project

Contents ❦

Illustrations ✑

Acknowledgments ᴖ

L ike all large projects, this volume would not have been possible without the help of numerous individuals. My thanks to all and my apologies to anyone I inadvertently leave out.

While working on my PhD at the University of Maryland, College Park, I was fortunate to receive the guidance and mentorship of wonderful professors. Frank Hildy's passion for theatre history sent me digging into the past. Thank you to Catherine Schuler and Susan Haedicke, whose insightful comments on my work early in my coursework spurred me to streamline my writing and demand logical reasoning. Most of all, Heather Nathans, my advisor and now colleague, seemed to sense when I needed to be pushed, left alone, or sent out into the world. Her energy, love of the archives, unflagging confidence, and phenomenal generosity of time and spirit have proven absolutely invaluable.

From my home in Tallahassee, Florida, my gratitude goes to my colleagues at Florida State University. Lynn Hogan and Cameron Jackson provided administrative support and assistance as I worked toward my goal. Mary Karen Dahl has proven to be a valuable and caring mentor, helping whenever and wherever she could. A special thank you must go to Irma Mayorga and Natalya Baldyga, my good friends and generous colleagues, who served as brainstorming companions, editors, and cheerleaders, graciously offering their time, expertise, and support; you have helped me push my work to a higher level, and I greatly appreciate it. Thank you to Bryan Schmidt, a graduate student at Florida State University, who offered heroic assistance and a persistently positive attitude while helping me to prepare the final manuscript, and to Scott Knowles for his help processing thousands of images. Finally, I would like to thank Florida State University for its generous First Year Assistant Professor Award and Small Grant Awards, which provided financial support for my research.

I have many other colleagues to thank as well. In addition to his fascinating and impeccable scholarship, Barry Witham has proven to be a generous supporter of my work and a tireless advocate for the Federal

Theatre Project; I thank him for blazing the trail that I now follow in my own research. Don Wilmeth, Christopher Bigsby, Brenda Murphy, John Frick, Jonathan Chambers, Cheryl Black, and many more scholars of the American stage have served as inspirations. Lorraine Brown and John O'Connor helped to make research on the Federal Theatre Project possible when, in 1974, they discovered the Library of Congress's collection of Federal Theatre Project documents in an airplane hangar in Baltimore. The American Theatre and Drama Society has provided an intellectual home for me as well as a community of engaged and invigorating scholars. I also thank those who have supported my work at conferences and in publication: Susan Kattwinkel, Heather Nathans, and Rhona Justice-Malloy have all enhanced my work with their suggestions, questions, and critiques during the editing process.

Many archivists generously gave of their time and wisdom at the National Archives and Records Administration, Library of Congress, George Mason University's Special Collections & Archives, and the many other archives, universities, public libraries, and historical societies throughout the country that became a part of this study. Their knowledge and willingness to share it repeatedly astounded me. Special thank yous must go to Walter Zvonchekno (Library of Congress), Eugene Morris (National Archives), Leah Donnelly (George Mason University), Pamela Madsen (Harvard Theatre Collection), and Karen Nickeson (Billy Rose Theatre Collection). Individuals at the Oregon Historical Society and the Friends of Timberline also graciously offered their time and assistance during the process. Joanne Bentley, Hallie Flanagan's stepdaughter, kindly granted permission to use items from her stepmother's estate. I also appreciate the assistance of Jane Pinzino, Caley Cannon, and Faye Jones at Florida State University.

I must also thank the anonymous peer reviewers who offered such supportive and thoughtful advice on my manuscript. I am indebted to Don Wilmeth, the series editor, and Samantha Hasey, my editor and contact at Palgrave Macmillan, for their sage advice, encouragement, and tireless work on this project!

Finally, I am grateful to my family and friends for their help and confidence. Tim Osborne searched through microfilm, made thousands of copies, and graciously offered his photo and graphics expertise. Erin Smith stepped in when I needed her support as well. Special thanks to my immediate family for their love and support through this process, particularly my parents, Jack and Mary Ann Stees. My father earned a PhD in Microbiology, worked for 25 years and retired, only to become my research assistant and editor. My mother picked up where I could not, caring for my son when I attended conferences, dashed off to the archives, or labored in the depths of writing. Last, but certainly not least, thank you to my son Connor, whose entire lifetime has been occupied by various stages of this project. Your unconditional support and willingness to leap with me into the process has been more valuable to me than you could ever know.

Abbreviations ❧

CCC	Civilian Conservation Corps
CIO	Congress of Industrial Organizations
CWA	Civil Works Administration
FERA	Federal Emergency Relief Association
FTP	Federal Theatre Project
GMU	George Mason University
LOC	Library of Congress
NARA	National Archives and Records Administration
NEA	National Endowment for the Arts
SWOC	Steel Workers Organizing Committee
WPA	Works Progress Administration/Works Projects Administration

When quoting from archival texts, I have retained the capitalizations, underlines, and spellings from the original sources. Many of the FTP documents underline play titles, while others use quotation marks or all capital letters.

Introduction: The "People's Theatre": Creating an Audience of Millions ❧

I am convinced that all these theatres, groups, and Federal stages in which the feeling of community is alive will lay the ground for an American national theatre, a real people's theatre, which is devoted to the cultural development of this great country.[1]

—*Ernst Toller*

If Federal Theatre had ever wanted to produce a cycle of plays epitomizing its own projects, New York would have been staged as a living newspaper, Los Angeles as a musical comedy, the South as a folk play, and Chicago as melodrama.[2]

—*Hallie Flanagan*

On President's Day in June of 1936, the Arkansas Federal Theatre Project joined forces with the Federal Music Project to create a spectacle in celebration of President and Mrs. Roosevelt's visit to Little Rock. A cast of 1,600 townspeople played to an audience of 50,000 in a "tremendous living mural" entitled *America Sings*. Created by and for the Federal Theatre Project, *America Sings* traced a broad history of the United States, beginning with a Native American ceremonial and progressing through the Civil War, World War I, and the Crash of 1929. It dramatized the protests, riots, and violence that plagued the Great Depression and ended with a broadcast of the calming opening words of President Franklin Delano Roosevelt's first fireside chat, which blanketed the audience in "new hope and new inspiration."[3] This monumental spectacle culminated as Roosevelt's voice—piped live through loudspeakers to the crowd—soothed the hoards of violent protesters, encouraging them to "re-form into lines of usefully employed."[4]

America Sings demonstrated many of the goals and possibilities of that sweeping organization known as the Federal Theatre Project (FTP). The FTP stands alone as the only real attempt at creating a national theatre in the United States. In the midst of one of the greatest economic and social disasters the country has ever experienced, and between two devastating wars, President Franklin Delano Roosevelt founded the FTP as part of the New Deal in 1935. Though it survived only four turbulent and exhilarating years, its programs touched nearly every state in the United States in some way. Under the leadership of inimitable National Director Hallie Flanagan, the FTP employed more than 13,000 theatre professionals throughout the country, brought theatre to an audience of more than 30 million, and fought to provide locally relevant theatre for the people of the United States.[5]

Legends of FTP adventures abound. Just as John Houseman and Orson Welles's infamous production of Marc Blitzstein's *The Cradle Will Rock* represents one of the best-known tales of American theatre history, the simultaneous openings of *It Can't Happen Here* in 18 cities across the nation appear as one of the FTP's most significant achievements. The Living Newspapers, colorful New York City projects, and the pitched battles with Congress and the Dies Committee have absorbed much of the scholarly attention directed toward the FTP. Yet these productions constituted only a small part of FTP activities. Thousands of actors produced hundreds of other plays across the country in cities as diverse as Portland, Tulsa, Omaha, Seattle, and Manchester. In many ways, these plays, produced and staged in locations beyond the confines of big cities like New York, better addressed Hallie Flanagan's ambitious intentions for the FTP and the potential of such a far-reaching project.

The case studies in this book examine selections from each of the FTP regions outside New York City, focusing on projects in Illinois, Massachusetts, Alabama, Georgia, and Oregon, and then moving beyond strict geographic boundaries by considering two of the FTP's touring ventures that took to the roads of America. These examples explore the essence of the FTP on its own terms, illuminating the tensions and dialogue between national, regional, and local identities and offering a more complete overall picture of the FTP's aspirations, actions, triumphs, and disappointments. As I will argue, some of the examples from this singular moment in U.S. theatre history even go so far as to resituate the FTP from its common characterization as a "successful failure" to a viable enterprise that in many ways attained its primary objectives: to achieve a theatre that could represent the nation while putting Americans back to work in their fields.

Unique in the annals of American theatre history, the FTP helped in part to reimagine the nation's arts. With the Federal Music Project, the Federal

Art Project, and the Federal Writers' Project, the FTP was one of four arts projects that comprised Federal Project Number One, the Works Progress Administration (WPA)–sponsored entity otherwise known collectively as Federal One.[6] Designed to serve as immediate relief to the unemployed, the programs in Federal One provided tangible evidence that the U.S. government would support its arts in heretofore unheard of ways during the Great Depression. For the theatre, this meant that the United States would initiate direct government funding in a way that mirrored the national theatres of Europe, though Flanagan was careful to distinguish between her own vision of the FTP and the reality of European national theatres. As she explained:

> The general policy and program would be outlined in Washington, but the carrying out, with modifications dictated by local conditions, would rest with the states. It was not a national theatre in the European sense of a group of artists chosen to represent the government. [...] It was rather a federation of theatres. That was the origin and meaning of its name.[7]

Flanagan's "federation of theatres" would be strengthened by its ability to exchange resources, pool experience, and enable each region to develop its own locally relevant theatre. This decentralized program would bring theatre to American audiences throughout the nation, even as it dramatized the stories of those Americans. As Flanagan would testify before Congress: "In stressing this material of the past and the present, we hope to help build a theater out of the fabric of American life."[8] This strategy would compel the creation of locally relevant drama, spurring a heady rush of creative activity nationwide.

The choice of Hallie Flanagan for the role of national director came directly from Harry Hopkins, director of the WPA and former classmate of Flanagan at Grinnell. Flanagan's work as a playwright and scholar earned her acceptance to George Pierce Baker's coveted 47 Workshop and a prestigious Guggenheim grant (1926). The Guggenheim funded a year of travel abroad during which she observed experimental theatre throughout Europe and Russia; upon her return, she founded Vassar's Experimental Theatre, through which she gained notoriety in the college art theatre scene for her restaging of classics and her focus on contemporary issues. *Can You Hear Their Voices?,* an original play Flanagan wrote with Margaret Ellen Clifford, was produced by several regional theatres in the early 1930s. Flanagan would bring a penchant for edgy works, a respect for theatre outside New York City, a noncommercial perspective, and an unflagging idealism regarding the possibilities of her "federation of theatres."

However, federal funding came with limitations. For the FTP, these boundaries would restrict the ways in which money could be spent, affect the day-to-day administration and bureaucracy, and open the door to censorship. Since the FTP was, first and foremost, a relief agency, federal regulations stipulated that 90 percent of all funding go toward salaries of workers eligible for relief. The occasional exception to this mandate could be made, but in most cases this left only 10 percent of the federal funds for publicity, costumes, scenery, equipment, space rentals, royalties, and the many other physical requirements of operating theatres. The salaries of any non-relief workers for positions of special expertise, administration, or leadership would count toward the 10 percent as well. To supplement direct government funding, many specific FTP units obtained donations of space, publicity, or equipment from local businesses or organizations, but this practice was inconsistent at best. Though 65 percent of all FTP productions were free to audiences, some productions justified small admission fees; these profits also provided additional other-than-labor monies for those units. All in all, the Federal Theatre Project cost the government just over 46 million dollars, 42 million of which went directly into salaries of workers the government qualified for relief. As Flanagan's incisive analogy informed Congress, supporting the entirety of the FTP for four years cost approximately the same as the building of one battleship.[9]

The vast bureaucracy required by the federal government of the FTP was often challenging for administrators as they struggled to open theatrical productions. As a subsection of Federal One, the FTP was categorized as a Professional and Service Project and under the jurisdiction of the WPA. For the FTP, this meant each individual state WPA director oversaw the expenditures of each FTP unit in his or her state. However, since WPA architect and head Harry Hopkins famously assured Flanagan that the FTP would be "free, adult, and uncensored," the state WPA directors had little control over the hiring of personnel, programming decisions, or general activities.[10] This arrangement, which gave the WPA fiscal responsibility but little power over programming, set the stage for a litany of conflicts between state WPA directors and their FTP administrators, not the least of which arose when theatre projects attempted to loan equipment or personnel across state lines or take productions on tours outside of the state. For those FTP units that enjoyed respectful working relationships with their state WPA directors, the benefits of smooth administration abounded; conversely, the unlucky FTP units that endured poor relationships with their WPA directors saw productions inexplicably censored and activities scuttled, and battled myriad bureaucratic irritations ranging from slow travel reimbursement to the surprise removal of all their typewriters.[11]

Hallie Flanagan also struggled with the double-edged sword of providing high-quality productions without alienating the theatre industry. Many theatre professionals derided the concept of the FTP for the seemingly contradictory reasons that a theatre composed of out-of-work actors could not possibly produce anything of artistic or commercial value, even as they decried the competition that these hopelessly bad productions would present to the commercial theatre.[12] The stigma against relief workers caused many critics, theatre professionals, and potential audience members to regard the FTP workers as charity cases who did not possess the talent to obtain a competitive job in the commercial theatre. Hiring stipulations directly prevented amateurs and hopefuls from gaining entrance into the FTP; nevertheless, many employees lacked extensive training or were past their performance primes. In the classic catch-22, when actors, designers, and directors performed poorly, private industry criticized the "horrible" productions; when they performed brilliantly, private industry stole them away. While this exchange undoubtedly helped many relief actors regain professional employment, it left the FTP with the task of continually training its workers so as to persevere in creating high-quality theatre.

The achievements of the FTP were many. The FTP created pivotal opportunities in professional theatre for actors, directors, playwrights, and designers by offering a steady paycheck and the opportunity to train with established professionals. It also instigated performance opportunities for African Americans, Jews, Hispanics, and many other ethnic and religious groups. The FTP nurtured emerging talents such as Orson Welles, John Houseman, Rose McClendon, Theodore Ward, Arthur Miller, Studs Terkel, and Marc Blitzstein, and employed theatre notables including Elmer Rice, Edith Isaacs, Eugene O'Neill, Clifford Odets, Philip Barber, Hiram Motherwell, Eddie Dowling, Susan Glaspell, J. Howard Miller, John McGee, and Rosamond Gilder.[13] Along with employment and development, FTP stages introduced the American version of the Russian Living Newspaper and featured performances of children's theatre, marionette shows, vaudeville, classics, legitimate theatre, circus shows, and modern dance.

In addition to putting thousands of unemployed theatre professionals back to work, Flanagan and the FTP struggled to provide some much needed emotional and moral support for a struggling nation. To this end, the project established five regional centers whose headquarters were situated in major metropolitan cities: Boston (Northeast); Chicago (Midwest); Los Angeles (West); and, initially, New Orleans (South), though this regional center was relocated to Atlanta. New York City served as its own independent region. Each center was designed to develop locally relevant theatre and to serve as a resource for the smaller cities and rural areas surrounding it. According to Flanagan, the dual objectives of the FTP focused on both the actor and audience; each of these groups was sorely in need of economic, physical, and psychological relief. When preparing to testify before Representative Martin Dies and the House Committee on Un-American Activities about the FTP in 1938–1939, Flanagan defined her goals as follows:

> Give employment to needy theatre professionals in socially useful projects which will rehabilitate them, conserve their skills, and at the same time, bring to thousands of American citizens not hitherto able to afford theatre going, a planned theatrical program, national in scope, regional in emphasis, and American in democratic attitude.[14]

As this statement revealed, Flanagan's intentions went far beyond simply employing theatre professionals during an economic downturn. She saw the FTP as an opportunity for American theatre to expand into a truly national enterprise that trained and employed out-of-work theatre professionals while developing a vast new audience—either uninterested in or unable to attend Broadway-style productions.

This audience would prove to be one of the great strengths of the FTP; as Flanagan articulated, "The greatest achievement of these public theatres was in their creation of an audience of many millions, a waiting audience."[15] New York theatre critic Burns Mantle began describing the FTP as the "People's Theatre," a term that came to depict an enthusiastic, working-class audience unfamiliar with standard theatre fare. David Weissman, a Los Angeles–based critic, concentrated on defining the audience as well: "The American theatre, through the Federal Theatres [*sic*], is becoming a people's theatre in the fact that it is making it possible for the public to see living drama at a price that it can pay."[16] These comments portrayed the radically different audiences that attended FTP productions in New York City and Los Angeles, and led to the common use of the term "People's Theatre" when referring to the FTP. Theatre critic John Cambridge similarly described the typical audience member for the New York FTP in the *Sunday Worker*. He highlighted the vast differences between audiences of the WPA theatres and those of the commercial Broadway houses:

> Most obviously, they are less prosperous in appearance. They look more like the people seen in the subways, and in the poorer residential streets, and for the very good reason that the Federal Theatre audiences are drawn from these people—in other words, the masses of New York, who have neither the money nor the time to waste on [...commercial American theatre].[17]

Cambridge went on to cite the 22 managers who comprised the central Broadway and commercial theatre producers in New York City, quoting these commercial producers as claiming to be the "creators" of the "bulk" of the American theatre. In sharp contrast, Cambridge's description of the WPA audience focused on those individuals who specifically did not attend Broadway theatre in New York City. Flanagan often referred to the character and demographics of the FTP audience when describing the organization's accomplishments. In fact, she was so deeply interested in this facet of theatre development that she created the Audience Survey Department, which distributed and analyzed thousands of surveys administered to audiences of dozens of FTP units across the country. While the Audience Survey Department was disbanded after two years, the contribution to audience analysis was monumental. In Chicago, for example, the Audience Survey Report for *It Can't Happen Here* documented the responses of 959 audience members. For nearly half of the audience, this performance represented their first experience with the FTP; many also cited their inability to attend commercial theatre because of the prohibitive expense.[18] This Audience Survey was only one of many that documented the important connection between the working class, otherwise "non-theatre-attending people," and the FTP. Of the 30 million audience members that the FTP reached in its brief four years of operation, more than 60 percent had never before attended live theatre.[19]

Despite these remarkable achievements, theatre professionals, political activists, and congresspersons lampooned the FTP for alleged indiscretions ranging from communism to homosexuality. The FTP was consistently berated by critics for its lack of quality and professionalism, by theatre professionals for infringing on their audiences and jobs, and by anti–New Deal politicians searching for a vulnerable target in the Roosevelt administration. As the most visible of the Arts Projects, the FTP frequently became the scapegoat for anyone hoping to make a name for him or herself by destroying part of Roosevelt's New Deal. When the FTP ended on June 30, 1939, it left behind hundreds of thousands of people and communities who clamored for its return and strove to continue their own local theatre movements.

While Flanagan cautioned against considerations of single productions or units as indicative of the entire organization, much contemporary scholarship is dedicated to illuminating the contributions of famous individuals or controversial productions—often at the expense of other FTP activities. At the same time, case studies for an enterprise as vast as the FTP are inherently valuable to scholars as they provide jumping off points that can gesture toward an understanding of the organization and its enterprises as a whole—particularly when one ranges outside of urban centers. Using productions in Boston, Chicago, Atlanta, Birmingham, Portland, and rural areas in the South and Northeast, I explore the myriad ways in which the work of the FTP both played to its audiences and was in turn shaped by those audiences. Each chapter considers and responds to the same overarching question: How did the FTP develop a relationship with its surrounding community, and what were the dynamics of that relationship? As I will argue, each region dealt with the question in a manner that was unique to its specific formation of an FTP unit and experience, which depended upon the political, social, cultural, and economic issues that made the communities themselves distinct. The differences between the FTP units provide insights not only into the communities they served but also into the FTP itself. In this, the analysis of this book allows the interrogation of the mythology of the FTP. As the chapters that follow will show, the FTP's methods reveal an organization that was ill-equipped to deal with the challenges of decentralization, yet also had difficulty conceiving of local FTP units as part of a cohesive national entity. Flanagan demonstrated the disconnect between the non–New York City units and the perception of the FTP as a whole in an exchange that followed the closing of the FTP:

Ten days after an Act of Congress ended the Federal Theatre a congressman telephoned my Washington office. I expected condolences, but that was not the intent of the call.

"I've always been very much interested in the Federal Theatre and its work in our State, and a few weeks ago I suggested that a certain fine professional actor of my acquaintance be considered for your rolls. I've heard nothing, and my friend, who is very much in need of work, is getting impatient."

I told the Congressman that I would look up the particular case and inform him, and then I added, "Of course, you know, however, that the Federal Theatre is no longer in existence."

There was a stunned silence and then an ear-shattering, "WHAT!"

"Surely you know, Congressman, that the Federal Theatre was abolished on June 30 by Act of Congress?"

Again a loud silence. Then a shocked and heavy voice said, "Was that the Federal Theatre?"[20]

That this Congressperson failed to link the *Federal* Theatre Project with the smaller units in the cities and towns of his own state demonstrates both the strength and weakness of the FTP: some local units acted as "miniature" New York City units while others separated themselves from the national organization almost entirely. Newspaper articles regarding units across the country suggest that this oversight was not confined to members of Congress. In town after town, critics commented on their local productions, but failed to connect their local FTP to the challenges that the FTP as a national entity faced. While this lack of cohesion allowed these smaller, individual units to connect more readily with their audiences, it left the larger organization—associated generally with controversial work in many urban areas—vulnerable to attacks that would not be repudiated by audiences and critics across the nation.

Extensive archival research at the National Archives, Library of Congress, Harvard Theatre Collection, Billy Rose Theatre Collection, and the WPA Oral Histories Collection at George Mason University provides the foundation for this study. Rich secondary sources complement this primary research, including works by renowned FTP scholars such as Barry Witham, Jane De Hart Mathews, and Lorraine Brown. Memoirs of the era like Hallie Flanagan's book *Arena* and studies of the New Deal and the Federal Writers' Project's extensive *American Guide Series* provide further perspectives on the cultural moment. My investigations have been influenced not only by print resources such as newspapers, diaries, scrapbooks, scripts, memos, and letters but also by what Natalie Zemmon Davis refers to as "associational life and collective behavior," evidence that Davis points to as "cultural artifacts."[21] As Robert Darnton similarly suggests, by placing the playscripts, correspondence, and other historical evidence of the FTP within their cultural frameworks, the historian can "tease meaning from documents by relating them to the surrounding world of significance, passing from text to context and back again until he has cleared a way through a foreign mental world."[22]

This book, like the FTP itself, is divided into regions. This strategy clarifies the relationship between the FTP and specific communities in the Midwest, South, East, and West—both urban and rural. The integration of a wide breadth of material, from play texts and playbills to inquiries into the government structure, institutional power formations, and dominant discourse, shapes this study into a detailed cultural history of the FTP and its surrounding communities. While the chapters focus on the same overarching questions about the FTP's relationships with specific communities, the unique needs of each region dictate the particulars of the chapters. The case studies that follow show some of the FTP's most important successes as well as its failures; often, the productions discussed in this book were deemed defining moments for the various companies and projects, and they invariably represent the few pieces that were created specifically by and for the FTP. While the examples presented may seem to have little in common, I would argue that they each provide a point of entry to discovering the ways in which "cultures shape ways of thinking, even for the greatest thinkers."[23]

Chapter One, "Danger, Disease, and Despotism: Balancing on the Tightrope of Chicago," traces the evolution of two groundbreaking productions in the "Windy City." *O Say Can You Sing* (1936–7) and *Spirochete* (1938) represent two very different agendas that characterized the division between the administration and the workers and their respective understandings of success. Administrators such as George Kondolf and Harry Minturn led Chicago with an eye toward commercial triumphs, while many of the writers, actors, and designers employed in Chicago looked to artistic innovation and experimentation as the contribution the FTP could make to American theatre. *O Say Can You Sing* began as a wicked parody of Chicago's infamous democratic machine, gangsters, immigrant populations, and even Mrs. Roosevelt; yet by the time the show opened, an innocuous revue had replaced the parody. In contrast, *Spirochete*, a public health play spotlighting the national syphilis epidemic and garnering the strong support of Susan Glaspell (Midwest Play Bureau) and numerous public health officials nationwide, received mixed support from the FTP administration and saw relatively poor box office receipts; however, several critics designated *Spirochete* as the single greatest justification for all money spent on the FTP. Placed into conversation with one another, these two productions illustrate the results of wars between artistic and administrative personnel and varying definitions of commercial success. The Chicago FTP had the potential to create exciting, innovative, and highly relevant theatre but struggled to do so without rousing the rancor of local censors. In the end, their attempts to please all effectively pleased very few.

The second chapter, "Demythologizing America: Past and Present Collide in Boston," analyzes two pieces written exclusively for Massachusetts audiences, *Created Equal* (1937) and *Lucy Stone* (1938–9). According to Flanagan, the FTP found its niche in Boston with John Hunter Booth's *Created Equal*. Tracing the themes of freedom and equality as well as the struggles of the working class against the landowners, critics praised *Created Equal* as "the stuff that makes history a vivid study for those unmoved by textbooks," even as they criticized it for romanticizing the role of the masses.[24] *Created Equal* inverted the traditional story of American History in a city famous for its role in nation formation. In sharp contrast, Maud Wood Park's *Lucy Stone* portrayed the Massachusetts suffragette's efforts to bring about racial and sexual equality. Written by a former president of the League of Women Voters and based on Alice Stone Blackwell's biography of her famous mother, the FTP's revision of *Lucy Stone* altered the portrayal of the great suffragette so that she would be more in line with Boston's grudging acceptance of women in the public eye. This traditional history emphasized Stone's contributions while ensuring that she was treated as a "woman," and as such bridged the perceived gap between the public figure and domestic wife and mother. These two productions point to an underlying struggle that the Boston FTP (and much of the eastern region) faced throughout its lifetime. Constantly overshadowed by the edgy, groundbreaking activities of New York City, the Boston FTP fought to attain legitimacy in the eyes of its audience by offering drama important to Boston audiences while circumventing the city's notoriously active censorship committee.[25]

Chapter Three, "'The Great American Theatrical Desert': Federal Theatre in the South," brings my focus to FTP activities in the southern United States. The FTP never established itself in the southern region with the intensity seen in places such as New York, Chicago, Los Angeles, Seattle, or any number of smaller cities or towns across the rest of the nation, a fact many scholars ascribe to both the southern audience's inability to relate to popular Broadway-style productions and the lackluster regional drama available during the period. However, this assessment only skims the surface of the FTP's efforts in the South. *Altars of Steel* (1937) is an example of a production that was, in fact, dangerously relevant theatre. Described by Flanagan as the Federal Theatre's "most important southern production," this southern social-labor drama premiered in Atlanta to hot debate, critical acclaim, and sold-out houses.[26] *Altars of Steel* both reflected and challenged the social, political, and economic hegemony of the South. Similarly, the so-called Georgia Experiment served as an example of the grassroots form of "folk theatre" that was believed to be directly germane to the people the FTP hoped to serve. Though the Georgia Experiment ended after a brief 90-day trial, this innovative program became part of the mythology surrounding the public face of the FTP, revealing the tensions inherent in Flanagan's goal of creating locally relevant, high-quality theatre in a country as culturally diverse as the United States. As this chapter will show, looking outside of urban centers' theatrical activities is vital to understanding the idealized, decentralized FTP that Flanagan privileged in her own writing.

In Portland, Oregon, the FTP operated a conservative program on a comparatively small scale, but unlike the majority of the FTP units in the country, the Portland companies created theatre that capitalized on the strengths of the company members and the region. Chapter Four, "The Fading Frontier: Excavating the Portland Federal Theatre Project," studies the FTP in Portland and Mt. Hood, Oregon. In many ways, the Portland FTP is an example of an FTP success story; it employed the relief workers in Portland (and grew as the relief population increased), created and performed drama engaged in pertinent local issues, and recruited new audience members by offering entertainment that they enjoyed for little or no admission fee. Flanagan cited the Portland FTP repeatedly as the example of an ideal administrative relationship with the WPA and as a project that consistently created theatre connected to its audience. Two productions, *Yellow Harvest* and *Timberline Tintypes*, and the unfortunately unrealized Paul Bunyan Festival, provide insight into the workings of the Portland FTP. Yet any study of the Portland FTP is challenged by the paucity of the archive itself, requiring scholars to work within a limited pool of primary evidence and very little secondary evidence. Thus, in addition to analysis of the aforementioned productions and special events, this chapter explores the inner workings of a project that exemplified the ideals of the FTP and considers potential ways to work through and around negative spaces in the archive.

Tent theatres, traveling troupes, and the many small companies that performed through the more rural sections of the country brought theatre to the FTP's targeted audience. In "Theatre 'In the Wilderness': The Federal Theatre Project Tours America," I argue that the heart of the FTP—the plays and projects that had the potential to be both national and local in scope—beat in the wilds of the theatre world. Chapter Five focuses on two touring entities. First, the FTP companies that toured throughout hundreds of Civilian Conservation Corps (CCC) camps fulfilled Flanagan's goals for a locally relevant, audience-centered national theatre in a unique way through performances of Grace Hayward's *CCC Murder Mystery*. Written specifically for the young male audiences at the CCC camps, this engaging comedy adapted easily to the needs and limitations present on the road. Performances of the participatory *CCC Murder Mystery* proved to be specialized, malleable, surprising, and, by all accounts, terrifically entertaining theatre. In counterpoint to the raucous fun of the *CCC*

Murder Mystery, the FTP also sent companies to tour in the wake of disasters. At the invitation of the American Red Cross, Major Earl House of the FTP's CCC Division and community drama expert Herbert Stratton Price organized an expedition into the depths of one of the most devastating and costly floods in U.S. history. Price departed with a traveling company and a single truck in February of 1937, producing performances in camps throughout Tennessee, Arkansas, Illinois, Indiana, and Ohio. These touring activities, largely ignored by both contemporary scholars and the FTP administration, demonstrate vital components of Flanagan's goals and offer new methods to examine the role of the FTP without limiting its diverse activities to specific states or urban areas. Instead, I draw focus to the ways in which the FTP was able to adapt to the needs of its audiences, regardless and in spite of geographic locale.

Flanagan's expectations for the FTP were high. When she took up the mantle of its directorship, she knew that her audience would not come easily. Yet under Flanagan's leadership the FTP grew from a relief agency into an organization that had the very real potential to become a national theatre with a vital connection to its audience members' lives:

> Our most urgent task is to make our theatre worthy of its audience. It is of no value whatsoever to stimulate theatre-going unless, once inside our doors, our audience sees something which has some vital connection with their own lives and their own immediate problems.[27]

Flanagan's task—to create a theatre that was "worthy of its audience" in quality and devoted to their lives and "immediate problems"—demanded a decentralized program that would allow the project to capitalize on local talents and themes with thoughtfulness and innovation. Hampered by a multitude of problems, Flanagan's FTP struggled valiantly through its four years of existence to do exactly that. The case studies that follow reveal that many of the so-called failures might more correctly be designated as successes according to the FTP's stated mission. They describe and analyze historical turning points, bringing much needed historical attention to some of the many pieces that were created specifically for the FTP to play in various communities across the country.

Throughout its lifetime, the FTP served a nation in desperate need of entertainment and expression. The case studies included here provide a unique lens through which to view the FTP on its own terms. By applying Flanagan's ideals for the FTP to the study of these specific projects, these examples provide a more nuanced understanding of some of the many FTP units outside of New York City. Through detailed readings of key plays and events, the integration of FTP correspondence and administrative factors, and the interweaving of the complexities of surrounding cultures, this study complicates and deepens the overall picture of the FTP's aspirations, actions, successes, and failures. The productions and companies discussed in the chapters that follow provide fertile grounds for an exploration of the FTP as the national theatre that it was—rife with regional, national, and local tensions.

1. Danger, Disease, and Despotism: Balancing on the Tightrope of Chicago ৩

Chicago Federal Theatre started like a detective thriller with farcical elements, worked up through a series of what Mr. Webster's dictionary calls "sensational incidents and startling situations," and reached magnificent heights of absurdity over the *Swing Mikado*.[1]

—*Hallie Flanagan*

In the 1920s, when Harry Minturn ran his own stock company in Chicago, Al Capone was one of his chief subscribers. During his brief time as director of the Chicago FTP, Minturn bemoaned the changes he observed in theatre. He explained, "The theatre's too safe now. It used to be quite a dangerous pastime in Chicago—you never knew when you'd get mixed up with a first-class shooting."[2] Capone, an ardent supporter of the theatre, always purchased 16 tickets, two for himself and 14 strategically placed throughout the theatre for his bodyguards. During the 1920s, theatre in Chicago was, quite literally, fraught with danger. Capone's 1929 arrest coincided with a meteoric shift from the wild age of jazz, prohibition, and gangsters to the joblessness, economic despair, and grim reality of the Great Depression. Chicago theatre reflected this shift as well; by the early 1930s, Chicago theatre had been stripped of its political (and physical) "danger." In many ways, Chicago was a political minefield for theatre during the Depression era. Topics such as crooked politicians, organized crime, and the city's economic collapse—even worse in Chicago than in many other cities nationwide—required careful treatment. As a result, city officials began a censorship campaign to end immorality in the theatre. Experimental, controversial, and otherwise edgy works gradually disappeared in this environment.

The excitement of the FTP's arrival in Chicago could not be overstated. Here was an opportunity for the city's many out-of-work theatre professionals to find employment in their own field again. Home to a formerly thriving theatre community, Chicago offered a wide range of equipment, facilities, audience members, and—most importantly for the FTP—skilled personnel. Yet Chicago also maintained a very specific set of political and social expectations that the FTP would need to understand and embrace before it could become a local institution. Flanagan described Chicago as a melodrama. Obstacles frequently appeared that required negotiation, ingenuity, and metaphorical spectacle to overcome. From the FTP's perspective, the heroes and villains were often clearly demarcated, and the epic battles sometimes required sacrifices in the form of entire productions.

Even as political battles over the content and form of various productions raged, the biggest challenge the Chicago FTP faced centered on determining its own identity. Flanagan argued that the FTP would have to earn the respect of its audience with a theatrical success to gain admittance to this thrilling, sensational, and magnificently absurd city, but the form of that success remained hotly debated. The series of local project heads focused on popular, commercial work that would bring in large audiences and receive at least lukewarm reviews from the generally hostile press. In contrast, the Midwestern Play Bureau (led by Susan Glaspell), its developing playwrights, and many of the actors sought an avant-garde, experimental program that would push the boundaries of the theatre. A clash between these two forces—one pursuing box office receipts and the other pushing the aesthetic envelope—was to be expected. While the conflict between commercial and experimental works infiltrated nearly every unit of the FTP (and remains a common thread of contention in many contemporary theatres as well), the ideological disparity was particularly strong in Chicago. Worse, this battle happened under the proverbial thumbs of Chicago's censors. How, then, would the Chicago FTP make a splash that would impress and attract audience members, while refraining from incurring the wrath of the city's censors?

In this chapter, I will examine two major Chicago productions, *O Say Can You Sing* (1936) and *Spirochete* (1938). Created by and for production by the FTP in Chicago, these productions offer two very different approaches to the ways in which the project would define itself and locate an audience in the Windy City. With *O Say Can You Sing*, the Chicago FTP found a popular, light-hearted hit that relied on political humor, music, and patriotism to endear itself to local audiences. In contrast, *Spirochete* capitalized on a major contemporaneous event—Chicago's war against syphilis. My examination of these two plays reveals the conflicts and tensions that characterized the FTP experience in Chicago as it struggled to find its own identity in a city that would force the FTP through a grueling initiation process before offering grudging acceptance.

The ideological controversy regarding the goals and identity of the Chicago FTP began with the personnel—particularly those individuals chosen to lead the project. From its commencement in late 1935 through the summer of 1936, the Chicago FTP produced revivals of safe, commercially successful shows, vaudeville, and the occasional dance piece. Flanagan remained unimpressed by this conservative approach and repeatedly noted the lack of a real "hit" in the city while it operated under its first director, Thomas Wood Stevens. The internal struggles of the three major local units—Americana, vaudeville, and Negro—regarding the type of theatre they wanted to present only exacerbated the problem. Local newspapers tended to operate rather strictly along party lines and displayed a clear love/hate relationship with Roosevelt, the New Deal, and the FTP rather than encouragement for their new FTP program.[3] In a pivotal meeting in May 1936, Flanagan introduced George Kondolf, a young Broadway producer, to the publicity and promotional staff as the new director of the Chicago FTP. In the ensuing discussion, Flanagan focused on the "temperament of the city" and concluded that the FTP should "cash in on the fact that Chicago likes entertainment." She went on:

> If you prefer to have no experimental theatre—very well, but I would like to stress again that the only chance the theatre has to make a success is to do something exciting. I would hate to see in any city a complete barring of experimental plays because of box office, although we need it to some extent. But unless we do some of these experimental plays, what is the use.[4]

This statement, and Flanagan's seemingly contradictory assertion about needing a popular hit in Chicago, illustrated one of her strategies for expanding the FTP nationwide. Flanagan planned to lure new audiences away from the movies and into the theatre with exciting, accessible work that spoke to local interests. In this way the FTP would become a national theatre with the potential for a life beyond the WPA and relief.

Kondolf's personal taste tended toward commercially successful, popular productions rather than political or controversial dramas. When asked about his intentions regarding the FTP as a whole, he replied, "I hoped that it might eventually become a national theatre. I thought it was a good opportunity for that. And I think my interest in it was primarily to make it as good as I could, to create shows that people would want to see." He specifically noted that he found political overtones untheatrical and harmful to the production quality and that he wanted his productions to be theatrically (as opposed to politically) successful.[5] For Kondolf, the FTP would gain respect as a national theatre through well-produced, commercially successful programs. He pursued openings enthusiastically. Through the summer and fall of 1936, Kondolf launched a series of plays in quick succession, including *Broken Dishes, Burning the Mortgage, A Cry for Life, End of the Row, Everyman, No Angels Singing, Quagmire, The Royal Family*, and *Youth Through the Ages*. In October he supervised *It Can't Happen Here*, part of the nationwide opening that made history when it opened simultaneously in 21 theatres and 17 states on October 27, 1936.[6] Once past the scandals that would arise surrounding productions of *Model Tenement* and *Hymn to the Rising Sun*, Kondolf's choices proceeded smoothly through Chicago's censorship gauntlet and into openings. Kondolf eventually graduated to a leadership position in the New York City FTP and was replaced by local stock company expert Harry Minturn as head of the Chicago FTP. Minturn was like-minded in his approach to commercially successful productions; his brainchild, the phenomenally popular Negro Unit adaptation of Gilbert and Sullivan's *The Mikado* entitled *The Swing Mikado* (1938), would move to Broadway in the midst of an FTP scandal that would lead to the firing of Regional Director John McGee.[7] Though *The Swing Mikado's* scandal was the most public, it was not the one that would reverberate throughout the Chicago FTP and affect programming for its duration. Local laws on censorship would take precedent in this regard and proved instrumental in defining the FTP that would and could thrive in the city. These rulings—and the ability to make such rulings—emerged from a very specific set of economic and social conditions that had begun to form during the 1920s and came to fruition with the arrival of the Great Depression.

When the Great Depression struck the United States, Chicago faced total collapse. Already in a far worse financial state than many of the nation's cities, the economic disaster hit as Chicago already teetered on the edge of bankruptcy due to the improper use of city resources and corruption that characterized Mayor 'Big Bill' Thompson's time in office (1915–1923; 1927–1931). Ranked by scholars as the worst big-city mayor of all time, Thompson's activities exacerbated many of the problems Chicago faced during the Depression; he accepted campaign funds from Al Capone, supported the Germans during World War I, led a campaign to censor school books, and threatened to punch Great Britain's King

George "in the snoot."[8] Thompson used Capone and other gangsters to fund his campaign and as a major source of income for the city in exchange for legal protection. During the 1920s, Capone virtually ruled Chicago and its more than 3 million people through a complex system of bribes and kickbacks. In the words of Herbert Asbury, "Chicago seemed to be filled with gangsters."[9]

In spite of the negative associations frequently made with gangsters today, it is interesting to note that Chicagoans often viewed their gangsters with equanimity during the 1920s and early 1930s. For example, in a positive publicity campaign that rivaled those of out-of-favor politicians, Capone instituted and paid for Chicago's first soup kitchen in 1930, distributing 20,000 meals a week through the early years of the Depression.[10] The regular presence of flourishing organized crime, gambling, and graft in Chicago during this period led to the wide-open, hard-boiled reputation that Chicago enjoyed for much of the early twentieth century.[11] Consistently under suspicion for various misdeeds ranging from taking kickbacks and bribes to defrauding the city, Thompson's tenure as mayor led to tax strikes, an explosion of organized crime, and a series of vicious court cases.[12] While the national unemployment average hovered around 25 percent, by May of 1932 Chicago's unemployment rate swelled to 40 percent, and more unemployed workers arrived in the city every day. By the end of 1932, Chicago was bankrupt.

Though Chicago's voters would dethrone Thompson in 1932 and elect Anton Cermak, the new mayor's efforts were cut short by his untimely assassination. When the Democratic party appointed Edward Kelly interim mayor of Chicago, he faced rioting schoolteachers and students, runs on banks, picketing in the financial district, and more. The city owed $40 million in back wages to municipal employees; one of the hardest hit groups—teachers—received paychecks for only three of 12 months in 1932. Clearly, even those individuals who had jobs in Chicago at this point had no guarantee of receiving a paycheck.

This volatile economic state placed enormous pressure on Kelly to take quick and decisive action. His first act as mayor was to sign $1.7 million in tax warrants that would provide the funds to pay thousands of municipal employees. He slashed the city's budget, secured legislation that would allow forced tax collection, wiped out much of the city's debt, and nurtured good relations with the recently elected President Roosevelt, thereby obtaining additional federal emergency funds. Furthermore, he combined these cuts with income and jobs by presiding over the extraordinarily lucrative Century of Progress Exposition (1933–1934), which repaid the city's debt, gave a 6 percent return on all city bonds, and accumulated a $160,000 surplus for Chicago's coffers. Kelly stabilized Chicago's financial situation as much as could be expected during the Great Depression, improving living and working conditions for hundreds of thousands of citizens. With the backing of influential factions and the popular vote, Kelly became the most powerful politician in the state of Illinois and commanded one of the most potent political machines in the country. By the mid-1930s, Chicago and the Democratic Machine were the key to Illinois elections.[13] Because he wielded this level of political power, Kelly's authority in Chicago was virtually unassailable; grassroots attempts to overthrow his rulings with regard to censorship were uniformly and quickly suppressed. For the Chicago theatre and the young FTP, this authority meant censorship.

The mayor of Chicago had exclusive rights to censor theatre, and Mayor Kelly exercised this right numerous times in the 1930s, often to the detriment of the FTP. As Kelly explained to Flanagan, "I can stop anything in this town I want to."[14] One of the most public closures occurred in 1935 when Kelly shut down the commercial production of *Tobacco Road* because of indecency and launched an investigation into all stage productions in the city of Chicago. *Tobacco Road*, which garnered complaints about its content in numerous cities across the country, was to open in Chicago just as the FTP began operations. Quoted in the *Chicago Daily Tribune*, Mayor Kelly declared: "We are not trying to make a church out of the city, but some things pass the bounds of being entertaining."[15] Kelly's closing of *Tobacco Road* sent shockwaves through the Chicago theatre community. While his choice sparked criticism across the city, his authority remained unquestioned. And so, when the FTP sought permission for a new experimental play—focusing on the controversial housing problem—the mayor's reticence was not particularly surprising. Meyer Levin's *Model Tenement* proved to be the Chicago FTP's first experience with censorship.[16]

The dispute over *Model Tenement* raged for months, and the implication was that the Mayor's office was avoiding the act of an official pronouncement either way. It may have provoked the resignation of Chicago's first director, Thomas Wood Stevens, and became the first major issue of Kondolf's reign.[17] But Kondolf picked his battles carefully and, faced with "the most beautiful stalling and shifting I have encountered in some time," decided not to pursue the Mayor's final ruling on *Model Tenement*.[18] Nearly a year later, Flanagan met with the mayor and broached the subject of *Model Tenement*. Baffled by Kelly's response—and under threat of a lawsuit from Levin—Flanagan wrote a detailed account of their conversation.

According to this account, Mayor Kelly said that he had neither heard of nor stopped the play and that no one in his office would have done so without his express consent:

> Mayor Kelly seemed quite exercised about this whole situation. He said that he was tired of being made a fool of on this subject of censorship—that he had closed <u>Tobacco Road</u> because it was an obscene play and because of the fact that during its run in Chicago attacks on women by morons increased sixty percent. He said that unless we did a play of this nature, he would certainly have no interest in even commenting upon it, to say nothing of stopping it.[19]

Flanagan pursued the matter further in a meeting with WPA state administrator Robert Dunham. He retorted that the play was "a lot of stuff written by a communist agitator" and stated Mayor Kelly had stopped the play personally. When Flanagan relayed the pertinent points from her conversation with Kelly, Dunham changed his story, stating, "Well, come to think of it, I don't believe it was the Mayor himself who gave the order."[20] The question of responsibility regarding the sandbagging of *Model Tenement* remained unanswered.

In October 1936, the Chicago FTP experienced another censorship setback; Paul Green's *Hymn to the Rising Sun*, a play that dealt with "'the brutality of the chain-gang' and [was] 'a powerful indictment of this anti-democratic institution,'" was mysteriously halted. On the evening of the opening, patrons who had gathered in the lobby were sent home; the cast did not seem to know anything and Kondolf offhandedly responded to queries by citing "technical reasons."[21] Inquiries by local newspapers led again to Robert Dunham, who confessed he had ordered the postponement because of the play's immoral subject matter and presentation. *Hymn to the Rising Sun*, one of the first productions of the Chicago Negro Unit, was certainly not for the fainthearted. Green's grim assault on racism graphically displays the intense claustrophobia of a southern work camp run by a cruel man who heaps violent punishments on the inmates.[22] The *Chicago Daily Tribune* reported that Fritz Blocki, Chicago theatre critic and liaison to the FTP, resigned his post because "he did not want to represent 'anything as vile as *Hymn to the Rising Sun*.'" Blocki was convinced, the paper commented, that the play would alienate people from the cause of legitimate theatre by its portrayal of nauseating brutality.[23] The production was postponed indefinitely.

These instances of censorship hampered the FTP's ability to operate in Chicago and altered the types of theatre it produced (or attempted to produce). Though citizens of Chicago would rebel against the mayor's stranglehold on local theatre—engineering a grassroots campaign in opposition to such political censorship—Kelly's control would not simply wane with time. In order to operate successfully in Chicago, the FTP would need to find productive ways to work within the boundaries set by Kelly and his political allies. In the cases of *Model Tenement* and *Hymn to the Rising Sun*, two powerful, locally relevant FTP productions were either in the rehearsal process or about to open when political forces halted them. These events forced the FTP to reconsider its place in Chicago, particularly with respect to risky or controversial work. I suggest that these actions led the Chicago FTP to adopt a specific identity, one that was ultimately shaped and propagated by the individuals chosen to direct the program once Stevens retired. Thus, in direct opposition to Flanagan's ideals for the FTP as a whole, light, commercially successful pieces took precedence over artistic, experimental, and locally relevant productions. Only in specific circumstances, such as the production of *Spirochete* in 1938, would the Chicago FTP break out of this predominantly apolitical, commercially driven model of success.

Indeed, it was important for the Chicago FTP to maintain the balance between amusement and danger—whether that danger was political, topical, or aesthetic. Chicago's structure and organization were extremely insular; city leaders, elected or criminal, did not embrace outsiders. This independence gave Chicago's leaders the ability to effectively make up their own rules; the FTP was not a part of this system, and so it struggled to comment on the goings-on with an outsider's sense of morality. Chicago politics repeatedly halted the FTP's moral agenda, either by censoring plays such as *Model Tenement* or *Hymn to the Rising Sun* or by causing administrative difficulties at the local or state levels. By the time the FTP arrived in Chicago, the systems that supported organized crime, abject poverty, rampant class stratification, and crooked politicians were firmly established; it was only when the FTP acknowledged and faced these issues that it was able to create producible and socially relevant plays and negotiate a relationship with local audiences. *O Say Can You Sing* stands out as the first real attempt—sometimes successful, sometimes not—by the Chicago FTP to deal with the idiosyncrasies of its community on stage.

O SAY CAN YOU SING: MAGIC, MAYHEM, AND A DASH OF NUDITY

A fictional FTP troupe is dispatched to the local nudist colony. They are unable to sell a single ticket to their show, in spite of the apparent skill of their star performer—a stripper. Upon realizing that they have been sent to perform a striptease before what would likely be an unappreciative crowd, the members of the company bemoan their fate, worrying that the failure of their burlesque performance at the nudist colony will somehow jeopardize their future within the FTP. They call the FTP director in desperation, and an idea is born: Miss Tillie Take-Off will change her striptease to the dress-tease of Miss Clarabelle Clotheshorse. Her performance, which climaxes with the donning of earmuffs, mittens, and a large hat, garners rave reviews from the nudists—even attracting enough attention to elicit a nudist police raid—and saves the fictional FTP from certain disaster.[24]

This sketch is from a musical revue by Sid Kuller, Ray Golden, and Phil Charig entitled *O Say Can You Sing*. As is the case with many FTP scripts, multiple versions of this play exist, though only two bear signs of production work, and only one was performed for audiences.[25] One of the reasons that *O Say Can You Sing* serves as such a rich piece of cultural history is that the revisions illustrate attention to far more than simple artistic integrity. The earlier version, located in the National Archives, is biting, fresh, and witty. This version contains numerous handwritten comments on the production details of the play, including the different stage drops that would be used for scene transitions, props, and extensive stage directions. The produced version is a bound copy housed at the Library of Congress and accompanied by a detailed production book featuring pages of director's notes, electrical diagrams, and many original production photos. When compared to the original version, the production script lacks intensity; its jokes are corny, the characters wacky but stereotyped, and the caustic bite has become little more than a nibble.

The original version of *O Say Can You Sing* exploited the amusing anecdotes that surrounded Chicago in all of its political glory. The musical revue alternates between catchy songs like "Fugitive From Rhythm," "A Pretty Girl to Love Me," and "The Show Must Go On," and scenes featuring the wise-cracking comic stylings of the secretary of entertainment (also known as the director of the FTP), Augustus Q. Hamfield. Hamfield is pitted against the cheap, antagonistic secretary of the budget, Robert J. Ratcliffe. Hamfield's adventures entertain the masses while he tries to keep the fictional FTP in business in spite of Ratcliffe's attempts to have Hamfield jailed for Communist sympathies and the FTP declared unconstitutional. Highly topical political and social references to the state of Chicago abound in this version of *O Say Can You Sing*. The deletions, additions, and rewrites suggest a volatile milieu in which certain FTP activities were inexplicably halted. It also shows a number of ways in which the FTP adapted creatively to its environment in Chicago, a skill that was vital to its success in the city, whether that success was to be artistically or commercially based.

The brainchild of George Kondolf, *O Say Can You Sing* made history as the first large, original FTP production to run for eight months. Replete with stunning dances, catchy musical numbers, spectacular sets, and more than 600 ornate costumes, the show was phenomenally popular with "young men and their best girls," and cost an estimated $80,000; much of this price tag went toward salaries for the 250 actors, dancers, and production personnel required to operate such a lavish show.[26] It capitalized on Chicago talent as well, making use of acrobats, jugglers, magicians, tap dancers, singers, and vaudeville stars, and integrated actors from the popular Americana unit with those that would move to the Negro Unit. When asked how this production differed from previous FTP fare, Kondolf explained that *O Say Can You Sing* offered massive employment opportunities and engendered "local excitement."[27] Kondolf's comment implies that *O Say Can You Sing* not only generated an audience connection but also marked a change in the direction of FTP productions in Chicago. Its use of actors' special talents, racial integration, and topical interest for Chicagoans distinguished it from the previous "stock favorites" that the FTP favored under Minturn.

Exciting and innovative though it may have been, Chicago's critics remained unimpressed by *O Say Can You Sing*. The *Chicago Daily News* described the show as "strong on dancing, long on gaiety and short on humor"; the *Chicago Evening American* referred to many of the protagonist's lines as those that "cried out, or, I should say, stank out for immediate burial"; and the reviewer from *Time* magazine pointed to the audience's tendency to "wince whenever [the protagonist] opens his mouth." The *Time* review continued, "When it was good it was very good, when it was bad it was awful."[28] In spite of these less than stellar reviews, *O Say Can You Sing* generated interest and laughter among audiences. The production poked fun at the practices of the federal government, the FTP, and Chicago itself—vexing Democrats, Communists, and Republicans alike. The popular appeal of the show was due, in large part, to the ability of the production to laugh at the characteristics that made Chicago unique—organized crime, political corruption, and incredibly high numbers of immigrants. As Flanagan reiterated, "The best thing about *O Say Can You Sing* was that it was as Chicago as Chicago. No anti-administration paper could laugh more at Federal Theatre than did Federal Theatre itself."[29]

The original version of the play opens as newsboys happily broadcast Uncle Sam's entrance into show business. A series of blackouts and quick transitions between scenes show the impact of this announcement on the lives of various individuals. A magician is contacted by his agent with the news that the FTP wants to see the act in which the magician pulls the rabbit out of his hat; he replies, "This is a fine time to tell me! [...] We had the rabbit for dinner last night!" The script then cuts to a scene in which a German family of acrobats struggles to rehearse while lamenting their lot in life; news of the FTP arrives and the Father hollers, "Hooray for Uncle Sam! I knew he wouldn't forget uns [*sic*] 100% Amerrrrrrrrricans!" The third flash is movement-based. A young actress, evicted from her home, despairs; she wanders across the stage until she meets a "hard-boiled, wise-guy type, smoking a cigarette. He gives the girl the eye and the desperation of her position gives her an idea. She passes him cautiously, dropping her handkerchief. He picks it up and follows her rapidly, then touches her shoulder [and] pulls out a bill." Just as the young actress is about to accept the money a newsboy arrives announcing the FTP. Her face "lights up with joy" and when "the man taps her on the shoulder," she "motions him away without even looking at him and walks off."[30]

This opening mirrors and parodies the situations of several specific populations in Chicago. The occupations of the first man, both a juggler and magician, can be seen as a metaphor for the millions of struggling people forced to juggle bills, the needs of their families, their self-respect, and their relief checks and hoping against hope that they will have enough money and luck to pay for food and shelter. At this point in Chicago the ability to balance these needs was, for many individuals, an act of magic; even people who had jobs (particularly for the city government) were rarely paid. Ironically, this man had to eat the means of his livelihood; like many in the working class, he was trapped in an unending downward spiral of poverty.

If the magician represents the thousands of frightfully poor Chicagoans, the German acrobats remind the audience of the heightened challenges faced by the immigrant population—a population that had steadily increased until white ethnics composed the majority of the city (and voting power). The 1930 population of 3,376,438 people was broken down into the several major categories: African Americans (6.9 percent), white native Americans (27.9 percent; classified as such once they reached third-generation American status), and white ethnics (64.3 percent).[31] As the clear majority, the white ethnic groups were a powerful presence in the government, united by their shared histories and geographic proximity to one another. Many immigrants had moved out of the center of the city during the 1920s but established communities in specific areas that could be characterized by the religion or ethnicity of many inhabitants. Irish, Czechoslovakian, Polish, and Germans populated the southwest side, for example, while the south side was predominantly African American. These immigrant groups were the workers who allowed the city to function and ensured the continuation of the Democratic machine that ruled the city with an iron grip.[32] They were, in the words of the German acrobat, "100% Amerrrrrrrrricans!" and well-worth remembering in *O Say Can You Sing*.

While the previous opening scenes offer humor in the face of the pervasive heartache of the Great Depression, the portrayal of the young actress driven to sell her body to a man who appears to be linked with the area's infamous organized crime is a stark reminder of harsh realities. This striking scene graphically illustrates the effects of the Great Depression on the unemployed people of Chicago. It also referenced a serious local problem: Chicago was plagued by one of "the most notorious red-light district[s] in the country." Even after Al Capone's 1931 tax-fraud conviction, his network of prostitutes, "dope peddlers, and backroom bookies" was simply divided between his former competitors.[33] Perhaps most vital to establishing the role of the FTP in Chicago, these scenes portray an organization that employs Chicagoans. The people in these scenes, while frequently amusing, are all desperate—the FTP arrives in town and saves each from metaphorical or literal prostitution, eviction, and starvation.

This opening series of brief scenes would have occurred within the first five minutes of the production, setting the tone for the rest of the show as amusing, yet highly relevant entertainment. These scenes also use a variety of theatrical performers to represent the various situations seen in Chicago's populace, thus tying the immigrant and working-class populations directly to the theatre and the FTP. In a way, the FTP and its struggling theatre artists become one with the people in the audience. In the actual production, however, all of these scenes and many of these similarities disappeared. Instead of a series of desperate and representative individuals learning of the FTP, the production opened with nothing more than a brief scene in which three newsboys holler: "Extra!...Extra!...Uncle Sam going into show business! [...] Uncle Sam wants actors, dancers, singers."[34] The first major musical number, "O Say Can You Sing," followed:

> Through this scrim come the men and women dressed in Beaux Art costumes, as Elizabethans, 19th Century, in evening dress, etc. The women [...] go through a routine of the first verse. On the second verse of the song spotlights

light up behind the scrim revealing four girls on a six-foot platform in military costume, one specialty dancer, and four negro tap dancers. The scrim flies up, as they begin their dance. On the third verse, a contour gold curtain rises on a twelve-foot platform behind the first, revealing singers dressed in either red, white, or blue choir robes. The colors formed by the robes are, successively, the colors of the American flag.[35]

This revision illustrates a dramatic shift in the tone and apparent intent of this production. While the early version referred to real people and problems in the city, the revised edition focuses on spectacle, pretty dancing girls, and the creation of a representative American flag via music, movement, and costumes. Though the integration of white and African American actors remains, the serious themes of the original opening are replaced by peppy patriotism (See Figure 1).

The changes are not confined to the opening scenes. Throughout the play innocuous one-liners supplant topical jabs, and many scenes vanish entirely. The aforementioned burlesqued-burlesque scene at the nudist camp, for

Figure 1   Scene from the Chicago FTP production of *O Say Can You Sing*. Note the variety shown in this image—a southern belle, gentlemen in tuxedoes, leg dancers, a choir, and what looks to be characters from the Elizabethan and Restoration periods. NARA, Record Group 69, Work Projects Administration, 1922–1944, RG-69-TC, Box 21, "Illinois."

example, disappeared from the production. Likely a concession to Mayor Kelly, the revision removed a scene that was both amusing and a political jab. During the World's Fair just a few years earlier, Kelly was said to have turned "'bashful pink' at seeing women dancers scantily clad." Much to the dismay of the managers, Kelly promptly ordered all performers to wear clothes at the fair.[36] This mocking portrayal of a "scantily clad" female sexily dressing herself would likely have reminded the audience of one of Kelly's early embarrassments in office. In a political environment that had already witnessed the banning of several FTP shows (not to mention the commercial productions that experienced similar difficulties), the removal of this reference in deference to Mayor Kelly would not be surprising.

The character of Augustus Hamfield, newly appointed secretary of entertainment, sees a similar shift when revised for production. Initially, he is a fast-talking, wisecracking pickpocket who occasionally works in the theatre as an actor and director. In spite of this humorous description, the parallels in authority to Hallie Flanagan are many. As the reporters who consistently trail Hamfield explain, "Why, do you realize that the secretary of entertainment holds the destiny of the American Theatre in his lap?"[37] When asked about his professional theatre experience, Hamfield replies:

> HAMFIELD: Who do you think supplied the dirt concession to "Tobacco Road"?...Me!...Who inspired "Strictly Dishonorable"?...Me!...Who was timekeeper for "The Children's Hour"?...Me!...Who do you think really directed a "Midsummernight's Dream"?... [sic]
> RATCLIFFE: Who?
> HAMFIELD: Max Reinhardt!...And you ask me what have I done on Broadway![38]

Like Flanagan, whose professional experience consisted of her playwriting and the building and leading of Vassar College's experimental theatre program, Hamfield has little experience in Broadway theatres. The character of Augustus Q. Hamfield recreated for the revised version is more subdued and professional. He refrains from demonstrating his pickpocket skills the first time he meets Ratcliffe, begins a rather innocent romantic affair with his secretary, actually has professional theatre experience, and his comic remarks take on a softer, gentler tone.

Hamfield leads the fictitious FTP in a crusade against the stereotypically pompous and overfed secretary of the budget, Mr. Robert J. Ratcliffe.

Ratcliffe serves as Hamfield's funding nemesis: "I'm here to tell Mr. Hamfield, the moment that he come in, that no matter how little he asks for his budget, it's too much. Hm! The idea of spending money on actors!"[39] Ratcliffe accuses Hamfield of Communist sympathies and even hauls him before the Supreme Court. Unlike the majority of the play, the character of Ratcliffe remains remarkably similar in the two versions, though it is notable that he never accuses Hamfield—or any of the productions—of unbecoming or immoral content. When placed in the context of the Chicago FTP's many issues with Mayor Kelly and censorship, this choice suggests that the writers were, in fact, taking great care in the choice of targets for their barbs. In a sense, Ratcliffe is the personification of the many critics of the FTP; whether the FTP was wasting money on actors, producing controversial works (or meaningless fluff pieces), or harboring Communist sympathizers, these naysayers consistently found fault and sought ways to eliminate or reduce FTP funding. Flanagan spent an extraordinary amount of time refuting these allegations. In these ways, Hamfield confronts many of the same obstacles that Flanagan faced in leading the real-life FTP.

Ratcliffe regularly becomes the butt of jokes featuring both Communists and Republicans. In fact, he gains his position by taking advantage of one of Chicago's most well-known political scandals—voting fraud: "He's the captain in an election district with 12,268 votes and in every election he brings in the whole 20,000 of 'em."[40] Prevalent in the original script, political humor leaves no form of corruption (excepting censorship) unskewered. As prospective theatre professionals arrive in search of jobs, for example, they are introduced to the director of the fictional FTP:

> MISS FLIPCRACK: . . . there's a magician outside to see you. He wants to get on the government payroll.
> MR. HAMFIELD: He doesn't need to be a magician to do that. All he has to do is vote democrat. Shoot him in.[41]

Mr. Hamfield's remark refers to an all-too-common situation in Chicago. As far as most Chicagoans were concerned, relief checks arrived via the City of Chicago or Cook County, both of which served as unapologetic vehicles for the Democratic Party. Congresspersons frequently required constituents who requested relief via the WPA to document their party standing with a note from their ward committeeman. As political scholar John Allswang concisely explains, "There was only so much relief available, and the machine felt it was only reasonable that it go to Democrats."[42]

Another scene from the original version addresses the influence of the immigrant population. A Russian director, Mr. Stankovitch, arrives with an idea for the "most sensational, marvillious, gorgeous and colosy production in de history of de teaaaater. It will haf 1000 stage hands, 2000 actors, 3000 costumes and at least 4000 pieces scenery [sic]." When told that this concept—which will cost only a million dollars—is a bit pricey for the FTP, Stankovitch suggests a minimalist production of the quintessential American play, *Uncle Tom's Cabin*. The Russian proposes a production in the style of the "Stankovitch-Mamoulian-Boleslavsky School." For a mere 79 cents, he will turn *Uncle Tom's Cabin* into *Uncle Tomashevsky's Cabin*, a play that features the *absences* of both Uncle Tomashevsky and the cabin.[43] Instead the play focuses on the death of Little Eva, a sexy, blonde Russian woman who is able to foretell the winners of horse races until she dies of a fever that apparently could have been cured if only some high-quality vodka were available.

This parody of *Uncle Tom's Cabin*, directed and adapted by a Russian director who had been fired from every commercial theatre avenue in Russia and the United States, contains a number of potentially problematic elements for a federal organization battling accusation of Communist sympathies. In terms of the deconstructed play, Stankovitch's version would remove the elements that make the play a canonical piece of American history. The loss of Uncle Tom and the cabin (as well as any mention of slavery) negate the themes and historical implications of the play, as do the shifts in Little Eva's character. No longer is she the angelic child, representative of all that is good and Christian in the United States; instead, she becomes a blonde Russian woman with unbridled sexuality. Unlike the Little Eva from Stowe's novel or Aiken's famous theatrical adaption, this Eva embraces the very vice that destroys her father—alcohol.[44] She is neither angelic nor pure, and her death offers a quick laugh rather than a questioning of one's deeply held political and religious beliefs. And so, while this character may have appealed to some demographics with her sexuality and support of alcohol, her role in this distortion of *Uncle Tom's Cabin* simply added fodder to the fires of controversy.

This radical revision of *Uncle Tom's Cabin* was challenging for the FTP as a national entity as well. For an organization that was consistently accused of Communist leanings and un-American activities, plays that gave the appearance of Communist sympathies were anathema. The hiring of a poor quality Russian director, the replacement of an icon of American innocence and Christianity with a sexually appealing Russian woman, the questionable morality seen in the endorsements of gambling and the liberal consumption of alcohol, and the appropriation of this important historical work for a comic theatrical piece could well send the wrong message to detractors of the FTP. As the FTP began to draw more serious fire from WPA critics, Flanagan regularly encountered denigration because of the time she spent studying experimental Russian theatre with her Guggenheim Award in 1926. Because of this, the decision to allow Hamfield, the fictional head of the FTP in the play, to entertain thoughts of hiring an apparently untalented Russian director in Chicago would have been ill-advised.

In the produced version of the play, this scene undergoes immense changes and is made optional. Though the script fails to specify why the scene was elective, it does state that the Chicago production included it in production. The revisions paint Stankovitch as an amusing caricature of a Russian gangster. When the doorman attempts to prevent his speaking to Hamfield, Stankovitch shoots him and orders his henchmen to remove the body in a curious melding of English and the Russian-sounding suffix "-ovitch," "Inovitch—haltovitch—grabovitch—upovitch—outovitch." The scene from *Uncle Tomashevsky's Cabin* is cut to only two pages and a "blonde with a southern accent" plays Little Eva. Hamfield announces that Stankovitch is a terrible director, appropriates the same mangled English/Russian used earlier, and orders Stankovitch's three henchmen to throw him down on the floor and sit on him. This image inspires Hamfield to drop *Uncle Tom's Cabin* from the season altogether so that he can replace it with a new show titled "*Three men on a horse.*"[45] This revision effectively neuters many of the potential problems in the earlier version. From the beginning, Stankovitch is an entertaining Russian killer rather than a tortured, unemployed artist seeking employment. An American actress plays Little Eva in the much abbreviated death scene, and all mention of alcohol and horseracing disappear. Finally, Hamfield's refutation of Stankovitch literally disarms and conquers the Russian. As the scene ends, Hamfield stands victorious before the prone Russian director. This shift demonstrates an awareness of the public perception of communism and the Chicago FTP's need to shape its image.

The revisions in *O Say Can You Sing* show attention to two specific factors—political cleansing and light-hearted, nationalistic praise of the United States and the New Deal. In fact, the dress-tease of Miss Clarabelle Clotheshorse is a lovely metaphor for the Chicago FTP as a whole; just as Miss Tillie Take-Off adjusted her risqué performance for her audience, ultimately stripping out the titillating and exciting bits, the Chicago FTP similarly took a witty, stimulating political parody and covered the most thrilling moments with metaphorical earmuffs. In light of the influence of Chicago politics—particularly the powers of censorship Mayor Kelly repeatedly wielded—it is not surprising that unflattering references to Kelly, his policies, and his allies would quietly disappear. As *Model Tenement* and Mayor Kelly's campaign against immorality on stage demonstrate, city censors regularly worked in concert with playwrights to ensure that the performed product would adhere to the unspoken code of morality required by influential leaders in Chicago. Though I have located no evidence that documents this interaction on this specific play, the majority of the plays produced in Chicago endured some facet of this process, and it is unlikely that *O Say Can You Sing* would have escaped the same scrutiny. The chain of events is suggestive, either of direct censorship by Kelly's office or, more likely, the self-censorship that frequently occurs in the presence of such imbalances of power. Recall that Kondolf replaced Thomas Wood Stevens as head of the Chicago FTP in the midst of *Model Tenement*'s fateful journey of censorship in the Mayor's office. When Kondolf arrived he dropped *Model Tenement* without hesitation, closed the controversial *Hymn to the Rising Sun* (on the day it was to open) without comment, and shifted the focus of the Chicago FTP to commercial successes. *O Say Can You Sing* was the first original production produced by Kondolf in Chicago. A fun, popular hit, it likely went far to mitigate any previously incurred ill will between Mayor Kelly and the FTP expressly because it avoided the political jabs that would have pained Kelly. *O Say Can You Sing*'s finale, "Out of the Red and Into the Blue," demonstrates the upbeat, optimistic nationalism inherent in the production:

> Wake up America!
> Awake and sing and show the world that we can take it!
> It's time—America–
> To climb—America–
> Into the Blue—this land is what we make it! [...]
> Everybody will rejoice–
> As a nation lifts its voice–
> And we'll sing the praise of better days in view–
> There'll be no more grief–
> We'll forget relief–
> When we're out of the red and into the blue![46]

And so, *O Say Can You Sing* shifted from a wickedly pointed parody to a nationalistic revue, emphasizing American pride, ingenuity, and strength in the face of adversity. This popular revue made audiences laugh, engendered long-term loyalty to and excitement for the Chicago FTP, and repeatedly reminded audience members that patronage of the FTP (both as a whole and in Chicago) improved the general well-being of the country. The underlying political and social pressures that led to these radical revisions would continue to haunt the FTP in Chicago, but the project had located its popular theatre audience. *Spirochete* would go on to cement the Chicago FTP's reputation for serious, topical drama.

SPIROCHETE: PLANNING FOR THE PLAGUE

In 1937, Chicago declared war on syphilis, quickly becoming the focal point for the national campaign against the nefarious disease. Initially driven by U.S. Surgeon General Thomas Parran, Chicago's public health officials, congresspersons, and mayor soon joined the call to arms. The *Chicago Daily Tribune* published a series of more than 800 full-page articles (with accompanying pictures) dealing with syphilis between 1935 and 1939. Local groups from the Lions Club to the Medical and Dental Societies, as well as young women, food handlers, and the Cook County Council of Legions appeared in the headlines supporting the city's massive efforts to eradicate the disease.

The FTP positioned itself within this dispute as a defender of scientific knowledge and public health. Susan Glaspell commissioned a living newspaper as a response to the massive anti-syphilis movement in the city. Though the FTP had been quickly dubbed popular entertainment for the poor, Glaspell and the FTP national administration hoped that the so-called "syphilis-play" would force local, regional, and national audiences to rethink the place of the FTP as both a creator of serious theatre and a national instrument for social change. Discarding the idealized America, the FTP would literally intervene in the battle against venereal diseases as it redefined the role of a government-funded theatre on a national scale.

Spirochete (1938) itself became the grounds for a pitched battle over the identity of the FTP as a whole. Would the FTP be a national organization that collected local pieces and turned them into an "American" identity, or would the small local and regional units themselves create a patchwork of identities that would reflect the American ideal? Fundamentally, would the FTP be a national theatre with many branches or a federation of local theatres united by a shared ideal and federal funding? This tension is seen throughout the operation of the FTP but particularly in those production units located in major urban centers outside New York City. *Spirochete* appeared at a time when the nation was beginning to turn away from the far-reaching WPA and toward the specter of a second world war. The FTP's position was tenuous; a new play with the ability to cause widespread social change and excite conversation had the potential to strengthen the project's standing enormously. *Spirochete* serves as a case study that complicates the FTP's struggle for its own identity as a national theatre as it negotiated American politics, morality, and culture.

In the fall of 1937, Glaspell asked Arnold Sundgaard, a recent graduate of Yale University's playwriting program and FTP playreader, to write a play about syphilis.[47] In this way, Glaspell hoped the FTP would respond to Chicago's massive anti-syphilis movement by creating a unique, experimental piece focused on one of the major political and health issues Chicagoans faced. Sundgaard wrote *Spirochete* in six weeks.[48] Glaspell's request for a play dealing with syphilis followed in the footsteps of the national opening of another play dealing with a contemporary social problem, *It Can't Happen Here*. This play would focus on a problem that was not only national but that was of special interest in Chicago because of its anti-syphilis campaign. As *Variety* would argue, "in SPIROCHETE the Federal Theatre finds its best argument for its existence; delivering a play of real social importance."[49]

The prologue opens as a young couple, Peter and Frieda, apply for a Cook County marriage license and are told they must provide medical certificates showing that they have been screened for venereal disease. Peter and Frieda respond indignantly, arguing that they are decent folks and will not be humiliated by submitting to a blood test for diseases that are "disgusting." The Clerk explains that the blood test has nothing to do with decency, and the Announcer notes, "a minute ago you two kids sounded pretty sensible to me. How come you're so prudish about this?" Frieda's reply addresses the general public attitude toward venereal disease, "We're not prudish. We'd rather not think about it." The Announcer decides that an education is in order and takes Peter and Frieda on a journey through the history of syphilis—how it began, how it spread, and how lucky modern society was to have treatment available.[50] With *Spirochete*, the FTP declared war on syphilis as well.

Spirochete appeared on the national scene at a crucial time. The "conspiracy of silence" that had hung over the unseemly topic of venereal disease since World War I had gradually broken apart. By the early 1930s, the commonly accepted figures estimated that nearly one in every ten Americans was syphilitic.[51] The American Social Hygiene Association

(ASHA), known for its rather liberal application of statistics, nonetheless serves as an example of public sentiment regarding venereal disease. ASHA attributed a litany of social ills (including the spread of syphilis) to the familial disruptions caused by the Great Depression, arguing that the spread of syphilis was merely the consequence of the decay of American family values. It was precisely this morally damning perspective that U.S. Surgeon General Thomas Parran and his associates battled with their public awareness campaign throughout the Great Depression.[52]

Many different populations in the city of Chicago called for action in the fight against syphilis; the disease was simply too widespread and too devastating to continue unfettered. This sentiment soon led to political action in the form of a new law. Though it had been shouted down in the Illinois state legislature just three years earlier, on July 1, 1937, the Saltiel Hygienic Marriage Law went into effect, requiring that all couples submit to a blood test for venereal disease before being issued a marriage license in the state. June 30, 1937, broke all records at the Cook County Marriage License Bureau; the office issued 1,407 licenses in a special, eleven-hour day, exceeding the day before the World War I draft went into effect by more than 300 licenses. After the law took effect, many couples avoided it by traveling to Crown Point, Indiana (where blood tests were not yet required) to marry.[53]

In late July, Chicago officials began a massive poll on the question of Chicagoans' willingness to submit to confidential, free blood tests for syphilis. The city mailed secret ballots to every family in the city. Sponsors included the U.S. Public Health Service, the U.S. Department of Health, the WPA, the Chicago Board of Health, and local doctors and universities. Officials asked religious, civic, and scientific communities to encourage everyone to take the blood tests in the hope that the ballots would provide the first accurate figures regarding the rate of syphilis infections in Chicago. National public health officials pointed to Chicago as "the first American city to attack the problem of syphilis in a realistic way."[54] Because of the combination of the survey and the Saltiel hygienic law, Chicago's head of the Committee for the Control of Venereal Disease, Dr. Louis Schmidt, declared that the city of Chicago had separated the disease from "superstition, ignorance, and false modesty and hence it was 'the logical city for the first popular referendum and actual abatement of syphilis.' "[55]

Within a few months, the *Chicago Daily Tribune* announced that it would require blood tests of all 2,700 employees. Dr. Herman N. Bundesen, president of the Board of Health, described the effort as a "great step forward because of the realization that it is good business to control syphilis" and commended the *Chicago Daily Tribune* for setting such a forward-thinking precedent.[56] Other major companies joined the march; soon Sears, Roebuck & Co., Carson Pirie Scott, Montgomery Ward, Bowman Dairy Company, and Charles A. Stevens & Co. required blood tests as well and promised that infected employees would not be adversely affected so long as they continued treatment. The Illinois Manufacturers' Association and the Chicago Association of Commerce also agreed to encourage private industry to use the blood test.[57] As Harry Minturn, who became director of the Chicago FTP after Kondolf relocated to New York City, explained:

> The law requiring a physical examination prior to issuance of a marriage cer-
> tificate has but recently been passed in the State of Illinois, and the matter is
> therefore a very timely subject. [...] In addition, Dr. Bundesen['s fight against
> syphilis] has the full support of Mayor Kelly, all of which lends strength to our
> belief that a Living Newspaper on syphilis within the near future, in Chicago,
> would tend to promote local good feeling toward, and support for, the Federal
> Theatre here.[58]

In light of the many problems the FTP (and Chicago theatre in general) experienced with Mayor Kelly and censorship, Minturn's attention to both topical relevance and public relations was understandable. The FTP needed something that would engender goodwill and capitalize on a relevant issue. Thus, Glaspell's choice to commission a play about syphilis—in the city that served as the national focal point of the war against the deadly disease—proved both timely and strategically well-founded. Inspired by U.S. Surgeon General Thomas Parran's 1937 public health book, *Shadow on the Land: Syphilis*, *Spirochete* documented the disease, its repercussions for unsuspecting patients, and scientific discoveries in diagnosis and treatment, finally concluding with a call to action. In spite of the public health campaign launched by the city and the *Chicago Daily Tribune*, syphilis remained a political landmine for a national, federally funded theatre. The response of the FTP national administration reflected their recognition of the hazards involved in presenting a play on syphilis.

One of the ways in which the FTP planned to circumvent the political and social problems inherent in a government play about venereal disease was to present the play in the style of a living newspaper. Facts, statistics, and rigorous documentation surrounding a specific problem and shaped around the dramatic presentation of its effects characterized the living newspaper as a genre. This documentation then served as a line of defense against critics that accused the FTP of forwarding a specific agenda with the controversial topics and ideas that frequently informed the living newspapers. In the case of *Spirochete*, Flanagan requested Sundgaard's bibliography, noting that "we have to answer searching criticisms, line by line, of every Living Newspaper...we must have documentation for every single fact given."[59] Because of these pressures, Sundgaard rigorously documented his collaborations with numerous medical luminaries regarding the accuracy of the content, citing Dr. Oscar C. Wenger (Assistant Surgeon General for the United States), Dr. Louis Schmidt (Chicago Board of Health and chairman of Chicago's anti-syphilis committee), Dr. Reuben Kahn (creator of the Kahn test for syphilis), Dr. Hermen N. Bundesen, and Paul de Kruif (novelist and microbiologist). According to Sundgaard, each of these respected scientists read the play, attended rehearsals, spoke to the cast, offered suggestions and corrections, or took Sundgaard on tours of local communities that had been ravaged by syphilis.[60] In a further effort for authentication, the FTP educated the actors playing in *Spirochete* and made free blood tests available to members of the production. Following his blood test, one of the older actors in the company happily announced what a "great feeling" it was to learn that his test came back positive; he was dismayed to learn that a positive result meant he was infected.[61] In fact, the cast eventually became so knowledgeable about syphilis and the painful, expensive, and time-consuming remedies that they gave the production an alternate and unofficial title—*One Night with Venus and Seven Years with Mercury.*[62]

De Kruif was particularly thrilled by the public spotlight that the FTP's production would throw upon the disease. In a letter to Flanagan, Florence Kerr, director of the Women's and Professional Projects Division, described a script meeting with regional WPA supervisor Howard Hunter, Paul de Kruif, and Dr. Wenger. De Kruif:

> Fairly bounced in his chair with enthusiasm and stated to the whole group that, in his opinion, the Federal Theatre had been and was now "knocking the spots off Broadway". Mr. DeKruiff's [*sic*] own conviction was that week by week, syphilis was getting to be hotter box-office, that the Federal Government should have complete control of this play, and that, furthermore, it should make plans to produce the picture which will certainly grow out of the play. [...] I am sure that with the powerful backing already evidenced the Chicago Production of this LIVING NEWSPAPER should go over.[63]

As the play rehearsed, local sponsors emerged. On opening night, the audience consisted of such locally and nationally prominent personages such as de Kruif, Dr. Wenger, Dr. Louis Schmidt, and Illinois Representative Edward P. Saltiel (sponsor of the hygienic marriage law).

Audience members entering the theatre walked through the Chicago Board of Health's free syphilis testing station, which was set up in the lobby. More than a dozen audience members submitted to testing on opening night.[64] Much of the audience consisted of health professionals; as the review in *Time* magazine noted, if one were to call for a doctor while in the theatre, "the audience would have risen as a man."[65] The national critical response was so positive that a series of letters and memos traveled between Chicago and Flanagan's New York office. An undated memo from Emmet Lavery confirmed Minturn's observation about the relevance of the production:

> To show the sweeping national potency of Federal Theatre shouldn't we launch a nation wide series of productions of *Spirochete* in conjunction with U.S. Health Service. It might mean the wiping out of syphilis—and would that justify the Federal Theatre! [...] I wonder if we don't take the success of *Spirochete* too calmly. Isn't this the biggest thing nationally that we have at the moment?[66]

In many ways, Lavery was correct in his assessment, and the FTP capitalized on the goodwill that the production generated. In spite of initial reservations about the piece, Flanagan frequently used it as an example of an FTP success story and a metaphor for the national organization. In fact, her 1938 introduction to an anthology of FTP Living Newspapers read:

> *Spirochete* [...] tells in Living Newspaper form the story of the fight against syphilis, tells it with such effect that the daily press, *Variety*, and *Billboard*, report it as sensational entertainment, while Paul de Kruif and the Assistant Surgeon General of the United States enlist its service in the nationwide struggle against the disease, even the nameless mention of which once put Ibsen in the pillory. [This] seems to indicate that the truth is not only stranger but often more entertaining and more dramatically effective than fiction. In fact, this conclusion might be said to apply to the entire history of the Federal Theatre.[67]

For many reasons—the support of the public health community nationwide, the timeliness of the topic, and the quality of the play as experimental theatre—*Spirochete* became one of the most frequently produced Living Newspapers in the country, second only to the hugely popular *One-Third of a Nation*. The FTP produced *Spirochete* in Boston, Cincinnati, Portland, Philadelphia, and Seattle and had scheduled productions in several other cities when Congress ended funding for the FTP in 1939.[68] The critical popularity and social importance of this play established the Chicago FTP as a distinct creative voice with the ability to create appealing, germane theatre. It also demonstrated the FTP's attention to a national profile that would literally intervene in the spread of syphilis while creating locally relevant theatre.

The Chicago premiere of *Spirochete* was the FTP's frontal assault on syphilis. A publicity blitz that was unprecedented in the history of the FTP accompanied the show by placing it squarely within Chicago's own battle against the unseen killer. Hundreds of newspaper articles, radio spots, and speeches dragged syphilis out of its secret silence and into the public sphere. The strategy posited by health officials, politicians, and news professionals focused on demystifying the disease, attacking the cultural mores that maintained the strict code of silence, and implicating the community as a whole in the disease's destruction. It is not surprising then, that Sundgaard and the FTP mirrored this methodology in *Spirochete*. Harry Minturn wanted a "bold" approach; as he told Sundgaard, "it was time to stop whispering about it and start talking out loud." Sundgaard adopted Minturn's turn of phrase as the curtain line for the play.[69]

Spirochete begins as Peter and Frieda, a young couple applying for a marriage license, become the foils for the larger community that has refused to discuss syphilis. When the county clerk asks for their medical forms documenting freedom from venereal disease, Peter and Frieda are shocked. Peter frets about the implied accusation that his fiancé has engaged in indecent behavior and leaps to defend her honor against the "disgusting" claim. When the Announcer finally confronts the young couple, Peter and Frieda admit that they are curious about syphilis, and that they have always been too embarrassed to ask questions.[70] This moment serves as the catalyst for the play; suddenly we are thrust back in time to learn about the history of the disease along with Peter and Frieda. Though Peter and Frieda do not appear again, their function is clear; they are the mouthpieces of the culture of silence who voice the moral outrage of "decent" Americans who refuse to discuss "disgusting" issues like venereal disease. This approach launches the attack on that "prudish" silence and urges the audience to join the young couple as the FTP demystifies syphilis.

As the announcer explains, the documented history of syphilis began in the year 1493 with the diseased sailors of Christopher Columbus.[71] The Spanish locals shun the sailors and their doctor is baffled. When Columbus explains that he and his men were "welcomed" by "native women with full warm bodies" in Española, the doctor decides the illness—"the sign of the devil"—is "a just penalty for sins;" he tells the men to wash the sores, let some blood, and go home to their wives. In the following scene syphilis spreads throughout Europe, largely the result of victory couplings between conquering soldiers and sexually enticing young women who serve as the spoils of war. A series of ill men blame their neighboring countrymen; the Italian complains of the Spanish disease, the Frenchman of the Italian disease, the Englishman of the French disease, the Turk of the Christian disease, and the Chinese simply says, "I'm velly [*sic*] sick and I was never sick before." Lenny, the Announcer, closes the scene:

> Thus in twelve years the disease had circled the globe and wherever white men went this new pox was his most adhesive companion. The doctors were appalled at first and were at a loss as to how to study the problems it presented. But they were surprisingly good scholars and learned many new things about their bewildered patient.[72]

These scenes demonstrate a curious juxtaposition between the implied immoral spread of syphilis and the attempt to historicize that information in a factual manner. The conquering soldiers agonize over the strange lesions that decorate the otherwise lovely bodies of the local young women, then flee in fear of the pox. Finally, one of the young women reveals her secret and a soldier rips away the bodice of another girl, revealing secondary sores. At this point, a large map of Europe appears upstage, obscured by the shadowy silhouette of "a woman dancing a slow, sensual dance"; it illustrates the proliferation of the disease onstage as "scarlet neon tubes spread like a feverish artery through the map of Europe."[73] Though Sundgaard clearly challenges the moral stigma that surrounds syphilis throughout much of the play, it is difficult to interpret this scene as forwarding that agenda. Indeed, it is all about prostitution and one-night stands. These individuals have no intention of marrying or settling down, and merrily spread the disease throughout the world in a mere 12 years. It is at this point that Sundgaard institutes a radical change in the path of the play. Instead of following the sexual antics of randy sailors and soldiers, he shifts to scientific exploration. For the rest of the play, earnest doctors endeavor to discover the source of syphilis and its treatments while the pitiable descendents of the morally questionable soldiers find their own lives destroyed by youthful passions, fleeting mistakes, or the actions of their parents.

A succession of scientists enters the play to follow the illness of a single, representative syphilitic patient, offering advice that ranges from rubbing mercury ointment on the sores to injections of the arsenic/chloride compound that became the foundation for the long-term treatment of syphilis. The first-act finale consists of Dr. Fritz Schaudinn's discovery of the corkscrew-shaped spirochete, the indicator of syphilis (See Figure 2).

Following scenes describe the series of medicinal advances related to the disease. The scientists are portrayed as kind, well-meaning men dedicated to ridding the world of this plague. The play proceeds to alternate between these scenes of scientific advancement and those of the personal tragedies that befall individuals infected with the disease, culminating in a demand for eradication. More importantly, the individuals that become the focus of these brief scenes throughout the rest of the play maintain their moral purity. A young man loses his mind and commits suicide rather than marry his fiancé when he learns that he has syphilis. A married man discovers that he has carried the disease for decades and that his disease likely blinded his young son. This combination resituates syphilis as an

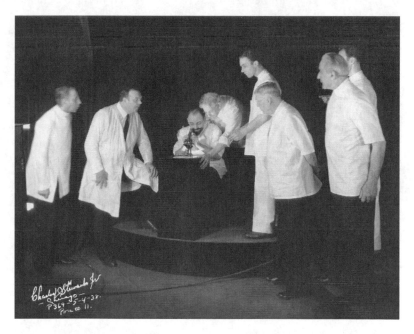

Figure 2   Scientists gather to observe as Dr. Fritz Schaudinn identifies the spirochete (the spiral-shaped indicator of syphilis) for the first time in the Chicago production of *Spirochete*. Federal Theatre Project Photographs, Special Collections & Archives, George Mason University.

equal-opportunity scourge affecting all classes, races, ages, and nationalities, and requiring scientific advancement and elimination. Interestingly, Sundgaard refrains from using young women as patients in the play; though women are infected with the disease, once past the nubile young women who cater to conquering heroes during the spread of the disease, the play represents only married women innocently infected by their husbands. As de Kruif argued in his comments on *Spirochete,* it was vital to focus on the widespread nature of syphilis in the play. In spite of studies and statistics that pointed to high concentrations of syphilis in specific populations, de Kruif and public health officials argued that anyone could contract the disease, and that its destruction would require the community as a whole to be a part of the cure. Thus, social responsibility became a pivotal element in *Spirochete.*

Sundgaard continues to challenge the prevailing morality in Act II, repeatedly reminding the audience of the costly errors of public perception. In the first scene a reformer arrives in the scientist's office and demands that a treatment be withheld from the public:

> REFORMER: Syphilis is the penalty for sin! You are about to remove that penalty and plunge the world into an orgy of sinful living. Man will be free to pursue his lustful impulses with no thought of any physical wrath being cast down on him. Think, Dr. Metchnikoff, what that will mean.
>
> METCHNIKOFF: You are a citizen, you say?
>
> REFORMER: Indeed I am.
>
> METCHNIKOFF: And you say that syphilis is the penalty for sin?
>
> REFORMER: Indeed it is.
>
> METCHNIKOFF: And it's a horrible ghastly penalty, you'll admit. A more horrible one could never be devised, could it?
>
> REFORMER: I could think of none worse.
>
> METCHNIKOFF: Then why in God's name hasn't it put an end to sin? [...] When all your moral prophylactics have failed to prevent the spread of this disease you wish to suppress a chemical one. [...] Telling people it's sinful hasn't stopped it from striking one out of every ten persons you meet on the street![74]

Here, science—personified in Dr. Metchnikoff—responds to the moral argument against treating syphilis. When the Reformer orders Metchnikoff to consider the future of American morality, he shouts, "Morals be damned! You think of their morals and I'll think of their illnesses. Now get out of here." After she departs, Dr. Metchinkoff refers to the reformer as a "prudish old witch" and a "fool, a stupid fool." In this moment, Sundgaard's public health statement parallels those that had been published widely by Parran, Bundesen, and de Kruif. For the scientists featured in the play and in real life, the moral imperative did not revolve around absolving sin; instead, their efforts focused on healing the physical ailments that devastated so many lives. Along with the eradication of syphilis, they hoped to stamp out the silence pervading the issue of venereal disease.

Sundgaard continues to attack the motivations for maintaining a collective silence regarding syphilis. Another example of this strategy appears in a series of short scenes played in quick succession in tight spotlights. These four exchanges again highlight the public perception of syphilis, this time from the woman's perspective. The women complain about the scientists, "respectable educated people" who print "silly articles in the medical journals" and waste their time seeking cures for the morally irresponsible. In addition to faulting the scientists for failing to "put their intelligence to something worthwhile," the women turn defensive when asked to take a syphilis test. Surprised and insulted, one young lady states, "They'd never dare ask a girl to do that. What do they think we are?" In the final monologue, a woman condemns the indecent politicians who would legislate venereal disease. She explains, "Just the other day someone was tellin' me that a guy named Saltiel was going to discuss syphilis right on the floor of the state legislature. Imagine that! My God, what's the world comin' to?"[75] These anonymous women express the common stigma against syphilis in a series of flashes that achieve multiple goals. First, Sundgaard reiterates the public perception, making it sound progressively more absurd each time it is spoken. The criticism is particularly pointed since these exchanges closely follow the Reformer's earlier defeat in the scientists' office. Sundgaard addresses the audience directly, ensuring that the audience becomes the pupil as its objections to a frank discussion on syphilis are systematically destroyed. As de Kruif suggests, Sundgaard extends the problem from the isolated population of syphilitics to the larger community.

Sundgaard raises the stakes in the next scene, intensifying the responsibility that the community as a whole—particularly those individuals who own and operate businesses—must take on in order to wipe out syphilis. No longer the task of the working class alone, Sundgaard implicates the business and manufacturing communities, holding them accountable for their failures regarding workers and their families. In this scene, a factory worker named John is fired due to inefficiency, falling behind, and causing minor accidents. Unknowingly infected with syphilis, John's health has declined, leading to these accidents; as his health goes, his employer, Mr. Thomas, fails him as well, firing him in spite of an otherwise successful ten years of employment. John leaves Thomas's office utterly defeated; he has a pregnant wife, a blind young son, and no means to earn a living.

The scene continues in John's home. His wife, Martha, reads a story to their son, Tony, in a gloomy portrait of domesticity. When John arrives, Martha sends Tony to bed then returns for her husband's disturbing news. In addition to losing his job, John has learned that his chronic fatigue is a symptom of a terrible illness:

> JOHN: Martha, I found out why Tony's blind!
> MARTHA: You—you found out why Tony's blind? Why?
> JOHN: Because of us. [. . . The doctor] said I've been sick for a long time, and most likely you've been sick, too.
> MARTHA: What kind of sickness?
> JOHN: The doctor said it's—it's syphilis. *(She stifles a scream while John continues.)* I didn't know I had it. I still don't know how I got it. I used to see those stories in the papers but I never dreamed it was me—me who might have it. He said it doesn't pain you at all. . . . It just comes quietly.[76]

The cruel reality of their situation is chilling. John and Martha discuss terminating her pregnancy and reveal that she has already miscarried twice; she says that they "couldn't have another Tony. Like Tony, he'd never have a chance." John replies despondently, "None of us had a chance, Martha, none of us had a chance!" and falls into her lap weeping.[77] While John and Martha go to the doctor and learn that treatment can give good odds to the unborn baby, irreparable damage has already been done; Tony is blind and John joins the masses of jobless in the Depression's relief lines. Sundgaard's original draft of the script, *Dark Harvest*, ends with this clear demonstration of the evils of syphilis and its victimization of otherwise good, hard-working people and their innocent children. In particular, the loss of John's job and the family's despair likely would have played to sympathetic FTP audiences, many of whom could have had similar experiences.

The produced version of the script adds an additional scene in which John's doctor confronts his former employer and explains that John's workplace difficulties were due to his illness. This frank discussion offers another opportunity to dispel popular sentiments about the individuals who would contract syphilis:

> THOMAS: I don't believe it. He's not the type.
> DOCTOR: The disease doesn't confine itself to types, Mr. Thomas. It's liable to strike anybody. John, in a rather unusual case, had gotten it innocently years ago. Because of ignorance of the symptoms he never even knew he had it.
> THOMAS: He must have.
> DOCTOR: No, he didn't.
> THOMAS: Well, I'm glad he's gone. We don't want any such men around this plant.[78]

Here, the doctor reminds both the audience and the employer that syphilis does not discriminate, and that the stigma against its victims is unfounded. In light of this, it is curious to note the doctor's specific statement regarding the "unusual" and "innocent" manner in which John contracted the disease; if the FTP is trying to remove the stigma, the implication that "usual" syphilis cases are contracted under guilty circumstances negates that effort. Regardless, the doctor continues to argue in John's favor, stating that the company could have played a role in curing John long ago if they had only required a blood test for venereal disease; this exchange also provides a forum for arguing in favor of the widespread implementation of corporate blood tests. In the time-honored argument for big business, the doctor finally points out that it is cheaper for a business to keep good employees than to continually train new workers and that businesses could save money by testing for syphilis as a way to screen for "potential inefficiency." He specifies that the process would only work if employees could be assured that their jobs would be in jeopardy only if they were diagnosed and failed to continue treatment. Thomas agrees to take the idea to the board of directors. John enters, "looking very strong and healthy," wins his job back, and the scene ends when the doctor assures John and Martha that their unborn child should be safe:

> Even the unborn are not beyond our reach. The baby will be all right. We can begin treatments as late as the fifth month and in ten cases out of eleven the child will be normal. The main thing is to test by the Kahn or Wassermann and find out where this disease is lurking. If John had been tested at the time of first employment he would have known this. If he had been tested at the time

of marriage it could have been prevented. Industry must do its part. The people and the State must do theirs...[79]

Here, the doctor not only informs the audience about the possibilities for saving unborn children from permanent disabilities, he again places responsibility for this action in the hands of the entire community. Employers, government, and the individual must all cooperate to stop the spread of syphilis and to cripple its far-reaching effects on the population. If any one of these community members had taken steps to test or treat those infected, John's illness would likely have been found early; he would not have lost his job, infected his wife, lost two unborn children, or caused his son's blindness. Notably, hope is restored. John's health returns, his job is reinstated, his wife undergoes treatment, and the unborn child's future is secure. With this scene, Sundgaard effectively addresses multiple concerns; he demystifies syphilis with the discussion about treatment options, reminds the audience that anyone can fall prey to the disease, and broadens the concept of "community" to include corporate entities.

The discussion on the legislative floor in the final scene again shows Sundgaard's attention to making syphilis a community and, ultimately, a national problem. Using rhetoric about truth and the "flagrant weakness of any system that allows its people to suffer year after year," the scene capitalizes on the strengths of the living newspaper genre by integrating these ideas with statistics comparing the dismal success rates of the United States to those of Sweden and Denmark. These European countries successfully dealt with syphilis; unlike the United States, Sweden "faced the facts and didn't try to hide them." Denmark likewise dealt with syphilis so successfully that only five babies were born stricken with symptoms annually, compared to 60,000 born in America. The legislators appeal to American—or at least Chicagoan—pride, "And I say that even if this isn't Sweden, even if this isn't Denmark, the things they can do, we too can do!" The Speaker calls for a vote and "everyone shouts aye in a great chorus which is taken up by the people." The Speaker bangs for attention and his request for "nay" votes is "drowned out."[80] In the midst of great applause, he announces that the amendment is adopted. He continues in the final words of the play:

Victory for this amendment is a battle just begun. Votes for a measure mean nothing unless translated into action by the people. This fight must go on until syphilis has been banished from the face of the earth. It can be done and will be done if you and you and you wish it so. The time has come to stop whispering about it and begin talking about it...and talking out loud![81]

Again, Sundgaard focuses the responsibility on the community as a whole, this time including the audience members as well. It is not hard to imagine this final monologue as the actor points to audience members throughout the theatre, shouting "you and you and you." Just like the disease, Sundgaard involves all levels of society, regardless of class, education, morality, or age; no one is free from the possibility of infection or the responsibility to contain and destroy that infection. The integration of knowledge and the obliteration of the culture of silence allow Sundgaard to shift the responsibility for the eradication of syphilis itself from a few "death-fighting" doctors to the community at large. This choice increased the relevance of the piece for the Chicago audiences and forced audience members to reevaluate their own perceptions of sexually transmitted diseases, their own responsibilities to their community, and their places within the nation.

CONCLUSIONS

The revisions in *O Say Can You Sing* point to a shift from pointed political satire to innocuous comedy. In contrast, *Spirochete* serves as a community indictment of those who would conceal knowledge, treatment, or action against syphilis. Both productions were wildly successful for the Chicago FTP, but for entirely different reasons. *O Say Can You Sing*, a conventional commercial success, broke box office records with the length of its run, if not with the amount that it earned based on ticket prices. It employed hundreds of actors, stagehands, writers, composers, choreographers, designers, and many more for months during rehearsal and helped the Chicago FTP to locate an audience in a city that had otherwise remained more or less indifferent to its efforts. More importantly, *O Say Can You Sing* integrated the talents of the FTP artistic personnel with content that was clearly created by and for Chicago. With this play, the Chicago FTP found an audience and a place in the community, rebuilding a troubled relationship with the all-powerful Mayor Kelly and ensuring the FTP could continue to operate in the Windy City.

Spirochete operated on a different level. It was not a box office success, though it did play for more than 30 performances and inspired a number of other productions throughout the country. Instead, *Spirochete's* success lay in its ability to gain a base of political and popular support; with *Spirochete*, the U.S. Surgeon General, the Chicago public health commissioner, public health author Paul de Kruif, Mayor Kelly's venereal disease control specialist, and even Illinois state legislators recognized the importance and potential of the FTP. Newspapers and magazines on both a local and national level lauded *Spirochete* not for its theatrical prowess (though some did reference that), but for its ability to educate the public; *Spirochete* "justified" the existence of the FTP, not only in Chicago but also in the United States. *Spirochete* demonstrated that a federally funded, national theatre could create socially vital, locally relevant theatre, and that these pieces had the potential to move between local and national venues. In spite of the admittedly commercial leanings of the Chicago FTP's administration, the project found itself in the midst of a work that made use of the exciting living newspaper form and pushed the artistic envelope (topically) while challenging preconceived expectations regarding the FTP's identity.

This exploration of *O Say Can You Sing* and *Spirochete* offers unique insight into the inner workings of the Chicago FTP as it attempted to establish itself in a city that was, at best, ambivalent toward its new FTP organization. The FTP faced difficult barriers in the Second City—often in direct opposition to those it would see in New York City—and only found its niche when it embraced the idiosyncrasies of the city itself. As I will argue in the following chapters, once the FTP stepped outside New York City, the challenge of locating an audience and a place within the community quickly became the highest priority. In Chicago, *O Say Can You Sing* and *Spirochete* effectively rose to the challenge; with these productions, the Chicago FTP demonstrated its potential to become a vibrant part of the local theatre community.

2. Demythologizing America: Past and Present Collide in Boston ᐁ

Boston is without an established theatre peculiarly its own. Those interested in the drama are dependent on visiting companies and are often disappointed when a play that has prospered in New York comes here.[1]

—*Philip Hale, Boston Theatre Critic*

In the summer of 1936, Flanagan formally requested the discontinuation of federal funds to the Boston FTP, and suggested that all personnel be transferred out of theatre and into recreation projects. The Boston FTP, the regional center of the Northeast, suffered repeated failures in its first year. In a letter to Massachusetts FTP director Leonard Gallagher, Flanagan could not quell her despair: "We have not one thing to show for a quarter of a million spent in Massachusetts [...] not a decent show, no equipment, no shop, no morale, no press, no research. The state director, under orders to keep peace, has been flabby and afraid."[2] This admission by the ever-persistent and optimistic Flanagan—that the Boston FTP was in such dismal shape that it would be more fruitful to abandon it entirely—speaks volumes about the severity of the obstacles faced in the city. Though her request to disband the Boston FTP was met with resistance on both the state and national levels, the project remained problematic. By 1938 the FTP had all but ceased to exist in Boston.

Flanagan devoted strikingly little attention to the activities of the FTP in the eastern region outside of New York City in *Arena*. Rather than promoting a program focused on original, locally relevant theatre created by and for Boston audiences, both Flanagan and contemporaneous critics focused on touring New York productions that captured audience attention along the eastern seaboard. Yasha Frank's famous adaptation of *Pinocchio*—a

Los Angeles creation performed by a New York City FTP—became "compulsory education for every child in Boston."³ Boston was, in many ways, the bastard child of the FTP; located far enough outside New York City that it was expected to act independently but close enough that it gained little in the way of attention or resources, the Boston FTP found itself constantly overshadowed by the New York City projects. While the Boston FTP certainly faced numerous problems ranging from a pervading anti–New Deal sentiment to censorship, its greatest challenge was in locating and pleasing its audience with high quality, locally relevant work. WPA officials worried that the Massachusetts FTP failed to earn the critical acclaim enjoyed by New York City units, even as they condemned ambitious or revolutionary work. Just as Mayor Kelly scrutinized the Chicago FTP for signs of political agitation, so too did the Massachusetts WPA monitor the Boston FTP for any hint of insurrection. As Paul Edwards, acting state administrator of the WPA, announced in the *Boston Evening Globe*, "The people of Massachusetts are going to have the type of plays they want—not the plays a small group wishes to promote. If there is any scandal on the federal drama project, I intend to get to the bottom of it and clean it up."⁴ An example of an antagonistic relationship between the WPA and FTP administrations, the Massachusetts FTP would find Edwards to be a formidable opponent.

This examination begins with a 1938 production that turned the proverbial tide for the Boston FTP, John Hunter Booth's *Created Equal*, and continues with Maud Wood Park's *Lucy Stone*. These productions demonstrate the Boston FTP's struggle for artistic legitimacy as well as its ability to capitalize on the rich history of Boston. *Created Equal* documents the promise of the Declaration of Independence and dramatizes the founding of the United States, while subverting the traditional approach to that history. *Lucy Stone* chronicles the life of one of the first suffragettes, the Massachusetts native Lucy Stone; it begins in her childhood and continues with her role as both abolitionist and women's rights advocate, her marriage to Henry Blackwell, the birth of her child, and the many struggles that characterized the early period of the women's rights movement. Both *Created Equal* and *Lucy Stone* serve as distinctive case studies, because they demonstrate solutions to some of the many challenges faced by the Boston FTP; these productions focused on dramatizing history rather than current events and did so in largely uncontroversial but newsworthy ways. More importantly, these productions promoted the Boston FTP for its audience—propelling it forward artistically while pleasing the Massachusetts WPA with their innocuous and respectable subject matter.

In order to fully realize the critical roles of *Created Equal* and *Lucy Stone*, it is first necessary to reveal key moments in the lengthy and traumatic journey to these productions. One of the first productions attempted by the Boston FTP was Maxwell Anderson's *Valley Forge*. A finalist for the Pulitzer Prize, *Valley Forge* documents General George Washington's frustration with Congress's lack of support as his troops starved over the long, bitterly cold winter—thus recording the darker side of the American Revolution. Flanagan hoped to send the play on a tour of New England "with a band in colonial costume playing colonial tunes in front of the theatre before curtain times, 'just as the old touring companies...used to do.' "[5] As Hiram Motherwell, regional director of the Eastern FTP, expressed in his regional report: "Don't think I've forgotten that we're going heavy on history and classics as well as straight entertainment. No experiments for New England!"[6] Motherwell's assessment demonstrated an acute awareness of the types of dramas that would eventually prove appealing to Bostonians. His emphasis on history, classics, and "straight entertainment," as well as the lack of experimentation, described a program that relied on conservative and proven successes rather than new works. While *Valley Forge* was certainly a well-respected theatrical piece that ultimately reinforced American patriotism, it also contained scenes in which major historical figures were portrayed as petty, cruel, and short-sighted, particularly when taken out of context. In light of this, the political and public reception to *Valley Forge* was unsurprising.

Boston had a strong and lengthy local tradition of censorship. The Watch and Ward Society, founded as the New England Society of the Suppression of Vice in 1873—and described by Will Rogers as "the Ku Kluxers of Boston literature"—institutionalized censorship in Boston.[7] By 1904, the Massachusetts State Legislature streamlined the process; it created a law that gave instant censorship power to city mayors, allowing them to "revoke theatre licenses for any reason whatsoever." When public support for the legislative power of censorship waned in the 1920s, the Catholic clergy stepped into the void. In 1927, Cardinal William O'Connor, one of the most powerful men in the city, launched a campaign against immorality in literature and the arts; this crusade saw works by Ernest Hemingway, Upton Sinclair, Voltaire, Henrik Ibsen, and dozens of others "Banned in Boston." One of the most infamous cases of Boston censorship occurred in 1929 when Mayor Malcolm Nichols targeted Eugene O'Neill's Pulitzer Prize–winning *Strange Interlude*. Though 50 Harvard professors banded together to protest the ban on O'Neill's play, Boston's reputation for literary prudery spread. Local newspaper critics worried that Boston would become the "subject of national and international contempt and ridicule" and noted that "Banned in Boston" was quickly becoming a national joke.[8]

Edwards envisioned his role as a mediator of public morality. When he received complaints about the upcoming production of *Valley Forge,* he appointed a board of censors to monitor the content of Boston FTP plays so that the good people of Massachusetts would not see plays that would offend their patriotic sensibilities. While Edwards withdrew his objections after hearing the evidence and approved the play for production, the public's reaction to the controversy was swift and severe. Rumors of scandal alienated the public and caused potential audiences to lose confidence in their newly founded Boston FTP.[9] Thus, it is not at all surprising that the people of Boston, ensconced within a city famous for—and fiercely proud of—its role in the American Revolution, responded in a less than supportive manner to this production that seemed to denigrate the historical figures they venerated. And so, even though Edwards recanted, the production of *Valley Forge* set the tone for the Boston FTP; Boston's primary FTP unit was damaged in both reputation and desire for creative risks. Two years later, when planning the production of *Created Equal,* a new play that would similarly question the political and social history of the nation, Blanding Sloan, director of the FTP's eastern region, would write, "Please bear in mind the VALLEY FORGE production, and the sad effects it had on the Boston public's attitude toward Federal Theatre Productions. The reaction in the public mind is bitter and very antagonistic."[10] Clearly the *Valley Forge* experience had long-term effects on the FTP in Boston. Flanagan maintained that this episode—which occurred so near the birth of the Massachusetts FTP—permanently scarred the project.

In addition to the potential for censorship, the Boston FTP also suffered from the stigma that affected many WPA projects in the Northeast—the humiliation associated with one's participation in WPA programs was so powerful that many of those who could have gained employment refused to have any part of it. Beginning in 1932, Boston city policy required anyone seeking relief to work for their unemployment checks in the city's Charity Building—nicknamed the "House of Horrors on Hawkins Street"—as frequently as four days a week, making it all but impossible to find external employment.[11] Worse, following the orders of Mayor James Michael Curley, the Boston Police launched a special probe that would investigate relief workers' bank accounts and pay surprise visits to families, effectively branding those on relief as "dishonest, parasitical, and without legitimate claim on public funds."[12] Jon B. Mack, FTP state director of Massachusetts, stated bluntly that the FTP "would never overcome the political stigma of the W.P.A." in Boston.[13] Local newspapers, most of which were vehemently anti–New Deal, similarly vilified the WPA and the arts projects, thus perpetuating the relief workers' disgrace. The *Boston Sunday Globe's* interpretation of a 1937 union picket of the WPA targeted the arts projects, stating that the "demonstrators yesterday were mostly members of the Federal arts projects"; though this behavior would have been more acceptable had the WPA cuts led directly to job loss for these individuals, the *Globe* explained that the arts strikers "were reduced in pay and were not given the kind of work they like to do."[14] While not openly hostile, this article painted relief workers—particularly those employed by the arts projects—as picky malcontents who demanded high salaries and particular jobs. Clearly, the newspapers would not help the Boston FTP adjust its public image after the controversy of *Valley Forge*.

Local newspapers contributed to a further public relations issue as well. In their description of the Copley Theatre, the Boston FTP's primary playing space, columnists emphasized the plush, classy surroundings. "Built for the elite of Boston," the *Boston Globe* explained, the Copley Theatre was remodeled expressly for the incoming "Broadway attractions" of the FTP.[15] Based on the former glory of the Copley Theatre, this impression was not necessarily historically inaccurate, but it misrepresented the FTP's goals as targeting "Broadway attractions" and the Boston elite, further alienating the FTP's intended audience. Between 1917 and 1923, when Henry Jewett directed the theatre and his own resident acting company, the Copley Theatre drew a "special audience, one interested in unfamiliar plays." Boston critic Philip Hale specifically commented on the audience's "genteel and sensitive ears" and emphasized their interest in a specific brand of high-quality, noncommercial, and pleasant play.[16] The Copley Theatre's location in the southwest corner of Copley Square, in the heart of Boston's Back Bay, and the fact that it had been home to this choosey audience suggests that the theatre catered to Boston's intellectual elite—those who had the means, desire, and daring to attend avant-garde, complex drama as well as clear opinions on appropriate subject matter. While it is certainly possible that some working-class audiences attended these productions, they were not the target audience, and had not been for decades prior to the arrival of the FTP.

Thus, the choice of the Copley Theatre as the Boston FTP's main venue created a contradiction in public perception and served as a metaphor for the battle that would plague the Boston FTP—the enduring struggle to attract its audience. Located in the wealthy Back Bay and in a theatre built by and for Boston's elite, the FTP seemed to cater to privileged Bostonians; yet Boston's elite, aside from offering the occasional endorsement or radio spot, would prove an unreliable support network for the Boston FTP. In contrast, the theatre's location and history as a privileged venue estranged the FTP's target audience—the working-class "people" who could not otherwise afford to attend the theatre. Effectively, both elite and working-class audiences shunned the Boston FTP because they felt that it had been created for the other. Simply overcoming the dishonor of relief work and producing theatre in places in which the working class would feel comfortable attending became a monumental task. When censorship, anti–New Deal newspapers, an unfriendly WPA state director, and a lack of confidence from the national FTP were added to the mix, the Boston FTP seemed to be headed for disaster.

DEMOCRACY CHALLENGED: RACE, CLASS, AND *CREATED EQUAL*

According to Flanagan, John Hunter Booth's *Created Equal* (1938) single-handedly turned the tide for the FTP in Boston, locating and speaking to Boston audiences for the first time.[17] Otherwise hostile theatre critics proclaimed that "every American should be shown this theatrical document."[18] This groundbreaking and contradictory production contested the foundations of American democracy even as it reinforced the prevailing racial sentiments of the 1930s. As a forerunner of "history from below," *Created Equal* reframed the history of the United States from the perspective of the masses, challenging audience members to reconsider their nation's past and minimizing the importance of venerated historical figures such as Thomas Jefferson and George Washington. At the same time, *Created Equal* failed to provide the same attention to the history of African Americans and slavery. Though slavery was certainly a pivotal issue leading up to and during the Civil War, and troubled race relations continued to plague the country through the twentieth century, *Created Equal* glossed over these problems and chose to focus on issues of class instead. Ultimately, these issues reveal the many competing tensions within the FTP—both as a local Boston theatre and as a federal entity—and its ability to critically address issues of class and race in American culture.

Created Equal stepped into a theatrical void for the Massachusetts FTP in 1938, playing to packed houses in Springfield, Salem, and Boston.

Created Equal tells the history of the United States of America, with an emphasis on the early period of nation formation. From the arrival of the Mayflower to the colonies' struggle against the tyranny of King George III and the English Parliament, through Shay's Rebellion, the Whiskey Rebellion, the Dred Scott Case, and ending with a visit to the Roaring 20s and the decline of the Depression, *Created Equal* condenses nearly 200 years of history into approximately three hours of stage time. Both the subject matter and the approach were particularly pertinent to Boston audiences.

Created Equal marked the beginning of the FTP's effort to create locally relevant theatre in Boston. With this production, the FTP took a chance by focusing on the history that was so ingrained in Boston's own identity as a city. The process of adapting this history to the stage capitalized upon and then destabilized that history so as to appeal to specific working-class audience members and their sense of national pride. Tracing the themes of freedom and equality, as well as the struggles of the working class against landowners, *Created Equal* placed the FTP's target audience squarely in the driver's seat of nation formation. It would be the working class that traded their lives for the new nation's freedom during the Revolutionary War, championed the rights of women and slaves, and battled the prop-ertied class for the rights promised by the Declaration of Independence. Hence, as the play underscored, the blood and sweat of the workers created the United States of America. Yet while *Created Equal* focuses explicitly on property ownership and class, exposing the hierarchical structure that takes power from the poor, the issue of race appears only sporadically, thus leaving this powerful influence invisible. Indeed, it is surprising that an organization that is often characterized as so progressive in terms of the representation of race on stage so clearly missed this opportunity. Since the FTP's famous Negro Units have garnered much scholarly attention as forward-thinking examples of race relations in the theatre, it is also vital to unpack the ways in which race was represented on stages of the main-stream units. *Created Equal* serves as a particularly rich case study for the exploration of the representation of race on FTP stages because it blended personnel from the Negro, Italian, and Vaudeville Units; in fact, Flanagan deemed this combination of units and peoples one of the great successes of the Boston FTP.[19] Hence, this analysis will juxtapose the treatment of class and race in the Boston FTP's production of *Created Equal*.

The intention of the FTP administration with respect to *Created Equal* was first broadcast in a publicity blitz that preceded the opening of *Created Equal* in all three Massachusetts cities. In addition to the typical promotions in newspapers, on the radio, and through the recruitment of local VIPs, activities for the Springfield premiere of *Created Equal* included an extensive speaking tour to local schools, women's groups, and service clubs, as well as a parade with eight drum corps (though only two appeared for the parade because of thunderstorms) and a squad of "motorcycle police." The parade marched up and down Main Street and directly into the theatre.[20] The ever-present radio interviews emphasized the play's basis in patriotism and history. As Jon Mack explained, *Created Equal* was:

> a historical cavalcade of the Birth and Growth of the American spirit—not only of 1776, but of 1938.... This intense drama, is a crowning achievement in stage annals, embodying an intensely dramatic flesh and blood parade of major events, which has colored the entire pattern of the Birth—the Growth—the America of Today.[21]

Though Mack highlighted the "Birth and Growth of the American spirit," *Created Equal* revolved around the presumption that American society was not, in fact, grounded in equality. FTP administrators from both the local and national levels challenged the execution of Booth's thematic purpose repeatedly, from the first moment that the play was accepted for FTP production until just a few days before it opened. Booth reiterated his premise each time, finally distilling it bluntly for the national administration:

1. The Declaration of Independence promised equality.
2. The Constitution established a propertied class.
3. Amendments to the Constitution are slowly fulfilling the promise of the Declaration.[22]

The failed promise of the Founding Fathers—equality—surfaced repeatedly, both in the dramatic text and in the rhetoric surrounding the production of *Created Equal*. Unlike the traditional mythologizing of American history, featuring a few individuals—often "great" white men— who bring about societal change through their intelligence, foresight, physical prowess, moral strength, and perseverance, *Created Equal* portrayed events and people in a way that simultaneously honored and challenged the Constitution, the Bill of Rights, and the ability of the American way of life to adhere to those founding ideals. It is interesting to note that, in spite of this potentially volatile revision of American history, the active censoring committees in Boston accepted the play without question. In contrast, the actors of a New Jersey production revolted over the play; they submitted a petition arguing that the unorthodox choice to make the central character the chorus of the working class was "Un-American."[23]

Even as *Created Equal* paid tribute to the contributions of the working class and enumerated their grievances with the classist system that dominated American culture and politics, it effectively removed representations of African Americans as sentient beings from the American history in the play. In order to delve into this contradiction fully, I will examine two versions of *Created Equal* below. The original and most widely available version does not match the production programs for Salem, Springfield, or Boston, and was probably not produced. The revised edition features stage directions that describe stage locations, specific lighting elements, and a floor plan that coincides with both production photos and critics' descriptions.[24] The two versions contain some fascinating changes in the handling of race and class. When complemented by the correspondence surrounding these changes, the two texts provide insights into the cultural perceptions of class and race in 1930s Boston, as well as the Boston FTP's ability and desire to transgress those views. The examination of the two versions of *Created Equal* allows an exploration of the ways in which "equality" is defined in this play, and by implication, in the FTP. It is particularly revealing to consider the ways in which class and race overlap even as they are pulled apart in this play. What comment does *Created Equal*, and by extension the FTP, really make on both the historical figures represented and the contemporaneous U.S. government of 1938, and, from this, what can we glean about democratic formation?

Booth's attention to resituating history from the perspective of the working class is clear before the play even begins. In the explanation that would so offend the New Jersey actors, the cast of characters lists the named roles in the production, then concludes:

> In addition to speaking "bits" listed are mobs and crowds with important omnes exclamations—soldiers, Supreme Court Justices, unseen members of the Constitutional (or Federal) Convention.
>
> It may be said that the mobs and crowds are the most important members of the cast.[25]

Mobs and crowds gather throughout the play; initially they worship and defer to those in power, offering their allegiance, contributions, and lives. As the play continues, the tensions between the landowners and the landless escalate; *Created Equal* thus becomes a play about economic and social divisions in a country that was supposed to have neither. It focuses not on the historical figures who write or ratify the Constitution, the president who unifies the newly formed country with the Bill of Rights, nor the president who emancipates the slaves, but on the masses of commoners—soldiers, villagers, and the proud, headstrong symbol of the American frontier spirit, a fictional everyman named Phillip Schuyler. The trials and tribulations of the common man are the heart of the play, exemplified by the efforts of several generations of Schuylers, all attempting to make lives for themselves in a country that (theoretically) accepts the weak, poor, and uneducated on equal footing with the powerful, wealthy, and educated leaders. Even the "Radio Talk" script of approved answers to standard interview questions reflected the populist spirit of the play. When asked, "Who are the principals?" the speaker was to respond: "Out of the past will emerge for the moment such figures as: Washington, Jefferson, Hamilton, Franklin, Lincoln, Grant, Roosevelt—Yet the author has made them secondary to the people who are actually the leading figures in this creation of a nation."[26] This pattern repeats throughout the play. Thus, while it began as a traditional story of American history, replete with the major leaders and events, *Created Equal* became a deviant drama that emphasized the contributions, exertions, failures, and successes of the working class and challenged the assumed rights of those in power.

Both the original and revised (produced) versions of *Created Equal* begin with an abstract prologue in which a group of tattered, underfed peasants gape at the "seat of Power," which is dressed on stage with the elaborate heraldry of a throne. A voice emanates from behind the throne, mocking the people for "Endowing with divinity/[their] own creation," while declaring that "the Many,/[are] trespassers on land that gave [them] birth."[27] Both versions of the play portray the peasants as witless automatons—"Fools and slaves!"—who arbitrarily advance certain people to positions of power in society; in turn, the people endow the chosen ones with both symbolic and actual power based on birth, the divine right of kings, and/or their own ability to take and maintain that power. With this opening, Booth presents a challenge—not to those *in* power—but to those who would offer up their agency to kings, presidents, the aristocracy, or other authorities. Whether or not these rulers prove to be good or just (however those terms may be applied), *Created Equal*, like the Declaration of Independence, implies that all citizens are responsible for ensuring that their leaders adhere to the inalienable rights that all people should be granted, regardless of class. It is important to note that, at this point in the play, class is the only distinguishing feature among the individuals present on stage; there are no representations of race, ethnicity, or religion, and gender is confined to clothing differences in this scene.

The seat of power displays visions of authority enforced by physical violence and intellectual oppression in both versions of the play. It stands in front of a "voluminous canopy of royal purple sprinkled with stars, crescent moons, bees, fleur-de-lis, swastikas, etc.," symbols of royalty and power over thousands of years. An enormous executioner, dressed in scarlet and leaning on a headsman's axe, and a soldier in full battle armor who rests "idly on his sheathed sword," grace either side of the throne.[28] The revised version, however, adds another class to the mix. In addition to the Seat of Power and the peasant subjects, a group of Beaux, Belles, and Substantial Citizens stand on a platform near the throne. They remain separate from the villagers, who are herded together on the lowest level of the stage. This addition heightens the class disparity present in the nonruling classes even as it implies that both working class and elite are guilty of blindly following condescending, pitiless leaders. This scene challenges the system that endows specific individuals with unassailable power, questioning the rights of those in power as well as the practices of those who relinquish power over their own lives. In this way, *Created Equal* interrogates the authority of the government, the class system (supposedly nonexistent in the United States), and the elevated stature of the landed class, but refuses to let the working class off the proverbial hook.

In a trend that he continues throughout the revised version, Booth further expands the group of powerless individuals by integrating the audience into the cast of landless peasants. Indeed, Booth makes a conscious effort to cast the audience as a character in the play at numerous moments. At the end of the first scene, when the actors are chanting "Long live the King!" and the Voice representing Power laughs mockingly, a stage direction suggests that "the audience be made a part of the above scene by placing loud speakers in back of the theatre auditorium, so that the chants and murmurs of the actors on the stage are reproduced out front, as if coming from the auditorium."[29] Stage directions further note that the poor, landless Villagers—like the audience—are located in darkness while all the other levels of society are illuminated by some degree of light. When characters announce the newly written *Constitution of 1787* to the townspeople in a later scene, they actually address the audience directly "as if they were the villagers at a town meeting." Finally, the working-class hero of the play, Phillip Schuyler, regularly enters from the audience while the Citizens, Belles, and Beaux remain on the stage throughout the play, thereby reinforcing the audience's identification with Phillip Schuyler and the working-class villagers. These textual choices, unlike the selection of the renovated Copley Theatre building, speak to a knowledge of the Boston audience; the FTP audience would likely have consisted of the Depression-era equivalent of the poor, landless Villagers—predominantly working class, uneducated Irish Catholics who had little political or economic clout until James Michael Curley's—the self-billed "Mayor of the Poor"—1922 election established Boston as "an Irish domain, a protected fortress against outsiders unsympathetic to an ethnic, working class community."[30] These political considerations extended only to the Irish though, leaving out women, non-Irish-immigrant populations, Jews, Protestants, and African Americans.

Created Equal accentuates class divisions; every scene in which the Citizens, Belles, Beaux, and Villagers are shown sees them grouped according to their relative levels of wealth, property, and power—the same stratifications that identified the Irish, Italians, Eastern Europeans, and African Americans in Boston in the 1930s. As rehearsals and revisions continued, Booth added lines and stage directions to reinforce the humanity of the lower classes; specifically, he did not want them to become a mindless mob. The director's report fleshed out the importance of the working-class "mobs" as well: "The careful handling of the mobs cannot be stressed too emphatically. Never let them become a noisy rabble. They are the Principals of the play. [...] They represent the spirit of America, protesting at abuses, striving towards the promised freedom."[31] As the director so succinctly argued, *Created Equal* painted the working class as the "spirit of America."

As the play progresses, Phillip Schuyler, farmer, soldier, and hero, emerges as a symbol of American idealism and the physical representation of the American frontier spirit.[32] In the search for unfettered freedom, he forsakes his role as a gentleman and captain in the Continental Army to move west and become a farmer in Pennsylvania. In a discussion with his love interest, Anne Hammersley, he explains his discontent:

> And this government is to be "the rule of gentlemen". I know. All I've heard since I've been [in the city] is talk of "courts", "Aristocracy", "upper and lower classes". I saw this coming when they gave us a new Constitution. That's why I went West. I was sick of the old world system. I wanted to escape from it- from this sort of thing. [...] And we had such an opportunity to do away with privilege and distinction.[33]

Though Phillip takes the opportunity to woo Anne during this exchange, he refuses to be dissuaded from his task; his community elected him to speak on its behalf in the matter of the 1794 Whiskey Rebellion. Unfortunately, Phillip's attempts to gain an audience with Congress or Alexander Hamilton (Secretary of the Treasury) are stymied, and he returns to Pennsylvania unheard. In both the original and revised versions of *Created Equal*, the military brutally arrests all the Pennsylvania farmers associated with the rebellion, injures many, and jails them in Boston for nearly six months without trial. In a last-minute revision for the Boston production—which is not present in either script, but which is attached to a letter in the NARA collection and included in the program—Booth replaces a scene in which military officers debate the use of force in the arrests of the tax-dodging farmers with a confrontation between Phillip Schuyler and Alexander Hamilton. In the new scene Phillip attempts to convince Hamilton of the validity of the farmers' claims. He argues that the tax is unjust because the farmers cannot afford to pay it and feed their families, but Hamilton remains unmoved; he coldly states, "Such is the law, fellow. You Western farmers will do well to obey it, - and without delay...If the tax is not paid immediately, it will be collected at the point of the bayonet. That is my last word."[34] Hamilton, a Federalist Elite, personifies the shortcomings of the Declaration of Independence and the land-holding class.

The parallels between Phillip Schuyler's complaints about the tax on whiskey and those of the Boston working class—particularly those who saw little in the way of government relief—are striking. In his argument with Hamilton, Schuyler complains that taxes are "a heavy burden for us," finally noting that "many of us lack funds. If we could be given more time...."[35] Boston boasted the dubious distinction of charging the highest taxes in the country in the 1930s, earning the state the nickname "Taxachusetts."[36] Not unlike the Whiskey Boys, nearly half of the working-class families in Boston lacked funds due to unemployment or underemployment during the Great Depression. Those who managed to keep their jobs saw their pay slashed repeatedly as the Depression deepened and employers reduced expenses. It is not hard to believe that a large portion of the audience would have sympathized with Schuyler's reasoning. Moreover, Mayor Curley's decisive and violent reactions to working-class demonstrations created an environment in which many Bostonians feared demonstrating more than they feared starvation. As one African American man explained when asked why he was observing (not participating in) an "indignation meeting," he replied, "We may need the bonus, but we're not crazy."[37] By choosing to voice working-classes concerns through the historical lens of the Whiskey Rebellion, writer/director John Hunter

Booth appealed to a suppressed need in his audience, thus bridging the gap between an audience that was largely working class and the Boston FTP. These decisions effectively demonstrate the class inequities in both general terms for the country and through specific allusions to the city of Boston.

While nearly every scene revolves around power and class in some way, race—certainly affected by both of these foci—is rarely mentioned. Indeed, given the fact that Flanagan touted this production as a triumph of collaboration because of the integration of members of the Negro and Italian units, this gap highlights the contradictions within the FTP regarding racial equality on stage. And so, while *Created Equal* successfully resituated the traditional American history with regard to class, the production failed to integrate a similarly transgressive history of the role African Americans played in the construction of American identity.

When Phillip Schuyler first appears, he is in the company of the wealthy Hammersley family. In the original version of the play, a young slave distributes tea in a silver tea set while Phillip and Upton Hammersley discuss the political ideas of the newly formed United States of America. Upton presents the Tory perspective, citing the sizeable amount of money that Jefferson and his fellow patriots owed the crown, and arguing that the revolution was little more than a way for the debtors to default on their loans. Schuyler's retort—that of the classic Stage Yankee—lacks Hammersley's sophistication, but demonstrates an almost naïve belief in his ideals; he replies, "There's somewhat [*sic*] in the air of America that won't let a man acknowledge anyone his superior, - except it be a better man." The irony of this affirmation of freedom, stated as Hammersley's slave stands quietly in the background, could not be lost on an audience. In fact, Booth reinforces this power dynamic following Schuyler's departure. A frustrated Hammersley takes a sip of his now cold tea, thrusts his teacup in the direction of his slave, and yells, "Here, you black symbol of American equality, - get me a fresh cup."[38] This powerful conclusion, focused on a compelling case study, draws attention to the distinct lack of equality for African Americans. However, Booth changed this scene entirely for the revised version, thus omitting any representation of an individual African American on stage.

In the revised version, Phillip remains in the company of the Hammersleys, but they walk together through the streets of Boston instead of meeting in the Hammersley home. In this scene the individual slave makes no appearance; he has been cut entirely and replaced by canonical images of African American slaves described only in the stage directions: "Three male negro slaves, each bearing a sack on his shoulder. [...] They are in [the] charge of an overseer who carries a whip. The procession files across platform, down steps, and off L.U." Little more than props, these slaves act as a group with no individuality or personal identity. Upton waves a hand at them dismissively as he indicts American equality: "All men are created equal! *(He snorts angrily)* Equal! And thousands of blacks in slavery to you Americans." Phillip simply replies, "Jefferson would free all slaves."[39] While the slave in the original version was named Pompey, the three slaves in this scene have no apparent ties to any of the major characters. They have no names, no voices, no characters, and have been reduced to little more than symbols. It is interesting to note that Schuyler's feelings on slavery seem to be linked to an institution in which individuals have little or no power over their lives, while Hammersley (a slave owner in the original version) uses the concept of slavery to criticize the hypocrisy of the newly formed United States of America. The two major changes between the versions—the replacement of the individual slave with anonymous representatives and the removal of Hammersley's own personal slave—suggest a movement toward the depersonalization of the issue. These nameless slaves have no opportunity to resist; instead, the critique of slavery develops in a roundabout way through Hammersley's attack on Patriot ideology.

Several scenes later, slavery surfaces again as a topic of discussion. It is 1787 and the delegates of the Constitutional Convention are in the midst of heated debate. The issue of slavery arises alongside debates over property ownership, voting rights, the right to defend oneself, and the composition of the U.S. government. North Carolina delegate Hugh Williamson proposes the infamous Three-Fifths Compromise, while Pennsylvania delegates James Wilson and Gouverneur Morris reject the concept. Morris asserts that he "never will concur in upholding domestic slavery. It is a nefarious institution." Finally, James Madison states the obvious; the states are divided "from the effects of their having or not having slaves."[40] Booth refrains from changing this scene in the revision. Again, note that no African Americans—slave or free—are represented in this scene. So while the topic of inequality through race is at the forefront of at least some of the scenes in *Created Equal*, there is reticence to engage it in its most antagonistic dimension—from the perspective of African Americans.

A slave auction scene returns the issue of slavery and race relations to prominence in a moment that remains unchanged between the two versions. A banner—"Prime Negroes for Sale"—hangs over a small platform. On it, three slaves are auctioned off to a group of wealthy, prominent citizens. The Auctioneer's descriptions of the slaves parallel those of livestock: "as fine a piece of stock as you'll find in New York"; "good natured, well-tempered, no marks"; a fine "specimen." A young woman is "tame as a lamb. She'll eat out o' your hand." The Auctioneer proceeds to show off her head and teeth and renames her Amanda. Juxtaposed against the slave auction is the arrival of General Washington and the imminent swearing-in ceremony of the first president of the United States. Like the slaves in the previous scene, these individuals never speak. The only independent action that any takes is the woman, who refuses to open her mouth to show off her teeth until the Auctioneer threatens her. According to the stage direction, she "meets the Auctioneer's threatening eyes, -hesitates, and then breaks into a loud, mirthless, laugh, throwing back her head and revealing her teeth." No one remarks on this challenge to white authority, as Washington's arrival cuts the auction short.[41] In the friction of this juxtaposition, it is almost as if Amanda laughs at the idea of equality available to her in this new, free country. Amanda's resistance—her "loud, mirthless, laugh"—lives as one of the only moments in *Created Equal* in which an African American character speaks of his or her own volition. Amanda's laugh serves as an eloquent rejection of the slave auctioneer's authority over her; her refusal to display her teeth and her subversion of his command demonstrates her ability to resist. Unfortunately, Amanda's strength and spirit stand out as unique in *Created Equal;* as the play continues, it returns to repeated representations of silent (and silenced) African Americans.

Slaves again appear as nameless and voiceless in the second act. In a brief prelude to the political battle that would end in the Missouri Compromise, a half dozen slaves cross the stage "in single file, chained to one another by ankle irons...ragged and barefoot," driven by two overseers who carry thick whips. Two young African Americans accompany the slaves on violins with "frenzied fiddling," capering around the slaves as the overseers demand, "Sing, you niggers, sing! Show folks you're happy, damn you! Sing, you black cattle—sing!"[42] They crack their whips to emphasize the point, and the fiddling of the children continues through the discussion surrounding the Missouri Compromise, and later, the Kansas–Nebraska Act of 1854, which repealed the Missouri Compromise and made slavery optional in territory north of the Mason-Dixon line. Again, none of these slaves are written as individuals. Each remains property—the commodity that has led to the system of the have's and the have not's—and thus symbols of the failure of the Founding Fathers and the Declaration of Independence.

To this point in the play, it is possible that Booth's representation of the nameless, voiceless slaves is an attempt to poetically represent the condition of the African American community during the era of slavery.

Though admittedly problematic, this removal of African American individuality and voice parallels the social and cultural situation in which slaves would have lived. Moreover, Booth's juxtaposition of horrific slave conditions, encapsulated within the "frenzied fiddling" and demands to "show folks you're happy," place slaves literally in the background of the congressional debates that would determine the fates of hundreds of thousands of African Americans. However, it is valuable to note that Booth seldom deviates from the silent enactment of traditional scenes of subjugation; with the exception of Amanda's act of retaliation, African Americans only appear when driven across the stage by overseers or auctioned to the wealthy elite. Though the reduction of African American representations to silent symbols that simply enact traditional scenes of subjection could be considered an attempt on the part of the playwright to embody the condition of slavery on stage, the final scene representing an African American demonstrates a departure from this potential interpretation.

The trial of Dred Scott offers perhaps the most potential for the representation of African American agency. This is the only time an African American character appears in *Created Equal* in a named role (other than Amanda, who was named by the Auctioneer) and the only time an African American character speaks in either the original or revised scripts. Dred Scott defers to his lawyer and introduces himself to the Supreme Court judges by saying, "I'se Dred Scott. But I dunno what for they're all makin' this excitement over a po' old nigger like me."[43] This suggests that Scott fails to understand not only why his case has come before the Supreme Court but also the larger social implications. In his own words, he is just a "po' old nigger" unworthy of "excitement." In the original version, Scott never speaks again. He hears and understands the ruling and ends the scene with a defeated slump of his shoulders. In the revised version, Scott speaks one more time. He asks his lawyer to interpret the Supreme Court's ruling, "Does that mean I'se free, boss?" When his lawyer tells him no, Scott's "head sinks, his shoulders sag."[44] The character of Dred Scott shows no sense of agency; he does not seem to have initiated this court battle and fails to understand the ruling on his own. Indeed, Scott must be told what the ramifications of the court's decisions are for his own life, even though he witnesses the ruling. This reaction again reveals the way in which the text continually disempowers the African American figures it represents. The emphasis in both versions of these scenes remains on the judges, who attempt to balance their tenuous positions of power with the rising national tensions preceding the Civil War. In the original version, Booth implies that the morally corrupt judges will make their decision based on the outcome of the presidential election. While this element disappears in the revision, the judges remain the center of the scene. Scott's presence is perfunctory. The reduction of this pivotal historical figure to a character that neither initiates nor understands his role in American history demonstrates that the Boston FTP was not yet ready to portray a nuanced, richly layered portrait of slavery.

Further complicating the representations of race in *Created Equal*, Booth draws parallels between the slaves and the working class. When Phillip Schuyler is arrested for his role in the Whiskey Rebellion, he is driven through a gauntlet of elite whites in a scene that is reminiscent of the chained slaves walking across the stage earlier in the play. This strong, independent pioneer loses his freedom, home, and family when he is arrested, and the officers beat him with guns and wooden sticks when he attempts to speak up for his own rights. Like the slaves, Phillip has no rights at this point. The jeers of the wealthy elite reduce him to an animal; they call Phillip and the other Whiskey Boys "vile wretches," "Filthy Swine," and "Dirty Dogs," then threaten them with a lynching.[45] After six months in jail, Phillip is released and sent home to die from his untreated injuries. I suggest that Booth's reduction of Phillip Schuyler and the working class to this level leaves the African American slaves with no place in this drama of American equality. The representation of slavery is effectively usurped by the white working class, again leaving the actual institution of slavery and the African American characters as little more than symbols of equality gone wrong.

The final scene of the play brings these issues into sharp relief. It serves as a blatant call to arms for the working class while avoiding most mention of African Americans as players in the creation of American history. Both extant versions of the play end in "any American city, 1938" and feature a veritable army of workers, each of whom has a job and a paycheck because of Roosevelt's New Deal. This, however, is where the similarities end. The original version of this scene is chanted as the workers hammer, saw, and dig in a rhythm that mirrors the forced cadence of the voices. Written in verse, the scene reads as if the workers are part of an assembly line, the individual voices unimportant:

1ST LABORER: Rich man!
2ND LABOREr: Poor man!
3RD LABORER: Beggar man!
4TH LABORER: Thief!

1ST CARPENTER: Doctor!
2ND CARPENTER: Lawyer![46]

Unlike the grateful WPA workers typically memorialized in FTP dramas, many of these men are not pleased to simply have jobs. They are the "Depression's victims"—a "warning" to all who would attempt to elevate themselves above their fellow Americans. Before the Depression they were doctors and lawyers, the "fat" and "sleek" who regarded the "lowly bum" or "hungry beggar" with contempt. Now they too are casualties of the whims of the Great Depression; they know "the bitterness / of poverty's despair." These characters believe that the problem lies with the system of government itself—a system that compromises the original ideals of the Founding Fathers. Because of these concessions, the "army of the unemployed," together with the audience:

> Have sought to solve with you,
> The problem of our national life.
> But this expedient, - *(He waves a hand towards group at back)*
> This sop to idle millions
> Is not the answer.[47]

These workers designate the WPA as a "sop to millions," "a compromise." Just as the Founding Fathers failed to follow through on the promise of the Declaration of Independence and made concessions in order to come to the terms stated in the Constitution, so too did the WPA focus on short-term solutions. Indeed, within the terms Booth defines in *Created Equal*, the WPA itself was the result of the Founding Fathers' failures. This scene lacks an overall sense of hope that the country can be redeemed without another revolution, this time fought as a class-based civil war. This ending, in its bitter condemnation of both the Founding Fathers and the current administration, and in its call to arms, is reminiscent of the grievances that brought the colonies to revolution to begin with; this time, though, if the most vocal rabble-rouser succeeds, the war will end in nothing short of a socialist utopia.

In contrast, the revised version begins with the workers "erecting a scaffolding on the spot where the throne of the first scene stood, and near it laborers are building a roadway with picks and shovels"; here, the WPA workers literally build the skeleton of a different power structure atop the old (See Figure 3).[48] While many of the workers are still former doctors and

Figure 3   This final scene from *Created Equal* shows the workers of the nation; former doctors, lawyers, and businessmen are now united with individuals from all professions and trades as WPA workers. They literally rebuild the nation in this final scene, as is shown by the structure they have created in the background. NARA, "*Created Equal* Production Bulletin, Boston, Mass.," NARA, E937, Box 441.

lawyers, they seem happy to be working and embrace the leveling of classes enacted by the WPA. They see themselves as "pioneers of the new economy," with a collective goal in their shoveling, picking, and sawing; these workers are clearing slums, building homes, and pioneering a new form of government scathingly referred to by the single malcontent as "The United States of Uptopia [*sic*]." This time, though, the workers shout down the complainer. They compliment Roosevelt's efforts on behalf of the working man, claiming that the great government clean up is already in progress as an "army of shovellers" clears away the broken profit system, uproots injustice, cuts down special privileges, and weeds out class consciousness. Even the argument that the government only provided jobs to prevent a worker revolution is met with an immediate defense of President Roosevelt and the New Deal.[49] The workers go back to work, harder than before, talking as they do so:

> 1ST GROUP: With pick, with shovel—Hi yah!
> 2ND GROUP: With hammer, with saw—Hi yah!
> 1ST GROUP: We'll build a Commonwealth
>   of true Democracy.

2ND GROUP: Where men shall live in peace,
thrive and know rich content
as brothers.
1ST WORKMAN: That was the original idea, brother, and
we're sticking to it. Yes, sir, we'll get there yet.[50]

The 1st Workman, the primary speaker in both the original and revised versions, shows the idealism and faith of the symbolic Phillip Schuyler with these words. Unlike the unhappy workers complaining of repeated compromises that damned the country in the original version, this group looks to the future with optimism. Certainly, priorities were out of line in the past, but the new American order, with President Roosevelt at the helm, places "human welfare before cash dividends;" the American spirit is "unconquerable!"

Returning to the play's link between slavery and the working class, the final scene refrains from any mention of inequities with regard to race. While the concept of slavery is referenced twice, neither occasion refers to African American history in any way. Instead, slavery becomes a metaphor for the ways in which the working class have been obligated to the wealthy: "Scorning the pettiness of money-changing. Demanding the full life—the life set free from what enslaves life." Here again, the play reduces the stature of the working class so that African American slaves have little or no place in the social structure. As the scene continues, the same speaker demands, "Is the American spirit the slave of gold?" A challenge to the characters on stage and the individuals in the audience, this question commands action. The final line of the play, shouted by all the characters onstage and broadcast to the audience via loudspeaker, orders the audience to prove their spirits are free from the dangers of unrestrained capitalism. To do so, they must show the world that "government of the people, by the people, and for the people, shall not perish from the earth."[51]

Created Equal was made for Boston. It capitalized on the national history that was relevant to Boston's identity, targeted the potential FTP audience, and made the Boston FTP a reality. In the reviews of *Created Equal,* several critics noted that the play was "one of the most ambitious undertakings of the Federal Theatre of Massachusetts" and "deserve[d] to rank as one of the most [...] successful enterprise[s] of the Massachusetts branch."[52] Like so many pivotal moments in history, though, its failings reveal as much about the contemporaneous society as do its successes. *Created Equal* certainly resituated American history in a way that appealed to the working-class audiences that had heretofore ignored FTP offerings in Boston, appropriating

American history in a way that allowed the voices of the working class to emerge from the silence. However, this success draws attention to the failures of representing race in *Created Equal*. In this way, *Created Equal* was a curious conundrum of the Boston FTP. In its ability to focus on American history and its approach to class disparities, the Boston FTP demonstrated a connection to and knowledge of its audience; its inability to forward issues of race in a similarly nuanced manner was a missed opportunity.

CAN'T GET BLOOD FROM A STONE: BOSTON'S PRODUCTION OF *LUCY STONE*

According to several newspaper articles, including one written by Flanagan herself, the success of *Created Equal* was to be followed with an entirely new type of drama. Because of the local interest in the historical significance of Boston dating back to the formation of the United States, the Boston FTP would continue to focus on the great American past. Again, the rich historical tapestry of Boston itself provided the impetus for the FTP's next dramatic innovation, one similar in many ways to that of the medieval pageant wagons. The FTP proposed a "progressive historical play in which the audience move[d] from Boston Common, to Fanueil Hall to Old South Church," and in which the FTP would evoke the history of the region by capitalizing on these specific locations rather than attempting to recreate them in the theatre.[53] While this particular pageant did not come to fruition, the Boston FTP continued under the twin constraints of creating exciting, locally relevant drama while refraining from controversial or potentially offensive pieces. Moreover, the national atmosphere was changing as 1938 became 1939; as the United States was drawn inexorably closer to World War II and the Depression showed signs of dissipating, anti–New Dealers sensed weakness in Roosevelt's pet program and began targeting the FTP. Because of this undesirable attention, the national administration was desperate for a show that would simultaneously attract crowds and demonstrate the vitality and social importance of the FTP in a manner that could become a suitable example for Congresspersons hoping to bring down the project. Maud Wood Park's *Lucy Stone* had the potential to satisfy each of these requirements.

Lucy Stone seemed to be ideal for the Boston FTP; as the program explained, among her many achievements, Lucy Stone was the:

First Massachusetts woman to take a college degree, became the champion of women's rights in this country, lectured to immense audiences all over the nation between 1847 and 1857, headed the call for the first national Woman's Rights Convention, [and] founded and edited the Woman's Journal of Boston which was the principal woman suffrage paper of America for half a century.[54]

Based on Alice Stone Blackwell's biography of her mother, *Lucy Stone* was an episodic play that dramatized the life of the great suffragette. Beginning in Lucy's childhood, Park first brings to life the moment in which Lucy reads Genesis 3:16, "Thy desire shall be to thy husband and he shall rule over thee."[55] Lucy's horror that the Bible would introduce and enforce such gender disparity is shrugged off by her parents and serves as the catalyst for her determination to ensure equal rights to all throughout the rest of her life. An educated and well-spoken woman, Stone gives numerous public speeches in favor of abolition, which in turn attracts the attention of William Lloyd Garrison. Lucy's speech-making prowess soon becomes integral to the abolition movement, but when her work for women's rights begins to alienate potential abolitionists, she chooses to focus on women's rights. The remainder of the play chronicles Lucy's struggle as she is courted by Henry Blackwell, marries, and gives birth to Alice Stone Blackwell while continuing her work as a strong public voice in favor of equality. Stone pioneered women's rights and, though she died in 1893, her dream of women's suffrage would eventually be realized in the Nineteenth Amendment.

Perhaps because of its potential historical and topical interest for Bostonians, *Lucy Stone* received nine different evaluations from the National Service Bureau, nearly double the number that most plays being strongly considered for production received. While a few of the readers appreciated the script as a historical account designed to memorialize this great American woman, the majority recommended extensive rewrites in order to develop characters, revise dialogue, and restructure the selected events so as to increase the staging potential. Converse Tyler, for example, wrote that the play was "an uninspired account of Lucy Stone's life," and that the character of Lucy, "that vigorous lady," was entirely "colorless" in the play.[56] The continued interest of both Flanagan and Ben Russak, supervisor of the playwriting department, eventually led to the FTP's extensive reshaping of the play for production. These revisions provide fascinating insight into the way that *Lucy Stone* would fit into both the Boston FTP's efforts to connect with its audience and the national FTP's urgent need to convince Congress that it was a viable and necessary part of the WPA. In fact, *Lucy Stone* premiered at a pivotal time for the national FTP—a moment in which the FTP would teeter on the brink of permanently losing its funding. Locally, the topical appeal of an independent-minded, well-respected Massachusetts woman who inspired major social change meshed well with the call for historical, uncontroversial drama. Even the personage of the playwright, famous suffragette Maud Wood Park, could be leveraged for publicity and social relevance. In addition to these encouraging possibilities in Boston, a solid production of *Lucy Stone* could serve as evidence that the FTP was doing the important work of a national theatre and that such efforts justified federal funding. Clearly aware of the importance this production could play in the national picture, one Boston administrator wrote to Flanagan:

> We are all working hard in Massachusetts to make the two weeks' productionof [*sic*] Lucy Stone a success both from the point of view of the play and for the help that we can give to the Federal Theatre movement through our active cooperation. [...] We may never have another opportunity to honor Miss Alice Stone Blackwell, and we'd like to have you see what Massachusetts can do both in the way of honoring our famous women and in building up a public for the Federal Theatre Project.[57]

This section explores the implications of the FTP's revisions to Maud Wood Park's *Lucy Stone*, as well as the role the production played within the Boston FTP.

Lucy Stone, revised by Robert Finch, opened in Boston on May 9, 1939, as the FTP—both nationally and locally—was facing its most difficult and, as many suspected, final battle with Congress. Discussion of additional productions outside Massachusetts permeated FTP communications regarding the script. Flanagan hoped it would become part of a national radio campaign focused on important women in American history, and that live productions could spread to other cities as well. Emmet Lavery confirmed this in a letter to Mack, in which he "recall[ed] distinctly that you mentioned the interesting exploitation possibilities for LUCY STONE and the way in which it would key in with Mrs. Flanagan's plans for a national spring drama festival."[58] In this way, *Lucy Stone* could have been relevant, uncontroversial, and easily defensible before Congress. The FTP's revisions would provide the key to realizing this effort.

Though famous for her writing of *Lucy Stone,* Maud Wood Park was better known as an articulate and active suffragette during the pivotal decade preceding the ratification of the Nineteenth Amendment. Park, chairman of the Congressional Committee, chief lobbyist for the National American Woman Suffrage Association, and newly named president of the League of Women Voters, played a pivotal role in the vote over the

Nineteenth Amendment. She effectively led the fight in Congress; charged with the difficult task of persuading reluctant Congresspersons to support women's suffrage, Park quickly became a renowned and respected figure nationally. She lectured professionally and remained active in civil rights affairs until her death in 1955.[59] Park followed in the steps of Lucy Stone and was instrumental in attaining Stone's goals. In writing *Lucy Stone,* Park reminded Americans of this great woman and invoked her own work as an activist and suffragette. She based the play on Lucy Stone's biography, *Lucy Stone: Pioneer of Woman's Rights,* written by Park's friend and Stone's daughter, Alice Stone Blackwell. Since Park also had access to much of Lucy Stone's personal materials, many of Stone's words in the play are taken directly from her speeches and writings. A brief preface by Alice Stone Blackwell preceded Park's play; in it she endorsed the play's "wit and ingenuity," as well as its ability to combine information about a vital struggle in history "with fun."[60] Park portrayed Stone as touched from birth, destined to be a woman who would lead others in the battle for equal rights. Here, Stone is a strong, fearless woman, able to consider the long-term consequences of her actions, convert countless individuals to her cause, and put her ideology into action in spite of personal hardship. This Lucy Stone, once a poor, uneducated farmer's daughter, rose to a position of influence and respect in the tradition of the true American hero. The combination of Lucy Stone and Maud Wood Park should have meant success for the Boston FTP. In fact, in a publicity coup, both Park and Lucy Stone's daughter Alice attended the first performance.

It is not surprising that the FTP would choose to perform a play about the great suffragette in her home state of Massachusetts. Stone's work on women's rights had been ratified to the Constitution in 1920, and so the subject matter would seem to be a safe and logical choice for a federal project desperately hoping to maintain its public support. Flanagan referred to the Boston production of *Lucy Stone* as one of the three "big productions [that] climaxed the success of a project which, by judicious suiting of play to community, and by expert direction, succeeded in triumphing over as strong political opposition as we met anywhere in the country," placing it behind only *Created Equal* and *Pinocchio.*[61] The FTP could exploit both the subject matter of the play and Park's own personal notoriety in the publicity of the show. Perhaps because of this ability to sell Park as the playwright, advertisements and public statements about the play listed Park as the sole creator; much to the dismay of Robert Finch, the man hired to rewrite the play for FTP production, his name was left off of everything except for the program itself, where he was designated as the script's adaptor.[62] As with *Created Equal*, the FTP could again capitalize on Bostonians' pride in their city's role of making national history. After all, if the FTP could convince skeptical Boston audiences to support its work, it could serve as a strong example of the popularity, strength, and longevity of the FTP. The FTP communicated their interest to Park late in 1938 and began making plans to complete the revisions they would require in order to produce *Lucy Stone*. Ben Russak, then supervisor of the playwriting department, oversaw the revisions, though Park would contract with and pay Finch independently.[63]

Finch's revisions to *Lucy Stone* would add scenes and highlight very specific changes in the characterization of the title role, though comparatively minor alterations abound throughout the text as well. In fact, many of the FTP revisions to Park's play consist of little more than juggling sequences and rewording lines. Park's original script, for example, opens as Lucy and her mother work side-by-side, Lucy sewing shoes and Mrs. Stone spinning thread. They discuss the heavy workload of women, consider the ways in which Lucy could spend the money she makes from the shoes, and prepare the evening meal while finishing their chores. Mr. Stone arrives to announce that his former schoolmate, Jim, has drunk himself into a stupor again and requires care. Mrs. Stone protests that Jim's behavior is not likely to change while people take care of his needs, that he sets a poor example for the children, and that he takes advantage of Mr. Stone's sense of duty, but she resigns herself to the task and continues her work. In contrast, the FTP version begins with the quick entrance of the drunken Jim. The incoherent drunk repeatedly humiliates Mrs. Stone; his complete helplessness forces her to help him remove his boots when he cannot figure out how, wash his filthy clothing and personal items, and even darn the holes in his repugnant socks. Moreover, these responsibilities are piled atop an already heavy workload that seems far from complete as the end of the day draws near, and Mrs. Stone shows signs of exhaustion. Finch's revision focuses on showing man at his worst at the expense of the women around him, as if to justify Lucy's devotion to women's rights. When Lucy's father finally appears, Mrs. Stone's protests, concerning the same issues as in Park's version, receive a sharp rebuke from her husband: "See here! You seem to be forgettin' I'm the head of this family!" At this moment, Jim hurls his grimy socks into the room, offering physical evidence of the men's dominance over the women; acquiescing to her fate, Mrs. Stone uses the fire-tongs to delicately pick up the socks and responds to Lucy's indignation by reinforcing the gender hierarchy, "You mustn't talk that way. It's your father's house and he's got a right to say who'll come here."[64] While these changes demonstrate an increased attention to characterizing the social and gender inequities, the majority of these moments are present in both scripts to some degree. Similar changes pepper the play; most of these changes clarify or deepen character, heighten conflict, or move the events of the play along more quickly, but do not alter the overall impression of the script.

In contrast, the more overt revisions suggest a specific agenda in which the character of Lucy Stone loses power and gains vulnerability. The first of these changes, seen throughout the FTP version, is the tenor of the romantic relationship between Lucy Stone and her future husband, Henry Blackwell. Park's original version portrays a Lucy Stone who is essentially married to her work; Lucy is in her late 30s when she agrees to marry Henry, expresses serious reservations about her ability to be a wife while maintaining her active advocacy for women's rights, and informs Henry that she has no intention of abandoning her career for marriage. This is most obvious in the first scene in which Lucy and Henry are physically present on stage at the same time. In Park's play, this occurs in Scene IV, entitled "Courtship and Cooking, 1853." At this point, Lucy is in the process of whitewashing the kitchen ceiling at her family's home in West Brookfield, Massachusetts. Henry, having walked the three miles from the train depot, appears unexpectedly, and the two discuss Lucy's recent speaking engagement, mutual friends, and the progress of the women's rights movement in general. Lucy and Henry have corresponded for some time and met on numerous occasions due to their mutual interests in abolition and women's rights. It soon becomes clear that Henry has come to visit Lucy with the intention of proposing:

> LUCY: I try to teach women's rights by pointing out their wrongs.
> BLACKWELL: It's one of the reasons why you are so successful—that and your sweet voice.
> LUCY: Thank you, Mr. Blackwell.
> BLACKWELL: But that wasn't what I came to talk about...
> LUCY: Is this your first visit to Massachusetts.
> BLACKWELL: Yes, it is. I made up my mind I wanted to see you again. But I didn't know I was going to have the good fortune of hearing you speak until I saw the notice of the hearing in the Boston paper. Miss Lucy, I-I—*(Hesitating.)*
> LUCY: *(In a second effort to get off the subject ahead.)* Was it about woman's rights you wanted to see me or about anti-slavery work?[65]

While it is difficult to tell precisely how unsettled Lucy may be by Henry's wooing, there are several points in which she takes control of the conversation and steers it away from personal relationships. Lucy speaks intelligently about her goals and methodology throughout the scene. She responds to his compliment about her "sweet voice" by graciously—and formally—thanking him and then referring to him as Mr. Blackwell rather than by his given name. When Henry attempts to change the subject, she interrupts to shift the conversation back to his journey. Lucy continues to stymie Henry's dogged attempts to woo her. It is only when he finally blurts out, "I want to share work with you all the rest of our lives, dear. [...] I want our lives to be shared. I want you to be my wife," that the power balance begins to shift in his direction. In spite of this, Lucy remains her steadfast, driven self. She responds, "I have made up my mind never to marry. I want to devote my life to the work I have undertaken. [...] A married woman can't possibly be so free to give her time as a spinster is."[66] Despite Henry's assertions that he would dedicate his life to helping her cause, Lucy refuses his proposal. Lucy's mother later reveals that Henry pursued Lucy for more than two years before she agreed to marry him; even then, she consented only after he arranged a lecture tour of the West Coast for her, thus proving his dedication to her cause. Park's Lucy is confident in her agenda; she chooses her path and defines the terms of her relationship with Henry Blackwell.

The parallel scene in the FTP revision offers a stark contrast. Lucy and Henry first meet in an added scene much earlier in the play. In it, Lucy enters pursued by young ruffians who jeer her bloomers and Henry rescues her by bringing her into his hardware store. According to the stage directions, Lucy is "wet, bedraggled, her hat wilted about her face." A "protective" Henry defends Lucy's honor and sends the boys away. Henry's brother then proceeds to praise his convictions about abolition, describing a situation in which Henry "made himself notorious by stealing two Negro slaves from a boat in the river!... and freeing them!" Lucy, in town to give a speech on abolition, admires his courage, apparently sensing a kindred spirit in Henry Blackwell. Henry also feels a connection; he is "struck by her beauty," chivalrously gives her his supper and only umbrella, and follows her the rest of the way to her speaking engagement (in a torrential downpour) to ensure her safety. In this short scene, Henry not only saves Lucy from a herd of young hooligans but also feeds her, cares for her, and impresses her with the strength of his own convictions; the old-fashioned chemistry between the pair is unmistakable. In the final moments of the scene, Henry returns to the store and announces to his brother that the "wonderful" Lucy Stone will "make an ideal wife."[67] This final moment emphasizes Lucy's lack of agency; Henry has already decided that he will marry her, regardless of her feelings on the matter.

Finch's next scene parallels that of Park's meeting between Henry and Lucy in her home. This time though, Henry plays the part of a confident playboy. As Lucy whitewashes the ceiling, Henry stands, dressed "neatly for visiting," and silently watches her work. He smiles, leans casually against the doorframe, and waits for her to reach as high as she possibly can before he says "May I help you?" He surprises her so that she nearly falls and he "rushes forward to help her" regain her footing; again, Henry rescues Lucy. Lucy begins the scene literally thrown off balance, and her level of control continues to deteriorate:

> LUCY: You must have enjoyed the convention. Mr. Phillips and Mr. Higginson spoke so beautifully...
> HENRY: *(Gazing at her)* Oh...did they speak too?
> LUCY: *(Embarrassed)* Of course! But...how did you get here from the depot?
> HENRY: I walked. It is such a lovely morning...
> LUCY: *(Trying to put on a company manner.)* Well! Father will be pleased to see you. Mother has gone to visit friends, but she will be back soon.
> HENRY: I came to see you, Lucy.
> LUCY: *(Self-conscious)* Oh!...well, I'm delighted...we have so little company here. Let us go into the parlor where Father is...[68]

In this exchange Henry openly woos a flustered Lucy. For her part, Lucy is embarrassed when he focuses on her speech and self-conscious when Henry proclaims his intention to see her personally. By the end of this brief exchange, Lucy thinks to flee to the parlor so that her father can rescue her from this confusing conversation. Lucy's attempts to change the course of the discussion are weak; her sentences trail off and she seems uncertain about what to say or how to respond. When Henry speaks of marriage, Lucy offers a response that seems as if she is grasping for a reason to reject the idea. She says, "Why...why...since wives are as subjected to rule by their husbands, by law and custom...I don't think of [marriage]. If the laws placed you, as a man, in such a position, would you?"[69] Finch's Lucy seems much less secure about her position on marriage; instead of clearly articulating her objections to the institution and its potential impact on her work, she asks Henry what he would do in her situation. She does not mention her dedication to her work, but rather claims that marriage is so fraught with arbitrary laws and inequities that she cannot consider it. This argument is one that Henry can easily deflect; he replies that women who are subject to the rule of their husbands really need only ensure that the men they marry will treat them with consideration and kindness, an answer that the Lucy Stone in Park's play would likely have refuted with an eloquent retort that would challenge Henry to reconsider. Here, however, Lucy seems as insecure as a teenager with her first boyfriend. The confident and controlled Henry befuddles her and the script suggests that she quickly agrees to an engagement. The power dynamics and priorities of this relationship are nearly opposites of the driven, career-oriented couple in Park's version.

The second major change in the FTP's version of *Lucy Stone* centers on the gravity of Lucy's mission as an advocate for women's rights and the abolitionist movement. This becomes particularly clear in the scene in which Lucy and Henry prepare for their wedding. One of the most important considerations for the couple is their marriage agreement, which they have revised in light of their concerns about the inequities inherent in the institution of marriage. In Park's play, it is clear that the minister, Reverend Higginson, is well-versed and supportive not only of the couple's plan for their marriage but also of Lucy's work in women's rights. When he arrives, he gives Lucy a bouquet of flowers and asks "How does it seem to a reforming woman's rightser, the morning star of the whole movement, to be on the eve of getting married?"

He recognizes that Lucy "is different from most young women and she ought to have a new type of husband."[70] Reverend Higginson describes Lucy's work as akin to a call from God, equating her to a missionary: "She's preaching the gospel of justice for all, women as well as men, black as well as white. And there are plenty of heathen right here in the United States."[71] In fact, Higginson implies that he considers himself a part of Lucy's work, saying "some of our opponents will be quite pleased to think that Lucy is married. Did any of you see that poem in the *Boston Post*?" The poem he references ends with a call for a courageous and self-sacrificing man, "Who with a wedding kiss shuts up / The mouth of Lucy Stone!"[72] Higginson does not approve of the poem or its sentiments, and fully supports Lucy's work in women's rights. In fact, Higginson and Lucy seem like longtime friends in this scene; they discuss mutual friends and Lucy's distant family, and each has extensive knowledge of the other's past work. Perhaps most importantly, Higginson wants the best for Lucy and states that he will refuse to perform the marriage ceremony if he thinks the groom is not up to Lucy's standards. He voluntarily omits the word "obey" from the religious ceremony and fully endorses the couple's desire to read their "manifesto" regarding the institutions of marriage during the ceremony, even suggesting the most strategic placement for it within the ceremony and offering to personally deliver a copy to the local newspaper for publication. Clearly, Reverend Higginson supports and values Lucy's work. This is the type of minister that one would expect to marry Lucy Stone and her fiancé.

In contrast, the Reverend Higginson in the FTP version appears to be little more than a kind, doddering, and conservative old man. Lucy's announcement of the marriage contract comes as a surprise to him:

> LUCY: [The marriage contract] is all written. We've even memorized it. Now we're making a lot of copies to send out to the newspapers.
> HIGGINSON: To the papers! It must be something very important. May I read it?
> LUCY: We shall read it for you, Rev. Higginson. At the ceremony tomorrow. *(Higginson puts his cup down in great surprise.)*[73]

Here, the Reverend is apparently unaware of the concessions he will soon be asked to make with respect to the wedding ceremony and Lucy refuses to show him the manifesto. When confronted with his agitation, Lucy simply states that if he does not approve, she and Henry will go to New York so that Henry's sister-in-law and Lucy's friend from Oberlin College, the Reverend Antoinette Brown Blackwell, can perform the ceremony. With this response, Lucy demonstrates her confidence and unwillingness to compromise; she will move the wedding to another state if Higginson refuses to play his role. Higginson also assumes that Lucy will be forced to give up her lecturing and campaigning for women's rights. When Lucy's mother corrects him, pointing out Henry's dedication to Lucy's work, Reverend Higginson replies doubtfully:

> A man will promise anything before he's married. Afterwards...well, I remember I promised Mrs. Higginson I'd never let her soil her pretty little hands in dishwater. *(He chuckles at the memory.)* At every marriage they say the same old thing. "Ours will be different." I hope Lucy's will be. But it's a big situation to change.[74]

While Reverend Higginson expresses hope for Lucy's future, he also demonstrates the attitudes that make Lucy's work in women's rights necessary. His unquestioned assumption that a wife will put aside her own needs and desires to serve her husband's fails to acknowledge the possibility that his ideas could be anything but ordained by God. In contrast to Park's portrayal of the Reverend, Finch's version seems to have little understanding of Lucy's work, and even less appreciation of it.

This shift in the characterization of Lucy Stone from a career-oriented woman comfortable in the public sphere to a more docile, emotional, and genteel female reflects a shift in Boston politics that began in the late 1920s (See Figure 4). When Boston's women officially entered the political arena, the public face of the female political candidate in Boston was not all that different from that of a man. Women publicized their roles in labor movements, women's rights controversies, social organizations, and anything else that might give the impression of a tough political candidate. Mrs. Grace D. Chipman, the sole female candidate for city council in 1921, appealed to public sympathies for the "fair and consistent" respect for women in the year following the ratification of the

Figure 4   Lucy Stone and Henry Blackwell sit together in Lucy's kitchen, shelling peas for the evening supper. Lucy is characterized here as excelling in both political activity and the home. NARA, Records of the Works Projects Administration, RG 69-TC, Box 27, "Lucy Stone."

Nineteenth Amendment, and Boston's League of Women Voters engaged in a vicious political battle against Curley in the 1921 mayoral election.[75] While the novelty of the situation initially garnered public attention and space in the newspapers, very few Boston women made it past the stage of candidacy.[76]

During the late 1920s, women began to alter their public persona in an attempt to gain votes. Gone were the vocal advocates of social equality, to be replaced by the public image of the refined housewife who happened to have political concerns. The first woman who served on the Governor's Council, Mrs. Esther Andrews, was appointed by the governor when the winning candidate died before taking office; she may have been a successful businesswoman, an advocate of equal pay and rights for women in the workforce, and a supporter of numerous public appointments, but "within minutes after learning of her appointment, Esther Andrews declared, 'No married woman has any right to go into politics, public service or the professions, if it means giving up her home.'"[77] Women who succeeded in Boston politics during the 1930s cultivated this image of refined homemakers, excellent cooks, and compassionate wives with well-mannered children, clean homes, content husbands, and a matron-like beauty. In 1931, Mrs. Eleanor L'Ecuyer ran for city council and compared the city government to "municipal housekeeping."[78] By the early 1930s women had great difficulty gaining even low-tier positions. One of the few who did, Mildred Gleason Harris, won a special 1937 election and replaced her brother when he passed away while holding a position on the Boston City Council. As Sara Deutsch argues, in spite of Mrs. Harris's repeated attempts to bill herself as a serious, experienced politician, the majority of the pictures published in *The Boston Globe* presented her as a homemaker, wife, and mother with "brilliant blue eyes," "thick bobbed hair," and a "ready smile on her small mouth."[79] It would seem that Boston was willing to support women in politics only as long as they performed socially acceptable gender roles.

By the time *Lucy Stone* premiered in Boston, the city was largely past the novelty of outspoken women in politics. Aggressive women were no longer attractive characters. Finch's revision of the play recognizes and incorporates this idea. He feminizes Lucy, giving her the same matronly qualities publicized by the women who succeeded in Boston politics; she is "beautiful," with a "sweet voice" and possesses the abilities of cooking, cleaning, and caring for a child. In this political and cultural environment, it is not surprising that the FTP—at a critical point in its brief lifetime and desperately in need of support—would choose to portray the character of

Lucy Stone in a more traditionally feminine manner. The play's director, Eliot Duvey, concurred: "Lucy Stone won her battles by her warm, human simplicity and sincerity. Lucy Stone was first and always a woman. There was nothing masculine about her as there was about some of the others who fought for woman suffrage." Even the lighting design focused on the creation of a "family album" on stage, again emphasizing Stone's domesticity.[80] Whether or not the director or lighting designer's perceptions of Lucy Stone (the woman) were accurate, both Alice Stone Blackwell's biography and Maude Wood Park's play contained a bare minimum of these traditionally feminine qualities, focusing instead on Stone's professional life.

The critical response demonstrated appreciation of these qualities in the character of Lucy Stone, as well as an awareness that these traits were at odds with the woman portrayed in Stone's biography. Elinor Hughes, writing for the *Boston Herald*, critiqued the chronicle play as a genre, discussed Maud Wood Park and Lucy Stone's activities, and wrote very little of the performance. However, Hughes mentioned Lucy's marriage twice in the short article. She explained that Stone's "happy marriage to Henry Blackwell was signalized by the omission of the word 'obey' from the service." She commended the demonstration of the couple's "devotion" to one another, appreciated the "frequent moments of humor," and praised the portrayal of Lucy Stone as a woman who was "human and admirable, not cold and remote."[81] Elliot Norton similarly described Stone as "kittenish in courtship," and noted that this choice marked a distinct departure from the biography on which the play was based: "The biography establishe[d] Lucy Stone as a serene, firm, clear-headed woman who was hardly likely to be goody in the presence of any man."[82] Similarly, a review in the *Christian Science Monitor* complimented Lillian Merchal's ability to portray Lucy Stone with "an unaffected cheerfulness mingled with sufficient degree of dignity to keep the characterization on the believable side. [...Lucy] dominate[d] the stage—quietly and pleasantly but firmly."[83] These descriptions of Lucy's character emphasized her serenity, amiability, and devotion to her husband. They bear a striking resemblance to the ways in which Boston's female politicians learned to publicly portray themselves during the 1930s. As further evidence of the link between *Lucy Stone* and the roles of wife and mother, the *Boston Herald* printed its review alongside a list of southern recipes, including Sweet Potato Pone, String Beans Brittany, and Beaten Biscuits. The biscuit recipe even included directions for treating one's mother on the upcoming Mother's Day.

In many ways, the life of Lucy Stone epitomized the American Dream; she began as the daughter of a poor farmer, struggled to overcome barriers against women attending college, and became a prominent public figure advocating racial and sexual equality. Her efforts, in concert with the great suffragettes of the late nineteenth and early twentieth centuries, changed the role of women in the United States. Maud Wood Park's own status as a famous suffragette, as well as her friendship with Alice Stone Blackwell, guaranteed that she would make every effort to portray Stone in an accurate and complimentary light so as to preserve the fading memory of an American icon and the early history of the women's rights movement.

The FTP production had a very different goal. Nearly 40 years after Stone's death and almost 20 after the ratification of the Nineteenth Amendment, the FTP was in desperate need of an uncontroversial, uplifting, and relevant drama for its Boston project. Finch's revision of *Lucy Stone* provided just that. With *Lucy Stone*, the FTP capitalized on Boston's fascination with history by recalling an influential and respected Massachusetts woman who helped gain women the right to vote. In a stark contrast to the professional, driven woman in Maud Wood Park's script, the FTP's production portrayed a soft, gentle, matron in the title role. *Lucy Stone* pushed no boundaries, ruffled few feathers, gained the sponsorship of the Boston University Women's Council, and had "local and historic rather than theatre interest."[84] In a final act of generosity and good politics, the FTP reserved the last Friday performance as a benefit for Boston's Morgan Memorial, an organization that gave summer outings to needy children and their mothers; the Morgan Memorial was housed in the Lucy Stone Home in Dorchester.[85] It was an ideal production for Boston's FTP during the fateful summer of 1939.

CONCLUSIONS

Plagued by anti–New Deal sentiments, constant threats of censorship, hostile WPA oversight, and the ongoing difficulties finding and connecting to an audience, the Boston FTP appeared to be doomed to failure. Flanagan's decision to withdraw funding and close down the program following the disaster of *Valley Forge* in 1936 certainly testified to the Boston FTP's many trials. In spite of Flanagan's misgivings, the program continued and offered innocuous productions that quickly passed muster with the censors, but which failed to kindle interest with local audiences. The original production of John Hunter Booth's *Created Equal* altered the face of the Boston FTP in 1938. In a trend that would continue with Maud

Wood Park's *Lucy Stone* in 1939, the Boston FTP discovered the formula for successful drama in Boston.

Both *Created Equal* and *Lucy Stone* capitalized on the rich history of Boston. Though they approached the material from different perspectives, the threads of American history permeated both productions. In *Created Equal*, the FTP challenged its working-class audience to fight for the realization of the rights promised to all in the Declaration of Independence; the production also restored the working class—whether soldier, farmer, or pioneer—to a pivotal role in nation formation even as it neglected issues of race. In contrast, the revisions to *Lucy Stone* chronicled the life of the great suffragette in a way that shifted emphasis away from her public achievements and toward the domestic sphere. Though well received by critics, the Boston FTP's production of *Lucy Stone* sacrificed the independence and strength of Lucy Stone to the public's preference for nurturing professional women. In fact, though both *Created Equal* and *Lucy Stone* brought history to life, both productions also surrendered the more controversial elements of that history. Thus, while the Boston FTP created locally relevant, uncontroversial theatre for its audiences, it did so at a significant cost.

3. "The Great American Theatrical Desert": Federal Theatre in the South ～

The South has sometimes been called "the great American theatrical desert." Even a casual survey of American theatre history shows relatively little organized professional theatre south of the Mason-Dixon line.[1]

—John McGee

And the other thing that we could have done with a little longer run of the Federal Theatre is gotten into experimental regional things that actually grew out of the region itself, rather than being controlled and sent down to us from New York.[2]

—Josef Lentz

In early 1937 John McGee, head of the southern region and deputy director of the FTP, and the employees of the region compiled a multi-volume scrapbook as a gift for Flanagan. Entitled *A Brief History of the Federal Theatre in the South*, its opening featured ten pages of hand-written signatures from eight different FTP units, including those in Atlanta, Birmingham, Jacksonville, Miami, Tampa, New Orleans, North Carolina, and Oklahoma City; all offered their support of the FTP as a whole, and Flanagan specifically.[3]

One of Flanagan's trusted assets and the former director of the Birmingham Little Theatre, McGee provided an overview of regional activities, difficulties, and suggestions for proceeding forward in the region that represented the greatest disparities the FTP would face, both internally and in comparison to the New York City hub. McGee was most troubled by the "paucity of talent" in the region, a concern that had initially halted efforts to establish the FTP in the South.[4] As Flanagan explained,

"We had in the South, due to the fact that for decades it had witnessed no professional theatre activity except an occasional stock company, or third-rate road show, fewer theatre professionals in need than elsewhere."[5] In addition to the implied privileging of specific legitimate forms of theatre in this remark, a lack of "theatre professionals in need" would fundamentally hobble any FTP activities. Flanagan justified activities in the South in two ways. First, the South's people and history presented rich materials for dramatic interpretation and a potential loss to American culture should it remain undeveloped. Second, federal tax monies funded the FTP; as Flanagan argued, "Since the project was financed federally out of everybody's taxes, we were reluctant to spend all the money in congested areas like New York City as long as there were even a comparatively few theatre professionals in need in the South, and the chance, through them, to make some contribution to these communities."[6] Therefore, if theatre workers qualified for relief in the South, the FTP should be there to support the rapidly deteriorating infrastructure and ensure that these individuals and their arts were resuscitated.

McGee recommended gathering theatre professionals in major urban areas and employing traveling talent to reach the smaller cities and towns throughout the South. Used in other regions with varying degrees of success, this method seemed particularly well-suited to the challenges that the South presented. Flanagan agreed and instituted the "flying squadron" method, which allocated directors, designers, actors, and theatre staff to whichever location was in need in the region. Though it was an efficient means to distribute skilled individuals and supplies, this method proved problematic for production teams tasked with creating locally relevant drama. Directors and writers often had little or no time to meet the people of the region, let alone create inspired drama that would speak to their lives. Further exacerbating these issues, the southern region's lack of qualified relief workers meant that the FTP was often forced to import workers from other regions to fill important gaps.

Indeed, I suggest that many of the difficulties the FTP encountered in the South were due to a fundamental incompatibility between the FTP's stated goal of producing dramas relevant to local communities and its own administrative structure. While the FTP's central locations in New York City and Washington, DC were a critical factor in many urban successes, the structural deficiencies created an intricate web of tensions and disconnects in smaller FTP communities throughout the country. In the southern region, where the FTP struggled for even a grudging acceptance, issues that were little more than nuisances in other regions expanded to become nearly insurmountable obstacles. Frustrations over administrative details peppered the memos, wires, and letters between the local and national administrations. Moreover, the smaller units possessed less strategic strength to push through the inevitable crises and garnered less attention and respect from the administration as a whole. As such, these units— particularly those relying on the "flying squadron" method to staff major roles in productions—were vulnerable to the whims of state WPA officials, newspapers, local politicians, and funding shortages. Perhaps most devastating to the long-term success of the FTP in the South was a foundational misunderstanding of the interests and needs of local communities. McGee explained:

> A stronger program must be evolved and aimed more consistently toward the likes and desires of the several communities, in which we operate. The past year has demonstrated many failures of our organization to analyze properly the public which we have set out to serve, and a careful study of these errors must be made to shape the future program.[7]

This chapter will concentrate on two theatrical excursions in the South, which exemplify the challenges and disconnects that McGee critiqued. First, I will delve into the infamous *Altars of Steel* (1937), which Flanagan referred to as the "most important Southern production" and critics described as dangerous, inflammatory, Communist propaganda.[8] *Altars of Steel* portrays a steel mill in Birmingham, Alabama, during the Depression. As the play opens, a large northern steel conglomerate, United Steel, forces the kind Southern gentleman who owns the mill to sell. When United Steel assumes control of the mill, their representative abuses the workers and ignores safety regulations, eventually causing an explosion in which 19 men die. The repercussions of this accident reverberate throughout the town, riot ensues, and the play ends in unresolved chaos. The latter half of this chapter focuses on the so-called "Georgia Experiment" in which the FTP sent five personnel into small-town Georgia to bring a localized theatre movement to individuals outside of major urban centers. Created with an eye toward future projects in rural America, the success of the Georgia Experiment would serve as a model for the potential of the FTP. *Altars of Steel* and the Georgia Experiment share a vital role in the formation of the FTP; both activities succeeded in finding ways to create locally relevant drama. Both also failed, for entirely different reasons, to create an ongoing connection with their audiences; these failures serve as case studies for the shortcomings of the southern FTP on a regional and national level.

YANKEE CONSTERNATION IN THE DEEP SOUTH: WORSHIPPING AT THE *ALTARS OF STEEL*[9]

Birmingham, Alabama earned the dubious distinction of being pinpointed by the federal government as "the city in America hardest hit by the Depression."[10] Residence of the newly founded southern branch of the Communist party, Birmingham was home to extreme poverty, starvation, sharecroppers, and the nation's single largest industrial conflict. Oppression was widespread, corrupt political and legal systems permitted lynching and mob rule, and violent terrorism was commonplace. Some Northerners compared Alabama to the fascist state of Hitler. Contemporary scholar Robin D. G. Kelley argues that Alabama "had the worst record of any state in the country on human and civil liberties and certainly one of the most wretched records in the annals of Western democracy."[11]

Worker organization in Alabama all but collapsed during the 1920s. As Neal R. Pierce explains, "It was a hard society of the survival of the fittest, in which money and power overshadowed all else."[12] U.S. Steel, widely known as "Big Steel," ruled the Birmingham area. As the single largest employer in the region, the behemoth could alter the city's economy, and with it the daily lives of the people, with a medieval-like "feudal sway." During the 1930s, Big Steel wielded such power that it freely defied both federal law and labor organizers.[13] While it may be difficult to believe that a single company could brandish so much power, it is important to understand the mammoth amount of money and steel produced by corporations such as U.S. Steel. U.S. Steel's mills in Pittsburgh, Birmingham, and Chicago produced more steel than all of Germany, the second largest steel-producing country in the world. Large conglomerates such as U.S. Steel typically perceived unions as threats to morale, production, and their bottom line and, as such, discouraged unionizing, particularly during the Great Depression.

However, legislation designed to protect worker rights between 1933 and 1938 gradually loosened the stranglehold the steel mills had on their workers. The National Relations Act (also known as the Wagner Act) of 1935 outlawed many of the traditional methods used by corporations to put down worker protest. In Birmingham, one example of this was the anti–sedition law (1935); under the guise of rooting out Communists and radicals, police and the "red-squad" could raid homes, harass suspected leftists, and enjoy virtual impunity if violence such as kidnapping, beating, or shooting into a crowd of radicals erupted.[14] In early January 1937, during the period *Altars of Steel* was to have opened in Birmingham, Congress of Industrial Organizations (CIO) chairman John L. Lewis and U.S. Steel board chairman Myron Taylor began a series of talks that would end several months later in a surprising agreement between U.S. Steel and labor; the largest steel company in the world agreed to officially recognize the Steel Workers Organizing Committee (SWOC) as a tool for collective bargaining on behalf of the workers. Likely due to a marked increase in steel orders and public sympathy for the plight of steel workers, Taylor argued that compromise would be better for business than the potential loss of public face and economic destabilization.[15]

In addition to the decades of labor strife that plagued Birmingham, the ubiquitous Ku Klux Klan (KKK) and the pervasive racism associated with that organization wielded considerable power during the 1930s. The city was known as "'bad, bad Birmingham, the murder capital of the world,' [...] a place where brutality had soaked into the fabric of the culture."[16] The infamous Scottsboro case (1931), which saw nine young African American men arrested, indicted, prosecuted, and found guilty by an all-white jury within six days, provided an opportunity for northern activist groups like the NAACP and the International Labor Defense Fund to make a national statement. The case pitted Jewish and Communist lawyers against the KKK, a social history of racism, and Alabama's hatred of northern influence. The Alabama KKK particularly despised the Communist leanings of the northern lawyers brought in to defend the Scottsboro Boys, as Communism threatened the racial and economic hegemony of the state by implying that class (and race) should be leveled in a modern society. The choice of Communist recruiters to focus on unionizing African American workers also did little to endear them to the KKK. Communism, particularly unionization of the working class, became a focal point for KKK activities in Birmingham. The Klan littered the city with leaflets proclaiming: "Communism will not be tolerated. Ku Klux Klan Rides Again."[17] These intimidation techniques frequently targeted African American laborers. One Klan flyer, distributed in Birmingham during the 1930s, warned African Americans against attending Communist meetings and asserted that "paid organizers for the communists are only trying to get negroes in trouble. Alabama is a good place for good negroes to live in, but it is a bad place for negroes who believe in SOCIAL EQUALITY." It went on to demand that all communist meetings be reported to the KKK via a local post office box.[18]

Those who attended union rallies endured attacks—particularly when the spectre of Communism was involved. Glenn Feldman documents the disturbing connections between the KKK, corporations, and the Birmingham police department. In one example, Klan representatives shot one man's wife because he attended a union meeting. In 1935, the Klan conspired with police and vigilantes to violently end a march of Communists and union miners designed to enhance solidarity. Tennessee Coal & Iron (TCI) joined forces with the KKK and police in retaliation against unemployment insurance demands; a series of beatings followed, each focusing on union and Communist leadership. The notorious Downs Ordinance (1935), which allowed police to seek out, fine, and imprison anyone possessing more than one "radical publication," provided an excuse for widespread terrorism. Protected by the law, police—often accompanied by Klan members—entered homes with impunity. In one instance of flagrant abuse, police invaded a man's home, claiming to be searching for Communist literature, then "stripped and flogged his two grown daughters." In another violent show of power, the Klan nailed an African American man's thumbs to his front door.[19] Unions, Communism, and racial equality were linked in the minds of Alabama KKK members; they were steps along the road to social and ideological disaster. The FTP production of *Altars of Steel* pitted the working class against the dominant hegemony, directly challenging the power of United Steel on social, racial, political, and economic grounds.

Altars of Steel's "United Steel" is both a thinly disguised reference to U.S. Steel, the enormous conglomerate that had purchased TCI in a forced buyout in 1907, and the abbreviated name for the national steel workers union, United Steelworkers of America. The forces that led to the formation of a national steelworkers union were well established by mid-1936. By the end of 1936, less than a month before the Birmingham production of *Altars of Steel* was to open, the massive organizing campaign of the SWOC had recruited more than 125,000 steel workers and the steel companies were taking desperate and violent measures to quell the workers. While *Altars of Steel* was ultimately performed only in Atlanta and Miami, it premiered amidst the heightening tensions that would result in the Memorial Day Massacre only a month later, as well as numerous "Little Steel" strikes throughout the country.[20] It is hard to believe that the Birmingham leaders of U.S. Steel would have been blind to these obvious parallels, and harder still to imagine that they would have made no move to preserve the hierarchy of power already in place.

The epigraph of *Altars of Steel* highlights the power of groups willing to fight for their beliefs: "The great questions of the times will not be decided by speeches and resolutions of majorities, but by blood and iron."[21] These words—foretelling a period of violence, coercion, and physical battle for supremacy—introduce the controversial southern social-labor drama that would prove to be a crisis point for the Southern FTP. *Altars of Steel* premiered in Atlanta to hot debate, critical acclaim, and sold-out houses and quickly became one of the most discussed southern plays of the 1930s. Two major city newspapers, the *Atlanta Constitution* and the *Atlanta Georgian*, ran a series of articles evaluating the merits and deficiencies of the play's political ideas. *Altars of Steel* was variously described as "the most impressive stage offering ever seen in Atlanta," "about as Communistic—as a health talk," and "infested with germs of hate and war." Hallie Flanagan depicted the play's reception as prophetic:

> Audiences crowded the theatre for *Altars of Steel*. They praised the play. They blamed the play. They fought over the play. They wrote to the papers: "Dangerous propaganda!"…Columnists fought over it. Mildred Seydell of the *Atlanta Georgian*, while calling it "magnificent, gripping, perfectly cast," found it as "dangerous as *Uncle Tom's Cabin*."[22]

This quote begs the question—was *Altars of Steel* really as "dangerous as *Uncle Tom's Cabin*" to the people of Atlanta and Birmingham? The flurry of debate surrounding the Atlanta production and the suspicious activity revolving around a cancelled production in Birmingham some three months earlier point to a play with great potential for social and political upheaval. While the FTP as a whole never caught on in the southern region with the intensity seen in New York, Chicago, Los Angeles, Seattle, or any number of smaller cities or towns in these regions, *Altars of Steel*'s powerful local themes and innovative style of production demonstrate just how relevant and timely regional productions could be.

In fact, of all the plays, musicals, circuses, variety shows, and other performances Federal Theatre produced in the southern region, *Altars of Steel* stands out as the event that *should* have laid a solid foundation for Federal Theatre in the South. Yet even as it drew its inspiration from regional sources and talent, *Altars of Steel* also challenged the social, political, and economic hegemony of the South. I suggest that the implicit and explicit attacks on the South's extant political and economic structure helped prevent *Altars of Steel* from laying that foundation for the FTP in the South. Unlike the projects in New York and California, which seemed able to absorb or ignore theatrical challenges to their political systems, the southern region seems to have regarded organized FTP units as unwelcome and dangerous intrusions (perhaps not surprising in a region occupied by federal troops during Radical Reconstruction only sixty years earlier).

It is curious that in *Arena*, Hallie Flanagan discusses *Altars of Steel* only briefly, first touting the media response, then focusing on an innocuous discussion of the monumental, expressionist set used in the show. Jane de Hart Mathews likewise skims over the show, referring to it only once in passing:

> Although the production of *Altars of Steel* a year earlier by the small Atlanta group had prompted *Variety* to proclaim that the 'spirit of Hallie Flanagan waves over Dixieland,' neither strong theatre nor strong public support had developed in this fast growing metropolis of the New South.[23]

The distinct lack of commentary regarding *Altars of Steel* in Flanagan's and Mathews's accounts is noteworthy. The Atlanta production created such a stir that newspapers and magazines throughout the country wrote about it. It was uncharacteristic of the politically savvy Flanagan to avoid capitalizing on the publicity goldmine that the production created both in the struggling South and nationally. While it is possible that Flanagan simply disliked the production for some reason, it is more likely that her response was related to the overall message that *Altars of Steel* conveyed to the city of Birmingham, the southern region, and the country. How, then, did the combination of *Altars of Steel* and the city of Birmingham both promote and contradict the mission of the FTP as a whole? To answer this question, it is necessary to first examine the play's uncertain genesis.

Thomas Hall-Rogers, the alleged playwright of *Altars of Steel,* was a mystery man with close ties to the city of Birmingham and the southern steel industry. Several contemporaneous newspaper accounts suspected use of a pseudonym, alluding to the playwright's fear of violent repercussions:

> The only information obtainable was that he prefers to be known only as Thomas Hall-Rogers, although many believe him to be connected with a steel mill in Birmingham, Ala. We have instructions to keep the identity of the author an absolute secret. [...] I don't think anyone in Atlanta and very few persons anywhere know who he is.[24]

The playwright's identity remained a closely guarded secret for more than 70 years. In her comprehensive chapter on the reception of *Altars of Steel*, Susan Duffy suggests that one possible identity of Thomas Hall-Rogers is Birmingham lawyer and newspaperman John Temple Graves II. Though my recent discovery of new evidence proves this hypothesis untrue, Duffy's explanation of the origins of the "steel play" demonstrates that the subject had gained great interest in the South. Duffy cites the subject matter of

Graves's keynote speech at an FTP conference in which he proposed that the FTP attack social issues that spoke to the southern condition; specifically, Graves discussed the abject poverty of the tenant farmers and their land, the place of African Americans in southern institutions, and the new political economy dictated by cotton and steel.[25] Following Graves's call for "a play about steel," the Birmingham FTP produced a staged reading of *Altars of Steel*. The play made such a "profound impression [...] on the assembly" of FTP administrators and directors that the southern branch of the play bureau submitted *Altars of Steel* to the New York office for reading and production approval a mere six weeks later.[26]

While Duffy's construction of the circumstantial evidence creates a logical and convincing historical narrative, my own archival research has discovered a series of previously unknown letters that identify the playwright of *Altars of Steel* as Josiah W. Bancroft. When not working in the theatre, Bancroft was a physiotherapist at the TCI Hospital in Fairfield, Alabama. U.S. Census records demonstrated that he was working at TCI in 1930, and he received at least one letter from John McGee at TCI Hospital in 1936.[27] Approximately eight miles southwest of Birmingham and founded by TCI in 1909 to attract skilled workers to their Birmingham mill, many steelworkers made Fairfield their home.[28] In his role as a physiotherapist for injured steelworkers, Bancroft would have come into repeated contact with the wounded or maimed victims of the steel industry; every day he would have seen the repercussions of steel mill accidents and the often futile struggles of the workers to regain pieces of their former lives.[29]

Bancroft so impressed McGee with his writing and his dedication to theatre in the years prior to the FTP that McGee suggested Bancroft and Francis Nimmo Green (who would become the director of the Southern Play Bureau) as potential regional supervisors. According to McGee, Bancroft had "intimate knowledge of the creative workers in the state and [...had] made important strides toward the establishment of an indigenous theatre." In describing the candidates, McGee noted that Green's unparalleled and "courageous struggle to develop a serious expression of Alabama life in terms of the theatre" would likely garner her a warm reception from the Alabama WPA but that Bancroft's history of dealing with incendiary topics had left fewer supporters. "[Bancroft's] selection may not be universally popular, but with nine-tenths of the people who are sincerely concerned for the development of real theatre in Alabama, his name should be welcome. Any who oppose [*sic*] are likely to do so from purely personal interests."[30] The FTP passed over Bancroft in favor of the less controversial Green.

Bancroft's only other official appearance in the FTP was as the writer of the great "steel play," *Altars of Steel*. Though he was likely disappointed about being passed over for a leadership role in the FTP and could have benefitted from the publicity resulting from a great theatrical success, Bancroft adamantly refused any public association with *Altars of Steel*, probably due to fears for his own personal safety. His connection to the play is established through three previously unknown letters. In the only letter addressed to J. W. Bancroft, McGee described the play as an "opportunity [...] too great for us to miss."[31] McGee noted that he had located the ideal actor for one of the lead roles in the play, Mr. Worth, and went on to discuss the promise of an FTP operation in Fairfield, Alabama, and the interest of directors in other cities throughout the country. Though the letter implied that Bancroft would be one of the top choices for the role of director, this project never came to fruition. Francis Nimmo Green filtered the rest of Bancroft's FTP communications so that he received no personal mail regarding the play (or showing any connection to the FTP), a practice that McGee described to Green at Bancroft's apparent request, noting that "there is no reason why the correspondence cannot be carried on strictly under his pen name. In fact, the New York Bureau does not know him under any other name."[32] McGee's assessment of the knowledge of Bancroft's pseudonym was correct; as far as the archives show, only McGee and Green knew of Bancroft's association with *Altars of Steel*, and both protected his anonymity; without the single letter addressed to Bancroft, identifying him as the playwright would likely have proved impossible.

McGee's enthusiasm for the project notwithstanding, *Altars of Steel*'s development would remain troubled. In a fit of frustration, McGee wrote to Green regarding the most recent version of the play:

> I am also very discouraged about Joe's new version of <u>Altars of Steel</u>. He has deliberately gone back to some of the earlier scenes and has thrown away much that we already gave him. [...T]he thing quite distresses me because here is one of our great chances, and certainly a great chance for Joe, but he seems to be frittering it away. Maybe he just hasn't got it in him—I don't know.[33]

Even before the FTP production of *Altars of Steel*, McGee realized its potential importance. In this letter he asked Green to locate a copy of the version read at the conference earlier in the fall and send it to him so he could work out further revisions on his own. In spite of some truly damning criticism from the National Play Bureau, McGee refused to give up on *Altars of Steel*.

Altars of Steel is agitprop theatre; it paints a cruel picture of the lives of the people who would be watching the play, assigns blame, and calls for action. Thus, while it may be a "simplification of a complex problem," it is also a highly effective piece of theatre.[34] The play moves quickly from one scene to another, an effect that was improved by the versatile, representative set used in the show. The characters have some level of psychological depth but are not complex; there are clear heroes and villains. With this in mind, it is interesting to note the striking contrast between the almost melodramatic style of the play and the FTP's handling of the production. Josef Lentz, who would ultimately become the regional director of the South, designed the set and sound effects to mirror the strength and power of the steel mill in a way that would cast a shadow over the proceedings. Created on a materials budget of less than 50 dollars, Lentz engineered an enormous door that appeared to be made of steel to open and close in lieu of a curtain, built a stage of cogs and gears, and recorded noises from a local steel mill for the soundtrack. Throughout the production, the cacophony of the steel industry combined with the large-scale machinery of the mill, creating a design that literally towered over the workers.[35] The choice to mount this production with this expressionistic flair demonstrates an attempt to tie an aesthetically edgy production design to the controversial subject matter of the play. Topically, *Altars of Steel* would have been an ideal—if dangerous—play for the Birmingham FTP. Verner Haldene, director of the Birmingham FTP, scheduled *Altars of Steel* for production in January, a mere three months after the idea first arose in Graves's speech at the conference of southern FTP directors.[36]

It is curious that the unanimous decision to strike *Altars of Steel* from the list of potential Federal Theatre productions was made in New York only a few days before the production opened in Atlanta, and months after it was scheduled to open in Birmingham.[37] While it is easy to dismiss this apparent inconsistency in approval and production as symptomatic of a large federal organization plagued by bureaucratic administrative procedures and poor communications, correspondence between Flanagan, McGee, and Lentz makes it clear that all three knew and approved of the production; in fact, McGee and Lentz both helped mount the production. A letter dated March 16, 1937, from McGee to Flanagan anticipated an "exciting production [that] should break all records in the South" when it opened in Atlanta on March 29.[38]

Bancroft's dynamic 16-scene play was set in Birmingham, about the social issues relevant to Birmingham audiences, and intended for the Birmingham FTP; initially, it seemed like a match made in Federal

Theatre heaven. *Altars of Steel* went through an extensive workshopping process in Birmingham, received several public readings, and despite some concerns about the script, southern FTP administrators touted it as a shining example of the possibilities of local drama.[39] Early October saw the Birmingham FTP—not the southern regional center of New Orleans—hosting the Southern Conference for the FTP and performing numerous pieces for the visiting theatre dignitaries. The Birmingham FTP appeared poised for breakthroughs with both the national organization and its local audience. On October 27, 1936, Birmingham participated in the national opening of Sinclair Lewis's *It Can't Happen Here*; the Audience Survey Report completed for the production noted public support for the continuation of the project as a community theatre even as local critics and the FTP administration recorded the opening as a major success.[40] Yet as 1936 drew to a close, the future of the Birmingham unit appeared surprisingly uncertain.

In a brief November article in the *Birmingham Post,* Verner Haldene, the director of the Birmingham FTP and former director of the Montgomery Little Theatre, told reporters that the local FTP theatre would be dark for the remainder of November, and likely through early January, so that plans could be decided upon. In the meantime, he had tentative plans to take the Birmingham production of *It Can't Happen Here* on a tour of Alabama while the Tampa FTP might play in the Birmingham FTP's theatre for a month or more. Haldene's announcement that the theatre would remain dark for at least six weeks, the lengthy visit by the Tampa FTP, and the subsequent unplanned schedule were ominous. The unnamed author of this article goes on to note that the Birmingham FTP would "begin work on *Altars of Steel*" for production in January, and highlighted its relevance to local Birmingham audiences.[41] Haldene's tentative program for the first quarter of 1937, sent to the national FTP administration for approval, confirmed these plans: "The first production, 'Altars of Steel,' by Thomas-Hall Rogers [Bancroft], to be prepared as quickly as possible and staged during the month of January."[42] From McGee's correspondence regarding royalties for the play, it was clear that he also planned to produce *Altars of Steel* in Birmingham in early 1937. In a letter to Green, McGee agreed to pay royalties for two weeks of performances in Birmingham; he went on to note that he felt it would run longer and that a number of other projects would compete for further productions throughout the country, thus increasing royalties for Bancroft.[43] The FTP never produced *Altars of Steel* in Birmingham.

Part of the explanation may lie in a series of letters between McGee, Lentz, and Blanche Ralston, regional director of the Women's and

Professional Services Division, which discussed an unspecified "situation" in Birmingham. The letters imply that McGee, Lentz, and Ralston had taken part in an ongoing conversation over the viability of Haldene's continued employment with the FTP. As early as November 5, 1936, three weeks before Haldene's statement to the press about the upcoming season, McGee wrote an apologetic letter to Harriett Adams, amusement supervisor of the city of Birmingham. In this letter McGee noted that he had already canceled one of the productions of which she did not approve, Ayn Rand's *The Night of January 16th*, and reassured her:

> For your private information, however, the entire responsibility for the Federal Theatre program in Birmingham is now vested in Mr. J. L. Lentz. [...] I have asked him to come and discuss the entire matter of program with you. Please rest assured that we wish to do everything possible to conform to the official regulations governing amusements in the City of Birmingham.[44]

McGee's letter suggested that the choice of FTP program violated Birmingham regulations and that Haldene was responsible for the infraction. While Haldene's impropriety was not named in official correspondence, he was publicly accused of homosexuality and communism. McGee, presumably with Flanagan's blessing, relocated Haldene to Detroit, "an entirely different situation from that which prevails in Birmingham;" there, Haldene would be "under continuous surveillance, and hence, [could] do no particular damage."[45] While McGee noted the importance of containing Haldene and the "situation," he seemed to feel that the change in leadership would avert any immediate danger to the Birmingham unit. Unfortunately, the damage was done. The disapproval of city and state officials continued to escalate, and when Congress cut the FTP's budget that January, the Birmingham FTP was shut down altogether; *Altars of Steel* disappeared from the city of Birmingham and opened in Atlanta less than three months later. As Hedley Gordon Graham, the director of *Altars of Steel* would state, "the drama project that they had in Atlanta was the aftermath of the Birmingham project failing."[46]

The timing of these events in conjunction with the silence of prominent FTP personnel is suspicious. Though the documented explanation for the play's physical removal from Birmingham is that the Atlanta Little Theatre Guild invited the FTP to join a cooperative community unit, the cancellation of an FTP production for political or social reasons happened more often than one might imagine in a "free, adult, and uncensored" theatre; *The Cradle Will Rock*, *Model Tenement*, *Hymn to the Rising Sun*, and *Ethiopia* are glaring examples of this practice and typically led to prominent personnel parting company with the FTP entirely. Was *Altars of Steel* an example of a text so riddled with social and political commentary and revolutionary ideas that it posed a threat to the social, political, and economic order of the Deep South? If so, why would Flanagan—who had a history of refusing to allow production of politically seditious plays such as this—allow the play to be produced by the FTP, particularly in a region in which the project was already struggling? On the other hand, it is certainly possible that Flanagan and local FTP personnel saw *Altars of Steel* as highly relevant, locally created drama catering to prominent issues in Birmingham, rather than a radical attempt to subvert the southern hegemony. Regardless, it is noteworthy that the troubled rehearsal and production experiences of *Altars of Steel* bear a striking similarity to that of Marc Blitzstein's *The Cradle Will Rock* (which would occur in New York City only a few months later). Perhaps the ideology inherent in a labor play revolving around worker rights, unions, the threat of company violence, and the uprising of a mixed-race working class was, in point of fact, so disturbing to the social and economic hegemony of the city that both the play and the Birmingham FTP needed to be eliminated; it was, quite simply, *too* relevant to the Birmingham social situation.

Altars of Steel dramatizes the story of the local Birmingham steel mill that is bought out by a large northern corporation, United Steel. A Communist worker, Draper, attempts to incite discontent amongst the workers, and the new conglomerate owner, Karl Jung, alienates the workers by demanding a work speedup, reducing wages, paying the workers in money that can only be used at the company store, prohibiting worker meetings and unions, and disbanding the safety department. He refuses to upgrade the worn-out equipment and confides in the management team that he plans to replace the old furnaces and machinery only when they break; at that time, he plans to drastically reduce the number of workers as well. In stark contrast to the benevolent reign of the previous owner, Mr. Worth, Jung clearly cares for neither the working men nor the community. In spite of repeated warnings by the former management—warnings that become so forceful that the entire team finally resigns in protest—Jung demands increased production. Nineteen workers die brutal deaths in the accident that follows. Urged on by the Communist upstart, the survivors riot and begin tearing the mill apart in their efforts to find and kill Jung. Trapped as he waits for the United Steel strikebreakers to arrive and deserted by the corrupt civil authorities, Jung begs Worth to reason with the men. Worth agrees, on the condition that Jung admits responsibility for the men's deaths and reinstate Worth's company majority. When Jung capitulates, Worth endeavors to reason with the men, but tempers flare, the Communist fires a shot at Worth, and Worth dies. Many more are killed or wounded in the ensuing bloodbath, and the play closes with the following announcement reported over a loudspeaker:

> The Special grand jury investigating the tragic death of nineteen men in the fatal explosion of Number Four open hearth at the plant of the United Steel, Iron, and Coal Company has returned a verdict absolving any individual from criminal guilt. The verdict recites that while the men were killed in the firing of a defective furnace, there is no evidence to prove definitely who gave the order to fire the furnace. There are charges and counter charges of political pressure and bribery to influence the verdict of NOT GUILTY.[47]

Thus, in spite of the clear portrayal of Jung's guilt in the play and the presumably damning testimony of Worth's safety inspector, foreman, and other employees, the courts absolve Jung of all responsibility. Nineteen workers are dead, United Steel retains ownership of Worth's steel mill, and the expectation of safe work conditions for mill workers disintegrates.

On the surface, the play appears simply to replay a series of events that actually occurred when Judge Elbert Gary (U.S. Steel's paternalistic chief executive in Birmingham) passed away in 1927 and new management arrived. As in the play, the new management was unconcerned with worker safety, took advantage of the workers, forced a company union on the men, and conspired with local police and government officials to prevent worker organization. During the early years of the Depression, steel production in Birmingham reached its all-time low; mills operated at between 40 and 60 percent of capacity, and the blast furnaces that once lit the nighttime sky with a continuous scarlet glow burned only sporadically. In a contemporary parallel and sardonic commentary, the character of Karl Jung serves as the villainous representative of United Steel in the play. In 1936, U.S. Steel appointed Arthur H. Young as the first vice president of industrial relations. Charged with negotiating a compromise between the company and the workers, Young's time at U.S. Steel ended in early 1937. His all-too-brief employment was a model of safety and worker advocacy; he was a safety expert for the U.S. Employees Compensations Commission, chief safety expert of arsenals and Navy yards during World War I, and consultant to the Secretary of War during World War II. A stark contrast to the profit-driven Jung in the play, the real-life Young abhorred the actions large corporations took against their workers; in 1935, Young was quoted in *Time* as stating that he would "rather 'go to jail or be convicted as a felon' than obey the provisions of the Wagner Bill."[48] Thus, while the possibility remains that the choice of "Jung" as the name of the parallel character in *Altars of Steel* could have been a coincidence, this comparison between Karl Jung, the play's two-faced villain, and Arthur Young, the real-life advocate for the worker, would likely have reminded audience members of the possibilities inherent in a caring management.

While the historical and contemporaneous references are apparent, it is also important to note the similarity of the play to the events of 1907. Prior to the financial panic of 1907, TCI was one of the major employers in the city of Birmingham as well as a leading producer of pig iron for the United States. The economic crisis caught TCI in the midst of expansion and associated debt, and the dramatic decrease in product demand left the company financially vulnerable. With Moore and Schley, a New York brokering firm heavily invested in TCI, close to collapse and amidst widespread fear of the repercussions of such a failure in the stock market, the executive board of U.S. Steel debated the purchase of TCI. After numerous conferences, the board sent an envoy to President Theodore Roosevelt to determine his position regarding the major problem associated with the purchase; the combined interests of U.S. Steel and TCI would constitute 60 percent of the iron and steel market, thereby creating a monopoly.[49] Roosevelt's tacit approval focused on the benevolent gesture proposed by U.S. Steel. He noted that the representatives of U.S. Steel:

> feel that it is immensely to their interest, as to the interest of every responsible business man, to try and prevent a panic and general industrial smash up at this time. [...O]f course I could not advise them to take the action proposed [but] I felt it no public duty of mine to interpose any objection.[50]

Buoyed by Roosevelt's support, U.S. Steel purchased TCI for approximately one-third of its market value.

U.S. Steel's "munificent" purchase of TCI is replayed in the early scenes of *Altars of Steel* with a careful attention to historical detail. As the play unfolds, the audience learns that Mr. Worth is heavily in debt due largely to his attempts to take care of his workers during the Depression. In spite of Worth's extraordinary efforts to raise money and take out additional loans, United Steel purchases every bank in the state of Alabama so as to call Worth's loans and foreclose when he is unable to pay. Worth's appeals to the federal government go unanswered: "With the acquisition of this property they will control over sixty percent [of America's steel business, but] the government does not feel called upon to intervene."[51] In *Altars of*

Steel, United Steel acquires the Southern Steel Company for one-quarter of its value.

While the parallels to the U.S. Steel procurement of TCI in 1907 and United Steel's hostile takeover of the Southern Steel Company in *Altars of Steel* are striking, the play goes on to reflect and challenge the social and cultural hegemony of contemporaneous Birmingham. At this point, TCI (owned and run by U.S. Steel) was struggling financially, as was the city of Birmingham and the state of Alabama. U.S. Steel's profits and productivity plummeted in the 1930s, dropping from earnings of 200 million dollars in 1929 to a loss of over 70 million in 1932.[52] Times were desperate in Birmingham.

One of the first scenes of *Altars of Steel* introduces the concept of unionization as well as one of the show's primary antagonists, a Communist worker who immediately sets out to inflame tensions among the other steel workers:

BILL: Then stand by the company. That's where you get your pay from. The more money the company makes the more time you'll work.

1ST WORKER: Ain't nobody going to talk me into joinin' no union.

CHECKER: Maybe not—but you ought to hear the talk that passes this window every day. Somebody ought to tell Old Man Worth.

DRAPER: *(who until now has been in the background)* Turn informer, would you? Don't you know enough to stick by your class?

(There is a sudden silence)

BILL: Who the hell are you buddie?[53]

This scene gestures toward several facets of the southern struggle for power during this period. First, the seasoned workers in this scene feel no need to join a union because they perceive their current employer, Mr. Worth, to be a reasonable, caring, and genteel man. When one of these loyal workers makes known Draper's Communist beliefs, Worth calls Draper to his office to discuss the matter. In the face of Draper's incendiary accusations, physical threats, and refusal to discuss his position rationally, Worth gives him an advance on his paycheck, allows the man to take both his Communist leaflets and his pistol back to work in the mill, and says simply, "He's so young…and he's a sick man—sick in his mind."[54] Worth's words not only show his kind practicality, but demonstrate a paternal concern and pity for the poor, mentally ill Communists that populate the city causing trouble. He does not take Draper seriously in spite of his loaded pistol and inflammatory ideas; this treatment effectively robs Draper of his political virility in the eyes of both the working men and the audience. Dennis Jerz, in his analysis of *Altars of Steel* within the context of machinery and technology, argues that Draper is "a drifter, a newcomer, [...] a murderer [and a] rhetorically effective agitator."[55] Worth's approach to Draper mirrors the "Golden Rule" philosophy adopted by TCI in the 1920s; by following a Christian model, employers took on the role of "fathers" with a "divinely sanctioned responsibility" for their children, or employees. While Worth is not referred to specifically as a "father" in the script, he clearly performs the role in the way that he attends to his employees; he cares for their welfare, encourages them to make their own decisions, and counsels good behavior and responsibility.[56] While it is certainly true that Draper, the man who ultimately shoots and kills Mr. Worth, is dangerous, it is vital to realize his role within the context of the social and cultural moment. Draper's Communistic beliefs in conjunction with his outspoken, irrational, and blasphemous remarks place him in a position in which he is seen as one who capitalizes on the tragic deaths of fellow workers in order to create chaos, not as a leader who will better the situation of the workers.

It is also interesting to note that, while the play makes no mention of the KKK, the men react with a careful vigilance once they learn that Draper is a Communist with an eye toward unionizing. Even Mr. Worth asks his foreman to "keep an eye on Draper."[57] While it is certainly possible that this reaction is due to a distrust of outsiders or anxiety related to unionizing and strikes, it is also likely that this reaction carries an undercurrent of fear with respect to a violent Klan backlash. The lack of Klan presence is conspicuous in the play, particularly when one considers that the play was written during a "wave of anti-Communist police repression" that reached its height with the beating of Joseph Gelders, an educated Jewish Birmingham native who had become the political liaison for the Communist party.[58] In light of this connection between Communism and Jews, it is notable that Draper espouses no particular religious affiliation in the play.

Finally, *Altars of Steel* calls attention to Southern pride and nationalism. In the play, southerners are characterized by well-mannered, courteous men like Worth and honorable, hard-working laborers. As long as Worth controls the steel mill, the men remain safe and basically content; it is only when United Steel purchases the company that trouble begins. Their reign ushers in a time of strikes, riots, and murder, a period that is capitalized on by Draper, the Yankee Communist. Again, the workers shun Draper until the northern management treats them poorly, thereby inciting the ensuing problems. In this agitprop drama, it follows that the southerners suffer at the end of the play. After raising the mob of angry workers to a fever pitch, Draper shoots Worth, leaving his son to reinstate the previous working conditions for the men (see Figure 5).[59]

Here, the Communist murders the beloved southern gentleman while the Yankee Industrialist's greed causes 19 workers to burn to death. The play ends as Jung escapes, the fate of the southern mill hangs uncertain, and the workers reach a state of anger and frustration that would make any steel mill owner wish to sneak quietly out of the theatre before anyone realizes his identity. This unsettling and provocative ending leaves one appalled at the outright injustice of the situation, and it is not difficult to imagine the agitated state of mind that could engulf an audience of Birmingham steelworkers, families, and friends. The lesson in the abuse

Figure 5 The riot scene from the Atlanta production of *Altars of Steel* provides a good opportunity to see the size of the cast, the expressionistic set, and the power of this climactic scene. Note the three men positioned between the owners and workers, pointing guns at the rioters and, with them, the audience. Federal Theatre Project Collection, Special Collections & Archives, George Mason University Libraries.

of power ends in a call for the South to rise from the ashes of the steel mill and regain its resources, people, and pride. In this way, *Altars of Steel* plays on southern pride, nationalism, and the potential power of the proportionally enormous working class in a way that clearly challenges the social, political, and cultural hegemony of Birmingham. Even though it was produced in Atlanta, *Altars of Steel* spurred weeks of controversy that spread quickly throughout the nation.

STORYTELLING, CHIGGERS, AND THE BIBLE BELT: THE GEORGIA EXPERIMENT AS THE PUBLIC FACE OF THE FEDERAL THEATRE PROJECT[60]

> Their feet are still in the mud. They live in indescribable want, want of food, want of houses, want of any kind of life. [...] Their one entertainment is an occasional revival meeting, so when I get excited, tear around and gesticulate, they think it's the Holy Ghost descending upon me. It isn't. It's a combination of rage that such conditions should exist in our country, and chiggers, which I share with my audience.[61]
>
> —*Herbert Stratton Price*

As I have frequently argued, no study of the FTP is complete without consideration of its many and varied efforts to take theatre beyond the primary urban centers in each region. After all, one of Flanagan's expressed intentions was to create a federation of theatres that was national in scope but regional and local in emphasis. She hoped to take this endeavor further than simply supplanting productions that garnered popular or critical acclaim in urban theatres into the smaller cities, towns, and countryside. For Flanagan, McGee, Lentz, and many other members of the administrative inner circle, these locales were opportunities to build a theatre that would reignite popular interest in what was widely perceived to be a dying art form. More than any other, the decentralized FTP units would provide fertile ground for a grassroots, community-based theatre. Ironically, since these performances are often the most difficult to research, they are the least likely to appear in scholarly analysis.

Though the "flying squadron" method described above served as a model for many FTP activities in the South, Flanagan encouraged conversations with other federal, state, and local relief agencies, hoping to engender relationships that would eventually return dividends in the form of locally relevant theatre for individuals outside of Atlanta, Miami, New Orleans, and a few other dominant cities. The Georgia Experiment built on these conversations and eventually became emblematic of the FTP's ability to connect with audiences in the country. In fact, one of the most frequently repeated stories of the FTP's rural activities centers on a community puppet theatre somewhere in Georgia:

> In many places in Georgia the children were taught to make puppet theatres and puppets, and one day Herbert Price made a discovery. A little girl tried to smuggle the puppet she had been making home under her ragged dress, and when it was discovered she refused to give it up.
> "Hit's mine. Hit's the onliest thing I ever had what was mine."
> The theatre changed its activity temporarily, and for the first time every child in the vicinity had a doll—a corncob doll dressed in gay clothes made of old sugar sacking dyed with the berries of the region.[62]

That FTP personnel were able to integrate themselves into this rural southern community to such a degree was testament both to the power of theatre as a universal device and the agency of the communities that embraced the project. This simple example showed the needs of a single child altering—if only temporarily—the activities of the local FTP; she stole a doll, refused to give it back, explained her reasoning, and soon all the local children had their own locally created dolls courtesy of the FTP. The veracity of this story notwithstanding, it is a charming tale of the FTP's effect on the small communities in Georgia, and an example of the mythology that surrounded the project's efforts.

The story of this young puppet-thief appears repeatedly in the FTP literature, and epitomizes the goals of the project on national, regional, and local scales. This section will examine the Georgia Experiment in terms of its goals and achievements, and then contextualize it within the mythology of the FTP as a whole. In the Georgia Experiment, three distinct threads became tangled, resulting in an example of slippage between stated goals, reality, and the public face of the FTP. Why was this story so vital to the public face of the FTP? Moreover, what does it mean that no archival evidence for this particular event appears to exist? In order to examine these questions, it is first necessary to flesh out the cultural context surrounding the Georgia Experiment with respect to Flanagan's goals nationally and in Georgia. I will then juxtapose the reality of the Georgia Experiment with the public mythology of the project in the aforementioned anecdote.

In the summer of 1936, an Englishman by the name of Herbert Stratton Price appeared in Flanagan's Washington office and asked for "something hard to do." Ideally suited for an adventure in community drama development, Price had experience in acting, directing, and stage management, as well as knowledge of sociology and interest in rural community drama.[63] He had worked as a liaison between the FTP and the Recreation and Resettlement Project; in this capacity, he traveled throughout 12 southern states attending conferences, demonstrating techniques, initiating and developing an extensive network of contacts throughout the WPA, and building up local and regional interest in recreational and community drama. Flanagan challenged Price to detail a viable proposal for an experimental recreational drama program. Price's plan would extend beyond the urban centers and into the vast countryside, focusing primarily on smaller cities and towns in the Deep South:

> The ideal achievement is for the plays produced by the Community Drama Groups to draw color and background from the life, desires, and ambitions of the community itself. The ultimate aim is not chiefly the production of plays, but the encouragement of the people in the free exercise of their imagination.[64]

Price emphasized the same traits that Flanagan herself highlighted in her plans for the FTP on a national level. The Georgia Experiment would draw from local issues and concerns in a way that invited community members to shape their own theatre, thus providing agency to a group of individuals who had received little opportunity to shape their own public personas since the Depression began. In this way, community drama would provide a form of recreation and develop skills, work, and talents, as well as much needed moral support to a struggling nation while employing only a few key individuals in leadership roles. While the Georgia Experiment itself relied on the strength of the foundation that Eugene Bergmann (Georgia's community drama consultant) and Price developed in their travels, the experiment could serve as a model for expansion to other communities in Georgia, the South, and the nation.

Once Price convinced the national administration that the project would satisfy a local need, employ theatre artists, and help to stabilize the FTP's unpredictable position in Georgia and the South, he received approval for a 90-day experimental collaboration with the Divisions of Recreation Projects and Women's, Service and Professional Projects. These drama consultants would retain their current project assignments and salaries but work locally in specific Georgia towns and cities for the duration of the Georgia Experiment; if successful in instigating the development of a community drama program, consultants would have the option to remain in Georgia to continue their work after the 90 days.[65] Price chose five individuals from the New York Community Drama Program with the assistance of the program supervisor, Madalyn O'Shea. Linked to a training program for community theatre directors, the popular New York Community Drama Program had personnel to spare. The FTP sent these five drama consultants—Mary Dirnberger (Savannah), Charles Carey (Columbus), Joseph Fetsch (Augusta), Howard Gantier (Albany), and Edward J. Hayes (Rome)—into Georgia communities in early 1937. Bergmann, an industrious Georgian who began his career with the FTP via a letter-writing campaign as an advocate for theatre in his state, was reassigned to Atlanta when the other five drama consultants arrived, thus bringing the total number of recreational theatre projects to six. The project mission was "to organize and develop Community Drama Groups."[66] More specifically, these six people had three months to travel into the small cities and communities of Georgia, incite or capitalize on local interest in theatre and create drama that the people of the community would support financially once the three-month experiment ended.

Many interested parties followed the Georgia Experiment. In addition to Flanagan and the national FTP administration, Frances Nimmo Green, Gay Shepperson (administrator in the Division of Recreation Projects), D. G. Nichols (district director of the Division of Women's, Service and Professional Projects), and numerous WPA officials requested repeated updates on the project. Early in the process, Shepperson expressed interest in a loose partnership between the FTP and the recreation projects. Her interest was apparent in her letters:

> I want to make a special trip to see the effects of this work personally, which I plan to do before long.
>
> On my recent trip North I stopped in the Washington office and found the entire office intensely interested in this Georgia experiment and are [*sic*] very anxious to get first hand information of the progress of the experiment. [...T]here seems to be no question about its ultimate success.[67]

Undoubtedly, the Georgia Experiment was buoyed by the optimism of the FTP, Division of Recreation, and WPA.

Though the Georgia Experiment varied somewhat based on location, the basic outline of the projects' goals and methods remained consistent. This section will focus on one of the five experiment centers in Rome,

Georgia. Neither the most successful nor the least successful, Rome appears to have been an average project in community response, challenges, and relative successes. Located in northwest Georgia, just a few miles from the Alabama state border, Rome was a leading industrial city and boasted a population of approximately 22,000 people.[68] FTP community drama director Edward J. Hayes arrived on February 22, 1937. Like most of the other drama consultants, he was sent from New York City and arrived in Rome with little more than a suitcase and the name of the local recreation supervisor. His belongings were in storage, he had no lodgings, and travel and expenses came out of his own pocket, as his travel reimbursement and paycheck were to arrive at a later date.[69] Hayes and his family stayed with the local recreation supervisor for a week, all the while seeking affordable accommodations and attempting to establish a rapport with the locals.

Certainly, Hayes encountered numerous challenges during his 90 days in Rome; yet he experienced a number of successes as well, as evidenced by his reports to Price and local newspaper records in Rome. Hayes's early reports to Price list many problems. Upon arrival he found the disorganized local Drama Committee and little overall interest in the project. As he described it, his invitations in the decidedly anti-Roosevelt newspapers went unanswered, forcing him to "go out into the highways and byways to secure members and arouse some enthusiasm."[70] Compounding Hayes's challenges as an outsider in a moderately sized southern town was the conspicuous absence of the project's supervisor, Herbert Stratton Price; instead, Price was spearheading a campaign to bring theatre to the thousands of flood refugees following the Great Flood of 1937 (see chapter five). Price had planned a series of staggered openings for the Georgia Experiment during January and February of 1937, which would allow him to make an initial introduction for each drama consultant locally and help to smooth his/her entrance into the community. Since Price conceived of the program and laid the foundation for its success with his numerous trips and vast network of local contacts, both at the community level and within the WPA state administration, his absence left a gap for those drama consultants who arrived in late January and throughout February.

It is interesting to note the contrast in Hayes's perceptions and those of the "poorly organized" Drama Committee and other citizens of Rome. In a letter to Price, Assistant Recreation Supervisor R. H. Elliott, a citizen of Rome, reported that the "first week's work by Mr. Hayes in Rome has produced much interest and much organization progress." According to Elliott, the Drama Committee built up Hayes's arrival in the newspapers, arranged for office and auditorium space, and secured initial funding for the program. Elliott personally introduced Hayes to members of the Drama Committee, radio stations, and newspapers, and as I have noted, invited Hayes's family to stay in his home until Hayes could arrange suitable accommodations at the local hotel.[71]

Elliott's perception of the local interest in the program appears to be validated by the accounts printed in the *Rome News-Tribune*, the only local Roman newspaper in the 1930s. The *Rome News-Tribune* printed a surprising number of articles related to the FTP's experiment in Rome and serves as one of the few remaining chronicles of those activities outside of the National Archives and Library of Congress. Though none of these articles were attributed to a specific writer, a pattern repeated throughout the paper with nearly all of the articles, the writer(s) did not seem particularly anti-FTP, anti-Georgia Experiment, or anti-Hayes (though the paper habitually decried Roosevelt's New Deal, the WPA, Social Security, the Supreme Court, and many of the more liberal political policies of the president's administration). The first article, printed a week before Hayes arrived in Rome, referred to the recent visit of the Atlanta Theatre Guild inciting local interest in the theatre and looked forward to Hayes's arrival with great anticipation. The advisory committee, which had formed months earlier to engage Price, the FTP, and the WPA in discussions about a community theatre in Rome, featured a number of prominent Romans who would eventually play major roles in the local FTP production of Channing Pollock's *The Fool* and in the numerous radio plays and religious dramas.[72] Repeatedly, the newspaper articles chronicled the community's excitement, the exotic nature of the New Yorker sent to their town by the FTP, and the fact that Rome had been singled out as one of only five points in the state for this "recognition and opportunity." As Hayes and the Drama Committee announced decisions and opportunities, the articles betray a distinct pride; according to the *Rome-News Tribune*, *The Fool* "made theatrical history" and the fact that their recreational drama program planned to take on "one of the most difficult of productions" placed Rome on a cultural footing parallel to Atlanta and Savannah. In fact, the paper predicted *The Fool's* opening as "one of the finest amateur performances in the history of Rome."[73]

By mid-March, the recreational drama unit in Rome had its own name—the Community Drama Players of Rome—and continued to appear regularly in the newspaper with tidbits about radio dramas, religious programming, and rehearsal updates. Articles pointed to the positive attitude of the town toward the players, the high quality of the stage sets (created by Romans for their production), the talent of their community drama director, and the skills of the Romans involved in the production. In fact, it seems that Hayes successfully won over the "anti-administration newspaper" he referred to in his initial report to Price by the time the 90-day Georgia Experiment concluded in Rome.

This disparity between the different perspectives is striking; Hayes insisted that the community's apathy jeopardized the project while the local perception, as demonstrated by Elliott and the *Rome News-Tribune,* was optimistic and pleased with the program's progress. About a month after his arrival, Hayes reevaluated his difficulties as follows:

> The principal obstacle or difficulty to the Drama movement in Rome, as I see it [...] is not the lack of interest, but the CLASS barrier[. T]here is a very distinct social strata in this town and it's going to be a hard job to hurdle it[. I] consider this the real problem, but I really believe that I [am] making some headway [...] and altho [*sic*] the results are not what I should like them to be, I think that I will eventually succeed in leveling the barrier to some extent.[74]

This statement points to several issues of interest. First, it is important to note that Hayes's impression of local apathy had transformed into an issue of class, and that he left out all mention of the highly charged topic of racial relations. Perhaps most illuminating, though, is the implicit assumption that the project was already enjoying success with one class and that Hayes wanted to expand his program across class barriers so as to include a larger portion of the community. Considering the obstacles Hayes faced upon his arrival in Rome, this speaks to an extraordinary level of success in a single month of work.

These widely varying initial impressions notwithstanding, it is clear that Hayes's success swelled as the experiment continued. In three short months, he produced *The Fool,* spoke at a number of local schools and churches, and created a radio broadcast that went out over the local radio station every Sunday. In addition, as the *Rome News-Tribune* explained, Hayes spearheaded a seven-week, free series of "religious dramatic presentations" on Sunday afternoons in a local community auditorium. "All plays," asserted the newspaper, were "endorsed by local ministers [...and carried] vivid Biblical messages."[75] A special Mother's Day production included exclusive seating and complimentary transportation for any mothers who wished to attend the performance of *A Mother's Memories,* based on the first chapter of the gospel of Luke, verses 40–48.[76] Other works included *He is Risen,* a radio drama designed to offer listeners insight into the transformation of the disciples from "perplexity and sorrow into belief and understanding" and to deepen listeners' "appreciation of the Risen Christ," as well as *The Prodigal Son, The Living Christ, The Widow's Mite,* and *The Stranger at the Gate.*[77] Each of these plays enacted and illuminated specific Bible verses. These religious plays were so popular with audiences that they carried on for several weeks after Hayes returned to New York City at the end of May. In his work with the Rome community, Hayes included a group of about 65 during the first month. He cast 37 Romans in *The Fool,* used more to build the production, and set up classes for those interested in playwriting, design, and other theatrical activities. Like the other recreational drama leaders, Hayes worked with children and saw interest spike in subsequent months.

As a testimony to Hayes's success in Rome, the citizens of a sister town sent an envoy to Hayes requesting that he organize and lead a similar community drama program in Marietta, a town about 50 miles southeast of Rome. Approval for their request arrived through official FTP channels, and Hayes described Marietta's enthusiasm for the program as dwarfing what he found in Rome. He chose another Channing Pollock play, *The Enemy,* cast it, and began the rehearsal process in mid-March 1937.[78] In fact, the *Rome News-Tribune* deemed Hayes's efforts to build a program in Marietta important enough to publish pertinent details; articles noted that rehearsals were being held at the Episcopal church and that "leading citizens" of Marietta were both interested and involved in the local community drama movement.[79] The situation in Marietta proved difficult for Hayes, though, as was shown in one of the few letters to Price from the latter period of Hayes's work in Rome. Hayes found it "absolutely impossible to serve the Marietta District under the present arrangement. [...] I can not [sic] see how I can give them any more time in Marietta as they are requesting without neglecting the Rome program."[80] Hayes cited two specific difficulties in this letter, including the two-dollar fare to Marietta (and the lack of timely reimbursement of these funds) and the time required to run two individual programs in two different cities. The issue of time aside, traveling the 100-mile roundtrip to Marietta for rehearsals of a production—even a couple of times per week—would have required approximately 15–20 percent of his pre-tax monthly salary. Hayes's involvement with the community drama program in Marietta appears to have ended around this time, as subsequent FTP correspondence demonstrated an unwillingness to fund his travel expenses and Hayes was unable to pay the fare.

Hayes's experience in Marietta evokes questions that cannot be satisfactorily answered by the archive. Why did members of the Marietta community choose to travel to Rome to invite Hayes to spearhead their community drama movement when Atlanta was a mere 20 miles away and possessed both superior resources and a recreational drama consultant in a position parallel to that which Hayes held in Rome? Eugene Bergmann of Atlanta had traveled throughout the state in his capacity as a statewide drama consultant, so it is probable that he was familiar with the Marietta community. Since the request received approval on both the state and regional administrative levels within the FTP, the choice of Hayes over Bergmann was likely a conscious one that was at least tacitly reinforced by the approval of the FTP. In what way(s), then, was Hayes a more appealing candidate than Bergmann? Second, local newspapers show no record of performances of Pollock's *The Enemy* in Marietta; there is, however, record of a community theatre group, led by Eugene Bergmann, rehearsing and performing August L. Stern's *The Hired Husband* in late May.[81] The *Marietta Journal* awaited the performance with great anticipation; it predicted "one of the best [performances] ever produced in Marietta" and noted the cast spaghetti dinner that celebrated opening night.[82]

While archival records and other primary sources fail to satisfactorily address these questions, I suggest that Hayes and Bergmann offered distinct programming choices to their respective communities and that Hayes was more appealing to the community of Marietta—until Hayes found himself unable to continue due to time limitations and financial hardship. Bergmann's choice, *The Hired Husband*, was a light, Broadway-style comedy. His own work throughout the state of Georgia was expansive, ranging from storytelling and holiday pageants to the staging of three original programs in the Slash Pine Festival (Waycross, Georgia); D. G. Nichols touted Bergmann's role in the festival, writing, "I think he did more for us in putting over the value of the recreation program to a large group of representative people from all over the state than anything we have done so far."[83] A notable accomplishment, this ultimately paved the way for the conceptualization and realization of the Georgia Experiment. However, it is clear that Bergmann's productions tended toward lighter fare, comedies, marionettes, and children's theatre being the most common.

In contrast, the program that Hayes offered in Rome consisted almost exclusively of drama with a respectful focus on religion, much of which (according to newspaper accounts) was actually approved by the ministers of the local churches; in fact, two of the five core members of Rome's Drama Committee—Reverend John H. Wood and Reverend H. F. Joynet—were local religious figures. The little that I have been able to glean of Hayes's personal background suggests that he would be uniquely suited to the creation of a community drama program with strong religious overtones. Hayes directed the Broadway Temple Players in New York City in a production of the one-act drama *The Widow's Mite* at the Broadway Tabernacle Methodist Episcopal Church in 1934, prior to his induction into the FTP's community drama program in 1936; he would choose *The Widow's Mite* for production in Rome as well.[84] Hayes also grew up in a theologically oriented family. His brother, Reverend Thomas J. Hayes, was a professor of philosophy at St. Anselm's College and his sister, Anna M. Hayes, became the Reverend Mother of the Western Province of the Order of the Little Sisters of the Poor, a Roman Catholic religious order for women.[85] Hayes's direction of the Broadway Temple Players demonstrated a link—whether or not his own religious proclivities tended in this direction—to the Methodist Episcopal Church. I suggest that this ability to integrate religion and theatre served Hayes well in his capacity as drama consultant in Rome. During the 1930s, at least 16 percent of Floyd County residents over the age of 14 were members of the various branches of the Methodist Episcopal Church. Another 25 percent were members of branches of the Baptist Church, all of which were categorized as evangelical protestant religions. According to the U.S. Census, Rome made up just under half of the Floyd County population. The statistics for Marietta (Cobb County) paralleled those of Rome in this area.[86] Certainly, religion could not be ignored as an identifying characteristic in these communities; Hayes's ability to unite religion and community drama deferentially was likely one of the keys to his success in Rome, as well as one of the factors that drew the community representatives of Marietta to him, rather than the light comedies of Eugene Bergmann.

In many ways, Hayes's experiences in Rome were indicative of the Georgia Experiment as a whole. With the notable exception of North Carolina native Mary Dirnberger, drama consultant to the highly successful experiment in Savannah, most of the drama consultants met initial resistance of varying degrees. Though Price knew it could pose a problem, he was forced to send New York directors and organizers to lead four of the five rural projects as he could not find any Georgians that were qualified as community theatre directors, on relief, and willing to lead the projects in these small towns. As Price would argue in his assessment of the program, "It is obviously difficult, if not impossible, to competently judge any experiment or project without personal knowledge of community problems, attitudes, and resources."[87] This lack of firsthand knowledge of the region, compounded by Price's absence because of the ill-timed flooding of the Ohio and Mississippi Rivers, stymied several of the projects during the crucial formative weeks. Moreover, Price noted that some of the projects took place in communities that already had some basic interest in theatre—and in some cases, infrastructures in place for the production of community theatre—while others did not. In Savannah, Columbus, Atlanta, and Rome, drama consultants built on the interest or organizations already in place; this was one of the keys to success in such an intense, brief experiment in recreational theatre.[88] Since the experiment only lasted for three months, the drama consultants simply did not have time to develop leisurely relationships with members of the community in addition to building a recreational drama program. Price highlighted the need to train local personnel and emphasized the importance of flexibility in theatre recreation projects:

> One thing which this experiment has revealed is the desirability of using more than one method of approach and more than one method of organization. There should be freedom to adopt that method of approach and organization which would appear to be the most effective in a community in light of local conditions.[89]

Price's argument—that each project director should be empowered to adopt the most effective method to approach his/her local community—recalled Flanagan's ideas regarding the need for a decentralized, locally relevant focus to the FTP as a whole. For both Price and Flanagan, these practices required personnel in each location to learn about their communities in visceral, individualized ways so that they could tailor recreational drama programs to fit those needs. This knowledge was particularly crucial in the South with its common use of the "flying squadron" method, which suffered the unfortunate side effect of distancing these traveling artists and administrators from the communities in which they produced FTP work.

Price's ideas were so successful, and coincided so well with Flanagan's goals for the FTP as a whole, that they excited interest in Pennsylvania, West Virginia, and North Carolina. WPA administrators from these states approached Price regarding the possibility of a similar recreational program in their states. With the approval of the national administration, Price began preliminary work in North Carolina and West Virginia. Applying the principles learned in the Georgia Experiment, Price sought professional FTP personnel native to each state to spearhead the movement.[90] In May of 1938, Price wrote of his success building a parallel program in North Carolina. It was only when repeated threats to Price's job coincided with prohibitive cutbacks in the FTP that these projects stalled.

The previous discussion of the Georgia Experiment considers the program's goals, execution, and achievements through a case study of Edward J. Hayes's activities in Rome. To return to my earlier question, what of the mythology that has grown up around the program? In a 1938 letter to Flanagan, Price described the success of his recent trip to North Carolina and broached a dilemma; the International Grenfell Association had offered Price a position in community organization in northern Newfoundland. Yet his reluctance to leave the FTP shone through: "As you well know I have pioneered in the field that now appears to be on the brink of real development. I should, of course, like to remain with you if you feel there is a spot for me in this new and broader program."[91] Two months later, Price did not hesitate to chastise Flanagan for her assessment of the Georgia Experiment:

> If we had followed through on our original plan in community drama in other sections of the country—servicing key communities outside of the larger cities—these centers would today be our outposts in the field and our touring companies would have representatives strategically placed.[92]

A hand-written note in the margin, presumably by Flanagan, stated only, "True."

And so, the Georgia Experiment was reduced from the proverbial apple of the FTP's eye—a golden opportunity for meaningful collaborations between the FTP and sister WPA agencies, as well as a chance to truly realize Flanagan's goals for a relevant, community-based national theatre—to a few apocryphal stories. But the mythology endured. Recall the story of the young girl who stole her corncob puppet doll and supposedly changed the activities of the entire community drama group. This story became representative of the Georgia Experiment and, with it, FTP activities outside of the large urban centers; yet there is no archival evidence of this specific event and the probability of the FTP supplying funds for a mass puppet-making endeavor is poor. This story is in Flanagan's personal history of the FTP, *Federal Theatre, Federal One*,[93] and in countless other locales (though its source is never cited). In fact, the story is so frequently repeated that another FTP worker named Herbert Price saw it in print and felt it necessary to write to Lorraine Brown and the George Mason University Oral History Staff to correct the record; as he explained, he had never traveled to Georgia, let alone "helped little 'hill' people to make good dolls, as a side issue of puppetry, for their first possession of that type."[94] Though research demonstrates that this Herbert Price and the

Herbert Stratton Price who engineered the Georgia Experiment were, in fact, two different individuals, this Price's insistence that he has nothing to do with this story is interesting.

Yet the problem of the anecdote about the poor little girl who allegedly changed the face of the Georgia FTP remains. What can the scholar make of this (very likely false) story serving as the public face of the FTP's rural exploits? It is easy to see why this story is repeated; if true, it demonstrated the FTP's versatility and suggested that the FTP was in the process of integrating itself into the community in a physical and ideological way. The corncob dolls, distributed to every child in the area, would serve as tactile reminders of the FTP's presence and interest in the local population. More than that, these dolls were actually created by the children and became their sole possessions. Here was a kindred spirit—a struggling, plucky, federal organization that cared enough to identify what local children needed and then found a way to give it to them in spite of the obstacles. The appeal cannot be ignored.

In a 2003 essay, Thomas Postlewait debates the place of anecdotes in theatre history:

> Even the most diligent scholars have recognized that the distinction between facts and anecdotes (or records and legends) is impossible to maintain consistently in any examination of historical documents; many records are not factual; many anecdotes not only contain a kernel of factuality but also express representative truths.[95]

While I cannot designate the story of the young puppet thief as fact, I also cannot dismiss it as fiction. It is certainly possible that the story contains a "kernel of factuality" and quite likely that in evokes a "representative truth." If this story is a "representative truth," what does Flanagan's inclusion of it in *Arena* say about the role she hoped the FTP would play in rural and national theatre?

I suggest that the story of the FTP adapting to the needs of a poor, young girl was chosen (or shaped) to show a specific relationship between the FTP and its audience. The child was poor—clearly a member of the impoverished "people" who made up much of the FTP's audience. In this story, the FTP not only listened to her needs, but adapted its own function to serve those needs. The FTP prioritized serving the community on its own terms; no mention is made of the extensive bureaucratic process required to change activities, the loss in potential box office revenue, or the expenditure of funds involved in making dolls that would then be given to the community (as opposed to being maintained in the service of the government). The mythological FTP, free from the constraints the real FTP was forced to operate under throughout its existence, was able to become the people's theatre without concern for the consequences. Hence, if this story is fabricated, it is easy to see why this slippage between the actual and the mythological FTP was so appealing. It is this slippage that makes the Georgia Experiment such an intriguing case study for examining both the "real" and the imagined FTP. While the reality of the Georgia Experiment laid a successful foundation for further community drama activities, both in Georgia and as a model for parallel structures in other states, the program itself did not survive the cuts to funding and manpower. Instead, the energy of the Georgia Experiment fizzled when the drama consultants departed for New York and FTP support evaporated.

However, if this anecdote is resituated as part of the mythological public face of the FTP, the program takes on additional significance. In this light, the Georgia Experiment becomes an ideal example of the decentralization and local relevance that Flanagan prioritized. It employed relief workers, cost the government very little, raised public morale, helped develop FTP audiences, and played to public sympathies. The story of the child puppet-thief is an icon of Depression-era America: an innocent and youthful American, put down by economic strife and struggling to maintain her individuality and imagination, stands up for her rights and single-handedly makes her corner of the world a better place. This represents the best that the FTP would have to offer—locally relevant and desperately needed activities for American communities. And so, while the Georgia Experiment itself sputtered into obscurity, its mythology provided evidence of the virility of the FTP.

CONCLUSIONS

Vital to the study of the FTP as both national theatre and as a reflection of the constantly evolving relationship between Federal Theatre and its surrounding communities, *Altars of Steel* and the Georgia Experiment serve as case studies for examining that richly nuanced and troubled region that was the American South. The play and the program, both very different in content and execution, ultimately characterized similar ideals. Both served as illustrations of the decentralization and local relevance that Flanagan idealized by focusing on themes and issues that spoke to the specified audiences—urban in the case of *Altars of Steel*, and more rural in the case of the Georgia Experiment.

Altars of Steel is an example of a play that was so relevant to its community that it threatened the dominant power and was forcefully ejected. The production—or lack thereof—of *Altars of Steel* on its home turf in Birmingham provides fertile ground for the study of Federal Theatre and its ability to inspire indigenous drama that was truly by and about the people of a given region. In this particular case, it appears that the production reflected the people of Birmingham so closely that it was deemed dangerous, particularly in light of the contemporaneous issues surrounding U.S. Steel and the American Federation of Labor. In its ability to incite change, the "intensely interesting" *Altars of Steel* provides a glimpse into at least a portion of the working-class minds in Birmingham during the tumultuous Great Depression, illustrating the fears of the dominant authorities and the potential agency of the working class in Birmingham.[96]

Was *Altars of Steel* as "dangerous as *Uncle Tom's Cabin*" to the hierarchy of power in place in the South? In Birmingham—quite possibly. Certainly, the play both reflected and challenged the political, social, and economic hegemony prevalent in Birmingham during the Great Depression. A product of a troubled time, *Altars of Steel* followed in the tradition of agitprop plays like *Waiting for Lefty* and *The Cradle Will Rock*. It offered no simple solution, refrained from glossing over tough issues, and forced the audience to contemplate the social chaos caused by powerless workers. While it may not have led to a riot in Birmingham, it likely would have provoked vigorous and animated discussion. Unfortunately, the Birmingham FTP was a promise left unfulfilled; *Altars of Steel* is evidence that the people of Birmingham were in dire need of an organization that would provide a forum for the issues of the working class. The FTP response to the pressures upon the Birmingham unit, and to the play as a whole, was one example of the local, regional, and national pressures festering within the FTP.

The Georgia Experiment was equally relevant, but did not elicit the same type of response; instead, as exemplified by Edward J. Hayes's work in Rome, it capitalized on the interests and needs of the community by sending a single FTP drama consultant into specific locales and then catering to those individuals who participated in the project. In so doing, the Georgia Experiment served as an example of the willingness of the FTP to engage in productive exploration with potential audience members and to depart from normalized definitions of "good" or "successful" theatre. The desire to investigate different types of theatre dedicated to serving multiple purposes in communities that did not otherwise have access to a national theatre illustrates an FTP that had the capacity to morph into varied forms as its audience demanded. This flexible, adaptable FTP hints at the potential of the organization.

Together, the Georgia Experiment and *Altars of Steel* represent the FTP at its moments of greatest potential—employing relief workers, entertaining the masses, and providing locally relevant theatre for specific communities in the South. At the same time, both projects failed to create a lasting change in the FTP's methodologies on a national level. *Altars of Steel* was never produced in Birmingham, the city for which it was intended. While it sparked impassioned debate at the time of its performance and was known for its innovative design, soundtrack, and style, Flanagan certainly did not emphasize it in her memoirs and the world of theatre has not immortalized the production or play in any way. Similarly, the Georgia Experiment initially capitalized on local interests but lost momentum due to funding cuts and personnel disruptions and was never realized as a long-term project. And so, while both *Altars of Steel* and the Georgia Experiment were powerful responses to the political and cultural issues of the South, they are remembered as icons of the possibility rather than the realization of the FTP.

4. The Fading Frontier: Excavating the Portland Federal Theatre Project ∾

While in New York we were always moving heaven and earth to get shows open, in the West we urged restraint.[1]

—*Hallie Flanagan*

According to Flanagan, the Western Region of the FTP was different from other parts of the country; it was "flamboyant," "free and easy," and "exuberant and gusty." FTP units peppered the West in Seattle, Denver, Portland, and throughout California.[2] In *Arena*, Flanagan characterized FTP workers in the East as perceiving themselves as diametrically opposed and fundamentally at odds with the administration; by contrast, workers in the West saw disagreements as "family squabbles," little more than minor issues warranting only minimal discussion. In comparison to the FTP units in the East, the Western FTP also displayed optimism about its chances for success and about the venture in general. Flanagan explained:

Perhaps the western attitude may be symbolized by a Christmas scroll six feet long containing the individually inscribed names of every member of a company of over five-hundred people. I unrolled this from the bottom up, and so inured had I become, at that point in project history, to the slings and arrows of attack, that it was a surprise when I reached the top and saw, instead of a demand for my instant resignation, the Star of Bethlehem and the hope that it would guide my destiny and that of Federal Theatre.[3]

Flanagan's description of the western units connote a far different feel than that of the comparatively cutthroat FTP groups in New York City and the East, or the politically complex Midwest and South. Her account of the Portland unit was particularly complimentary. As she described it, unencumbered by political controversy, additional regulations, and the interference of the national FTP administration, the Portland unit simply moved forward with its productions. Though there were certainly challenges, Flanagan repeatedly referred to the arrangement between the FTP and the Oregon state WPA as "perfect":

> Of all the states in the country Federal Theatre had its most perfect working conditions in Oregon, under Mr. Griffith. He ran the business and administration end completely but he left program and artistic personnel entirely to us. Under this arrangement it is noticeable that there was no censorship in Oregon in spite of the fact that we did a strong program, including three living newspapers.[4]

Though Flanagan paints a rosy picture, the history behind her praise is significantly more complicated. Based on the extant archival evidence, Oregon's program was neither particularly strong (in the ideological sense) nor entirely free of censorship, both of which will serve as fodder for further exploration in this chapter. While the Oregon program may ultimately have evolved into the epitome of cooperation between the FTP and the WPA, it certainly did not begin that way.

The FTP unit in Portland, Oregon, serves as a useful case study for addressing the ways in which the FTP successfully realized Flanagan's goals for a locally relevant, quality theatre that focused on the interests of its community rather than simply replicating Broadway fare. Productions spanned a spectrum of topics and themes, focusing on national, regional, and local issues in a style that was drawn not only from the skills of the local actors and directors, but that also spoke to local audiences. In spite of (or perhaps, because of) the conservative leanings of the Oregon WPA and FTP administrations, the Portland FTP gained momentum and strength even as the national FTP faltered under political attack. The Portland FTP's ability to resonate with community interests effectively realized Flanagan's nationwide—and locally centered—goals. In a city of approximately 300,000, the fact that nearly 200,000 seats had been filled by the time the project closed in 1939 speaks to the way in which the project ultimately found its place in the Portland community. Moreover, the administration associated with the Portland unit had time to mature, and by the time the FTP closed in 1939, state and local officials collaborated well; in many ways, as Flanagan argued, the partnership between the administrative and artistic sides of the Portland FTP was ideal.

Though Flanagan regularly highlighted its strengths, scholarship dedicated to the Portland FTP is all but nonexistent. I suggest that there are two major reasons for this persistent omission. First, the relative scarcity of archival documents presents a substantial challenge in piecing together the history of the unit. Records are scattered, missing, and incomplete in the major FTP collections at the National Archives and Library of Congress.[5] Correspondence, employee records, many production records, and some of the general administration records are simply gone in spite of specific listings in the finding aids. This is unusual in the FTP collections, even given the comparatively small size and level of productivity in Portland. Secondly, through the persistent privileging of 'highbrow' theatre forms from urban centers (common both in scholarship and in the hierarchy of the FTP itself), productions with local resonance, particularly those from the proverbial boondocks, are often ignored in favor of Broadway-style shows and the splashy controversies that consistently shadowed high-profile urban productions. The Portland FTP, like the Georgia Experiment, serves as an example of the FTP capitalizing on local themes and talents to create theatre that worked for the people of Portland. The Portland project also provides a case study for the FTP outside the major urban centers like New York, Chicago, and Boston. In this way, the Portland FTP offers a more sweeping view of the impact of the FTP on the rest of the country. To this end, I discuss two specific productions, *Yellow Harvest* and *Timberline Tintypes*, as well as the role Timberline Lodge and the proposed Paul Bunyan Festival were to have played in the establishment of the FTP as a Portland institution.

Based on the previous chapters in this volume, the reader might reasonably expect that the topic of this chapter should be the FTP of either Los Angeles or San Francisco. Chicago and Boston were regional centers, and the activities of the Atlanta FTP certainly revolved around a major urban center. With the exception of the Georgia Experiment, I have worked thus far with productions that occurred in large regional cities outside of New York City. FTP employment figures placed the Illinois and Massachusetts FTP's at almost identical levels, both employing just over 1,000 people per state at the height of the FTP in May 1936. Compared to these two regional centers, the Portland FTP unit was minute; the state employment figures began at 34 in 1936 and grew to 53 people in 1939. Further differentiating Portland from the regional centers in Chicago, Boston, and Atlanta was the availability of resources; regional centers drew from vast supplies in terms of talent, space, funding, and potential audiences. Essentially, they could target a specific subgroup of the population and sculpt their productions to appeal to that group. In conjunction with the range of talent available to these regional centers, this widely varied potential audience offered the freedom to create edgy or controversial pieces, even at the risk of alienating a segment of that audience. Though Portland was a reasonably sized city in the 1930s, its population of 300,000 could not compete with Boston's 800,000, let alone Chicago's 4 million. The Portland FTP would never rival Chicago, Boston, or Atlanta in terms of box office receipts, volume of produced work, or the creation of aesthetically edgy theatre.

According to Flanagan's summary of FTP activities on a national level, the Oregon FTP was one of the smallest in terms of total output, budget, and staff. Yet, of the 33 states included in the FTP, Oregon was one of only five that grew in size from the May 1936 figures (designating the high point of FTP employment numbers) to those of June 1939 when the project ended. FTP units in Maine grew by approximately 30 percent, Colorado and Oregon by 50 percent, and Louisiana by more than 100 percent.[6] The projects in states with large urban centers like New York, Illinois, California, and Massachusetts dropped drastically in size; many lost at least half of their employees. This growth among the regional units, when coupled with the radical declines in the urban centers, denotes a trend worthy of investigation. Perhaps due to their focus on learning about their audiences rather than engaging in national political controversies, these smaller units found greater opportunity and justification for growth than their major urban counterparts; this suggests that Flanagan's goal of creating a decentralized national theatre had the potential to come to fruition. The smaller units successfully integrated themselves into their communities, often so much so that the local audiences failed to identify *their* FTP with the *national* FTP. This dissociation was often intentional. As a case in point, in Portland, State WPA Director E. J. Griffith deliberately used alternative names for the local FTP including the WPA Players, the Federal Players, and the WPA Theatre. In fact, Griffith persisted in using these surrogate names for the local FTP even when corrected by FTP Regional Director Ole Ness and, eventually, by Flanagan herself. Examining the Portland FTP's battle to gain acceptance within the Portland arts community, as well as a loyal local audience, provides new insights into the feasibility of Flanagan's goals for the FTP and into the FTP as a national federation of theatres.

The challenge of focusing on the Portland FTP is that archival evidence is significantly rarer than in the copious volumes available for those larger, controversial, and comparatively less successful models in the regional centers. While differences in size and productivity certainly account for part of the lack of archival documentation, correspondence between pivotal local figures is missing, as are approximately half of the district and regional reports and many of the original scripts. Of the 19 original pieces created by and for the Portland FTP for performances to local audiences, only six scripts remain extant in the Library of Congress, National Archives, or George Mason University collections; only one production book with detailed information on the pieces created by the Portland FTP exists. In contrast, scripts and production books remain for nearly all of the Portland productions of the shows the FTP produced on a national level. Though one might assume that the small Portland FTP had fewer resources to devote to archiving and tracking paperwork, the fact that these ephemera remain for productions that could be categorized as legitimate theatre, but are absent for vaudeville and variety shows, implies a bias in the creation or preservation of these records. Since my intention here is to locate those plays and productions that reveal the politics, culture, and relationships present in Portland in this historical moment, it is the productions that are uniquely created by and for the Portland FTP that are the focus of my study—a prospect made more complicated by the comparative lack of an archival base.

The gaps in the evidence may reveal two fundamental—and seemingly contradictory—issues regarding the underlying ideology of the FTP. First, the targeted lack of documentation implies that the FTP administration may have placed less value on a project that created entertaining vaudeville sketches or musical revues rather than political dramas such as *The Cradle Will Rock*, socially committed pieces like *Spirochete*, or living newspapers that would advance a new genre on American stages. The Portland FTP was not invested in creating experimental works that would serve the FTP's long-term aesthetic goals. Instead, the Portland FTP built on the talents and interests of its company members and audiences, and frequently looked back to the theatre of yesteryear to create its success. Second, it may have been the very success of the Portland FTP that resulted in this paucity of paperwork. Unlike the New York, Chicago, Atlanta, and Boston units, which generated controversy so continuously, the Portland unit seldom required FTP officials to mediate or intervene in its activities, which meant that records for such exchanges were never created in the central administrative records.

In *Oregon: End of the Trail*, Federal Writers' Program authors described a friendly, uncontroversial FTP that staged a few living newspapers and the popular children's theatre of Yasha Frank, as well as popular entertainments. The account emphasized the regional appeal of the Oregon

FTP: "Dance skits given at Timberline Lodge in 1937, depicting flax culture, Indian life, and other regional folk activities, were followed in 1938 by *Timberline Tintypes*, sketches portraying Oregon logger life."[7] Based on the production records of the Portland FTP, this factual description appears to be much more accurate than does Flanagan's earlier comment about the "strong program," which emphasized living newspaper productions with controversial themes and other edgy programming. In fact, the living newspapers that the Portland FTP produced tended to occur long after the controversies inspired by their politically volatile premieres had faded in other cities. Nick Chaivoe, an actor and stage manager in the Portland FTP, characterized the project similarly in his oral history interview, explaining that he "always had the feeling that [the director] wasn't too happy to do the Living Newspaper [...because it] attacked all the things she believed in."[8] Though these descriptions of a comparatively uncontroversial unit may not seem to be entirely complimentary, this does not preclude the possibility that the Portland FTP entertained local audiences, put relief funds to use employing and retraining theatre professionals, and created pieces that became a part of the local artistic and cultural landscape. Rather than attempting to adhere to a general concept of "good" drama, the Portland FTP offered its community theatre that was based on their needs and interests.

Like the big-city units in Chicago, Boston, and Atlanta, the Portland FTP experienced a number of early setbacks. Initially, the Northwest had difficulty procuring funds to begin an FTP program because of a lack of theatre professionals on the relief rolls, difficulty obtaining local sponsors, and other bureaucratic hurdles.[9] The talkies hit Portland's theatre particularly hard, and many of the individuals who considered themselves theatre professionals hailed from vaudeville, tab shows, and the circus, but had not actually earned their livings in these venues for some time. When WPA Project Director R. G. Dieck asked for FTP support in Portland, Glenn Hughes (then-director of the FTP's western region) replied that the relief rolls did not appear to support such a request. By the time the FTP came into being, the remnants of professional theatre in Portland consisted almost exclusively of amateur and community theatre. Since these actors had not earned their living from the theatre for years, the WPA did not consider them "professionals," and so they were not viable candidates for skilled wages in the FTP. Eventually, the WPA certified enough actors to serve as the foundation for the company, but the perception that the Portland FTP lacked quality and professionalism would plague the company throughout its existence.

The FTP hired Bess Whitcomb, the politically conservative and anti-union former director of the Bess Whitcomb Players and the Portland Civic Theatre, as the state director of the Oregon FTP in early 1936, and the Portland unit began operations that spring.[10] Local and regional leadership decided on a proposal that featured two separate units operating out of Portland. Under this plan one unit would produce two original plays by Oregon native and Broadway playwright Frederick Schlick; the other would tour Civilian Conservation Corps (CCC) camps throughout the state with vaudeville shows.[11] While the CCC tours would prove logistically difficult in Oregon because of travel restrictions and the complications of allowing women to spend the night in entirely male CCC camps, WPA officials and the national FTP administration supported the idea wholeheartedly; the CCC tours would come to fruition in other locales, though the Portland FTP participated in these only infrequently.

Even as the Portland FTP grew in popularity, it struggled to maintain a professional level of quality in acting and production, particularly when producing legitimate theatre. Visiting FTP officials—including Flanagan herself—noted the amateurish quality of the acting in the productions. Mathews referred to the "one-time vaudeville, stock, and circus people" who participated in the "woefully bad rehearsal of *The Taming of the Shrew*."[12] In his oral history, Nick Chaivoe noted a similar distinction in the actors; he explained, "they weren't actors as we would think of actors on the legitimate stage" and stated that Whitcomb sometimes became impatient with those unable to portray their roles with the depth of character and believability that she wanted.[13] WPA State Director E. J. Griffith concurred as well:

> The project here was originally principally dumb-acts, and while legitimate personnel has been added in the last year we have to face the fact that only a small percentage of our acting group has educational background. While they have showmanship, they lack artistic background. We have found that they seem to be once removed from [a] folky environment in their own lives, and consequently they bloom in a folk type of script. [...] This is not to belittle the project but to make it clear that folk drama is the thing that they do with authority.[14]

Griffith's statement regarding the performers' ability to authoritatively perform folk drama, when placed in conjunction with those of visiting FTP personnel and Nick Chaivoe, indicated an awareness of the strengths and skills of the Portland FTP performers.[15] Interestingly, even though the project's larger goal was to develop organic theatre productions within communities regardless of their level of education and culture, Griffith still clearly saw education and formal actor training as prerequisites for a certain type of artistic success and aesthetic merit. Since the letter prompting this discussion is unavailable, it is difficult to determine Griffith's motivations in writing of the "folky environment," but whether he was apologizing for the performers' lack of talent or defending their growth, Griffith's diffidence to the "folky" may help explain why it was so hard for the FTP to establish itself in regions with less access to or interest in Broadway-derived theatre. These multiple, independent sources indicate that the Portland FTP was composed predominantly of vaudeville performers with little training in the legitimate theatre. Constituted in this way, the choice to create original vaudeville revues and other light stock pieces appears both logical and a matter of survival; in focusing on this type of entertainment, the Portland FTP capitalized on the strengths and talents of its performers.

However, it is also important to note that these derogatory statements regarding the quality of the acting derived from those who saw legitimate theatre as superior to vaudeville and other variety acts. Many Portland community members and FTP performers did not share this perspective. Lester Schilling summarized one of the interviews he conducted for his dissertation on the history of theatre in Portland, stating, "being vaudeville actors, they felt acting was beneath them, for it took years to work up a good vaudeville act, but anyone could act in a play." From this perspective, the Portland FTP was gifted with numerous talented performers, each of whom possessed the ability to excel in specialized audience entertainment; though they would eventually do what the job required, acting for the legitimate stage was perceived as a step downward. Shilling's interview with Bess Whitcomb also referenced a 1937 directive from Washington, DC that required the Portland FTP to "turn legitimate or it would be discontinued."[16] Though this order does not appear to be present in the archives and it is difficult to reconcile this assertion with the FTP's very public respect of vaudeville, minstrelsy, circus acts, and other forms of entertainment that are typically excluded from legitimate drama, this period marked a change in the general programming of the Portland FTP. In late 1937, the popular, loosely constructed plots designed to showcase miscellaneous musical, dance, or vaudeville talent were replaced by the plays of Shakespeare and Eugene O'Neill. This transition may indicate a fundamental shift in the mindset of the FTP administration from simply producing shows to protecting the FTP from the ever-popular criticism of WPA boondoggling with the creation of more traditionally accepted theatre pieces.

Yet this shift from vaudeville revue to legitimate theatre was not as dramatic as one might have imagined in Portland. The aforementioned "woefully bad rehearsal of *Taming of the Shrew*" highlighted this difference with a unique twist on the Shakespearean classic. According to the director's report in the *Taming of the Shrew* production bulletin, Whitcomb chose *Shrew* for two reasons: to see if Portland audiences would be interested in seeing a "colorful low-brow Shakespeare production" if it was free summer entertainment in the local park, and because it offered a vehicle for the integration of vaudevillian skills such as singing, dancing, acrobatics, and pageantry. Whitcomb proceeded to cut the play "drastically" even as she added in breaks for "specialized entertainment;" these moments would provide the opportunities the Portland variety actors needed in order to shine. The report admits that the production "was ragged in spots but was good fun" and emphasizes its success with local audience members. This early Shakespeare-in-the-Park event drew audiences averaging 1,200 per night; in fact, many young audience members returned to the show so frequently that cast members were embarrassed when children "shout[ed] their lines to them before the speeches actually came in the text."[17] Clearly, the Portland FTP's lowbrow rendition of *Taming of the Shrew*—complete with acrobats, dumb shows, and dance cameos—found a willing audience among the city's residents.

Though it would seem that this production concept would find a happy compromise between the expectations of the FTP administration and those of the variety show performers, it actually led to a series of minor revolutions. One performer, Hope Garner, apparently served as the leader of one of these small insurrections; during rehearsals of *Taming of the Shrew*, she and other cast members left notes scattered about the theatre stating that they hated Whitcomb.[18] Further revolt never materialized though, and Whitcomb's emphasis on legitimate theatre programming—with a vaudevillian twist—continued with only a few exceptions for the remainder of the Portland FTP's lifetime. After the success of *The Taming of the Shrew*, the performers apparently took to this unique style fairly quickly. In an early 1939 note to Whitcomb, Flanagan complimented the company's progress: "I have just written to Mr. Griffith, telling him how impressed I am by the great improvement of the Theatre Project under your direction and under Mr. Griffith's administrative control."[19]

In fact, the Portland FTP's administration overcame many of the obstacles that threatened other regional units: conflicts between personnel, lack of initial support, and uneven acting quality. The extant paperwork depicts a generally cooperative administration that worked well with the WPA, enabling growth and creativity in the Portland programming. Local administrators identified and addressed most of the political and civic issues that arose before they could cause serious problems and devised solutions when those pressures endangered the project. In one of the most controversial exchanges, Bess Whitcomb engaged in a long series of negotiations with the Junior League-Civic Theatre, which planned a conflicting production of *Pinocchio* with one already scheduled through the FTP. Though Whitcomb offered generous terms in her negotiations, proposing that the FTP supply costumes, scenery, and props, use all the actors that the Civic Theatre provided, and give the Civic Theatre the proceeds from the first performance, the Civic Theatre administration rebuffed her. They promptly lodged formal protests with the Junior League, the Parent Teacher Association, and the University of Oregon. Rather than further raise the ire of this locally respected company, Whitcomb capitulated and delayed the FTP production. Although this decision would serve as a point of contention between Whitcomb and FTP regional administration, her insistence that "the action [grew] entirely out of public relations" seems to be well-founded.[20]

Griffith's supervision ultimately served as the fulcrum of the Portland FTP; he consistently engineered situations so that the FTP emerged with greater support and facilities and was described as "extremely sensitive to the furtherance of art."[21] Early in the life of the Portland FTP, Ole Ness, regional director of the West, stated flatly that "a home location in Portland will never be secured without a commitment by Mr. Griffith."[22] Griffith would prove to be a valuable ally for the Portland FTP. In fact, his personal interest ultimately saved the FTP in Oregon as he found ways to negotiate the many difficulties that plagued units elsewhere. He paved the way for the exchange of resources between Los Angeles and Portland—an activity that would seem an obvious step for the much smaller Portland FTP, but which was complicated by regulations involving employees or government property crossing state lines—and was instrumental in securing administrative and performance space for the FTP. In fact, Ness described Griffith's efforts to secure a performance space for the FTP in downtown Portland in glowing terms, stating that it "should be recorded in the history of the Federal Theatre Project as an example of what can be accomplished through the interest and close coordination of the WPA and its State officers."[23]

Yet Griffith's support came at a certain cost. FTP unit leaders chafed under his close supervision. J. Howard Miller, a close friend of Flanagan and deputy director of the FTP, complained:

> The director of professional projects, who is also state director of art projects, is an older man, very congenial but quite dictatorial. His authority includes

censorship of all mail to or from the project. The State Administrator also reads all project correspondence. I am glad that we have a small and not a large program there or I would fear the consequences.[24]

It is worth noting that Miller specifically mentioned Griffith's tendency to censor correspondence, since it may suggest a reason that many of the records of the Oregon FTP have disappeared. The day-to-day correspondence, particularly the paperwork documenting Bess Whitcomb's direct activities, remains one of the primary areas of evidence conspicuously lacking in the archival records. If Griffith were interested in controlling the image of the Oregon unit, he would likely have taken pains to censor or eliminate any evidence that might reflect poorly on his tenure as a state leader.

Perhaps more importantly, Griffith was an "exacting person who require[d] more-than-ordinary cooperation" from the FTP. As Ness noted, Griffith felt justified in calling upon "his" performers and, regardless of their production schedule, requesting performances at various special events in the state of Oregon with very little notice. For Griffith, the FTP was a part of a personal domain that he could call on at will; as the archival records demonstrate, Griffith repeatedly called upon the Portland FTP to abandon other commitments to create special performances and productions for festivals and special events. Though he hoped that Griffith would soon note the differing levels of quality in quickly prepared pieces and the Portland FTP's regular programming, Ness dealt with this challenge by suggesting that the Portland units prepare a few versatile pageants that they could quickly adapt to many of the occasions Griffith was likely to request and which would remain in the repertoire virtually indefinitely.[25] And unlike the directors of FTP units in Boston or Chicago who often had difficulty in identifying and cultivating audiences, Whitcomb, Williams, and Griffith also thought of a plan to bring the FTP to larger audiences in Oregon by capitalizing on these large-scale festivals and special events.

THEATRICAL GOLD: HARVESTING A FLAX GROWER'S DREAMS

Outdoor pageants proved popular in Oregon, helping the project to find a place in the community and catering to Flanagan's goals regarding projects with local relevance. Celebrated before large local audiences admitted for free, these pageants typically located new and underserved populations and performed local history. Moreover, outdoor theatre was part of the

Oregon tradition. By the 1930s, the Portland Civic Theatre, the University of Oregon, and other local institutions engaged in outdoor theatre during the summer and fall.[26] This convention provided the FTP with a point-of-entry in identifying potential audience members, particularly when the players performed during festivals that would already attract large numbers of prospective attendees. Frederick Schlick's *Yellow Harvest*, the first of the Portland FTP's plays focusing on the flax industry, emerged as the first of many locally driven special events in the Portland area.

Griffith's requests for special FTP productions frequently paralleled dedications, festivals, or other events that highlighted major achievements of the Oregon WPA. The first example of this occurred when, in 1936, the WPA celebrated the opening of three flax manufacturing plants in Oregon. The WPA funded the development of these plants in response to mounting pressure for support of the Oregon flax industry. A vital component of the economy in the 1930s in Oregon's Willamette Valley, flax is a raw fiber crop that is used in the weaving of linen, twine, rope, rolling paper for cigarettes, linseed oil, and more. The opening of the Mt. Angel facility would serve as the inspiration for the first annual flax festival. Thus, when the WPA invested so heavily in the future of Oregon's economy by building these plants, Griffith tasked the Portland FTP with the creation of a piece that would celebrate this historic opening, drawing attention to the WPA's feat as well as the work of the Portland FTP. The FTP received Griffith's request only three weeks before the festival.[27] Fortunately, in light of the important role flax played in the local economy and the highly anticipated opening of the new flax processing plants, FTP administrators predicted Griffith's request. Because of this foresight, the Portland FTP had already commissioned Schlick to write a piece about flax. And so, when Griffith requested a pageant about the flax industry for the Mt. Angel festival, the FTP produced *Yellow Harvest*, a pageant/living newspaper focusing on the flax farmer and the development of the industry in Oregon. The production was well-received by the public, praised by the festival organizers, and commended by the national FTP as "an example of how Federal Theatre can function for and with the people of a locality in exploiting an important local cause."[28]

Yellow Harvest features a cast of five and a clearly focused plot. In the play, Lee Halmis, a respected flax farmer and the leader of the newly established local cooperative flax farmer association, Oregon Flax Incorporated, celebrates as his fields produce a stellar crop and his wedding to the lovely Julie Calhoun approaches. He and Belden, his field worker, prepare to harvest the crop, while James Kells and his wife Alice play the villainous business speculators who have purchased Lee's loan note. Though not billed as such, *Yellow Harvest* certainly demonstrated progressive tendencies. Fundamentally, the play pits the little man against the evil capitalist. In their first tense conversation, Lee challenges Kells's disregard for the Oregon flax industry; Lee accuses Kells of trying to break up the cooperative, finally stating bluntly that "we didn't build up the flax industry to have it exploited by one man—even if he is a highpowered [*sic*] business man."[29] Kells, the eternal capitalist, argues that the cooperative will decrease profits for many of the members and offers to purchase Lee's farm in what Lee believes is a plot to take over the Oregon flax industry. When their attempts to force Lee to sell his farm and interests fail, Kells and his wife set out to destroy the farm and any hope Lee has of resistance.

Though the play portrays big business as the nemesis of the Oregon flax farmer, the vast majority of the issues raised in the play related directly to the Oregon flax industry rather than a specific political agenda. For the audience at the flax festival in Mt. Angel, the situation portrayed in *Yellow Harvest* was so grounded in local events, fears, and challenges that it likely would have been perceived more as a fact-based living newspaper than a form of political drama. Since the Mt. Angel Flax Festival commemorated the opening of a flax-manufacturing plant sponsored by the WPA and funded almost entirely by the federal government, it was logical that the play would champion the hard-working Oregon flax farmer struggling to break even in difficult economic times and the government organization that would help him to do so. Though Oregonians had campaigned for the flax industry as far back as the mid-nineteenth century, it was a project that many scorned because of the lack of mechanization and extraordinarily high labor costs required to process the crop. The Oregon state government made several unsuccessful attempts to buttress the industry, even building a plant designed to employ state prisoners as nearly free labor in 1915. Even this did not prove profitable though, and it seemed that the combination of excessive labor costs and repeated damage from fires would doom the production of flax in the United States along with much of the Oregon economy. In fact, it was only in the mid-1930s that the federal government completed studies showing that the Willamette Valley environment was suitable for the growth of the flax crop at all.[30] Once the government documented and scientifically verified this fact, Oregon Governor Charles Martin engineered the deal with Griffith (a former advocate for and employee of the flax industry) in which the WPA would fund these three different flax processing plants. The WPA completed the construction and gave the plants to the state, which in turn leased them to the local cooperatives for one dollar a year. For a "common stock" purchase of ten dollars, any farmer could send his flax to these plants for processing. Thus, the cooperatives and the new flax processing plants—funded and built by the WPA—made the Oregon flax industry both economically viable and dangerous to the competition in the eastern United States and abroad. Aside from economic woes, the greatest fear of the flax farmer was fire; beginning in the early 1900s, fires plagued the Oregon farms in a pattern that locals argued suggested sabotage by a "secret linen trust" in the East.[31]

Celebrated on September 5, 1936, the first annual flax festival featured a series of speeches, athletic events, a parade (led by one of the earliest flax growers in the area), a concert by the WPA Music Project, a dance, and a fireworks display, as well as the sole performance of the FTP's *Yellow Harvest*. The festival attracted such political notables as Griffith, Governor Martin, Joe Carson (mayor of Portland), G. J. Hyslop (head of the Oregon Flax Board), and Harry Hopkins (key architect of the New Deal and head of the national WPA).[32] Griffith's choice to feature the Portland FTP and an original, locally relevant script by an Oregon native at such an important political and personal triumph demonstrated his commitment to a well-rounded state arts program in which the theatre would play a prominent role.

Like many of the Portland FTP's productions, Frederick Schlick's *Yellow Harvest* is a topical and largely uncontroversial piece. Perhaps the most striking element in the play initially is the great pride that Lee, the flax farmer, takes in the prosperity of his crops. As the play opens, he and his field hand Belden look out over ripe fields of flax, blowing gently in the breeze:

> BELDEN: *(Looking down on gold flax fields)* Sure pretty the way it riffles the flax.
> LEE: Yeah! *(Still admiring flax)* Pure gold, and the finest flax in the world! Ha, ha, guess that'll put the skids under my troubles, all right![33]

The staging likely took advantage of the fact that the actors could have been looking down the slopes of Mt. Angel and onto the flax fields of the local farmers. Their lines compliment the crops and industry of the audience. It soon becomes clear that Lee believes passionately in his chosen profession in spite of extensive criticism from "everyone" that the industry would fail. In fact, the flax industry appears to be poised on the brink of success in *Yellow Harvest*. Lee explains, "Remember in the old days when they tried to make us believe that we couldn't grow flax here?—Grow it here!—Why, Belden, old socks, a sight like that is the answer to a flax-growers dream!.... Now if we can only keep harmony in the cooperation, we'll be on top of the world!"[34] It is important to note that the Oregon flax industry had struggled to gain federal support for nearly 75 years at this point, but the locals continued to champion their crops in the face of all doubts. Like the farmers in the Mt. Angel flax community, the character of Lee perseveres in the face of adversity and skepticism, a commitment that pays off for him and his community.

Lee also organizes and leads the local farmers in a cooperative, thus ensuring fair sale prices to all members of the community and more efficient processing at the plant. Lee's plea to "keep harmony in the cooperation" serves as a warning to individuals who might be tempted to get greedy in anticipation of high profits at the expense of their neighbors; a cooperative worked only when all farmers agreed to accept the purchasing price the cooperative negotiated, even at the risk of losing income if that price was later found to be too low. Lee explains, "We've spent five years building [the cooperative] up.—We donated sites for the plants, and the Government built them! Why? Because we believe, and the Government believes in flax!"[35] Lee's description unites the struggling flax farmer with the government; with the opening of the flax production plants, the government put forth a good faith effort of support by choosing to invest in the flax industry and help the farmers to develop cooperatives. In this sense, the FTP's production of *Yellow Harvest* serves to solidify the bridge between the Oregon flax growers and the WPA.

Yet Lee's situation—like that of the Mt. Angel flax farmers—remains tenuous in *Yellow Harvest*. When Kells calls in Lee's note and attempts to force him to sell the farm, Lee fears that the sale of his farm—forced or voluntary—will lead directly to the dismantling of the already fragile cooperative. When Lee departs from his farm in a last desperate search for an emergency loan to carry his debt until the crops can be sold, Kells and his wife manipulate Belden into leaving his position as watch and set a fire in the gasoline-filled barn so as to obliterate the crop and Lee's hope of repaying the loan. Like the mysterious "secret linen trust" accused of repeatedly setting fires that ravaged and ruined the Oregon flax industry beginning in 1905, Kells exploits that universal fear of the Oregon flax farmers—fire.

Lee returns from his desperate wanderings with the blessing of both God and the state government. As Lee explains, he retreated to the Benedictine monastery on the top of Mt. Angel—a monastery that was founded in 1882 by Swiss monks, and that still exists today—to pray for guidance:

> LEE: I asked the Lord on my bended knee to save the flax farmers! *(He crosses himself, looks up, continues quietly and simply)* And then I [w]ent out and sat in the garden, and looked at the flowers.
> KELLS: *(ironically)* What did the Lord do?
> LEE: *(With antagonism)* Father Benedict came out, and sat down. We looked out across the valley, and I told him my troubles. [...] He put through a long-distance call to Salem, and talked to the Governor!...And tomorrow I'm goin' to get a loan![36]

In this happy union of church and state, the Catholic priest and the governor of the state of Oregon (who, not coincidentally, attended the performance at the flax festival on Mt. Angel) combined their efforts in what may have seemed to the flax farmers in the audience to be no less than a federally funded miracle. Lee, the virtuous leader of the flax farmer cooperative, refuses to give in to the villainous representative of the "foreign flax growers [who would] give their eye-teeth to get control of the Oregon Flax Industry."[37] He protects his colleagues and the Mt. Angel flax industry, even at the risk of his own future in the profession that he fervently loves. In so doing, he seeks out the help of the community and manages to obtain significant financial (and moral) support in very little time with only his honor and community standing as collateral, a feat that would likely have been perceived as even more impressive at the height of the Great Depression. This union of church and state in the play lends a certain integrity to the actions of the WPA; here was a federal organization that was effectively performing the will of the Catholic Church in Oregon. In a second round of *deus ex machina*–style miracles, Lee's farmhand manages to save the crop by chopping down the farm's water tower in time to douse the fire that the Kellses began. Lee's fiancé witnesses James Kells setting the fire, which gives Lee the ammunition he needs in order to blackmail Kells into burning up the loan note. And so, the crop is saved, Lee's debt is forgiven, Lee and Julie make plans to marry the following day, and the Oregon flax industry remains free and strong.

In this extraordinary ending, the WPA, the Governor, and the Mt. Angel monastery help the flax farmers to retain their economic and ideological independence in the face of seemingly insurmountable odds. *Yellow Harvest* was an ideal vehicle to tout WPA achievements and encourage ongoing, productive relationships between the Mt. Angel community and the New Deal programs. This production provided a forum for the FTP to play to an estimated audience of 2,000 in a style that was familiar to the Portland and Mt. Hood communities and that would become a hall-mark of the Oregon FTP—the outdoor pageant.[38] Though no production bulletin or reviews of this single performance remain extant, Griffith was apparently pleased enough with the performance to put forth a Herculean effort to gain a downtown Portland theatre space for the FTP, circum-venting WPA-spending regulations to do so. In order to secure this space, Griffith took over five floors of a building in Portland for the WPA and moved various departments into the space, then concentrated nearly all of the expenditures on the one floor occupied by the FTP. Though the FTP would be charged a significant monthly rental fee until the balance was repaid to the WPA, this was an unprecedented statement of support by a state WPA administrator and one unlikely to be seen again by the FTP. In exchange, Griffith continued calling upon the FTP for special events.[39] Indeed, the pioneering flax festival at Mt. Angel would prove to be the first of many occasions when Griffith required the Portland FTP to perform pieces sculpted to fit special events. More importantly, the pro-duction of *Yellow Harvest* demonstrated the Portland FTP's ability to cre-ate and perform locally relevant drama that suited its community while celebrating an event that would ease the burdens of many locals in the flax industry. *Yellow Harvest* was one of the plays made by and for this unit, and which established Portland FTP as an unsung success of the national organization.

"THEATRE UPON OLYMPUS," *TIMBERLINE TINTYPES*, AND PAUL BUNYAN

The opening of Timberline Lodge provided another opportunity for the Portland FTP to show its connection to its community. Widespread inter-est in recreational winter sports emerged in Oregon around 1930. The southern slopes of Mount Hood, located about an hour outside of Portland, became a prime tourist attraction for the state. For years, Griffith and a number of other prominent Portland businessmen had eyed the slopes above a tiny village called Government Camp. The site was ideally posi-tioned to avoid the worst of the winter storms while still maintaining a dozen or so feet of snow during the tourist season. When Roosevelt created the WPA, Griffith saw an opportunity to realize a project that was—in the words of the interior designer of Timberline Lodge, Margery Hoffman

Smith—"very dear to his heart."[40] He identified local business support and petitioned the Forest Services for permission to build a commercial hotel on federal land. In late 1935, the United States Forestry Service formally requested WPA funds for a hotel on the slopes of Mount Hood. Griffith completed the project application, which had an estimated cost to the WPA of $246,893. Timberline Lodge eventually cost nearly one million dollars.[41] Like the opening of the Mt. Angel flax processing plant and the first annual flax festival, Timberline Lodge would provide an opportunity for Griffith to call upon "his" FTP and for the Portland FTP to create original, locally relevant theatre for a specific audience.

The first mention of FTP involvement in the opening festivities surrounding Timberline Lodge appeared in a request for initial project funding in January 1936, prior to the official opening of the Portland FTP. At this point, the lodge was slated to open on May 15, 1936. Guy Williams, who came to Portland from directing the Seattle FTP, wrote that the Portland unit should create "a Pioneer Life Pageant to be staged on Mt. Hood:"

> The pageant will celebrate the opening of a huge new Mountain Lodge Hotel by the Forestry Service; that the site of this pageant will be alongside the old Pioneer route of the Oregon Trail; that Portland civic leaders are naturally keen on having it put on; that it would probably play to as many as 75,000 people; that [a] vital script employing the Paul Bunyan theme is being prepared by Mr. Schlick; and finally that the first period of WPA theatricals with the other projects [be] gauged so that the full FTP personnel will be assigned to the Mt. Hood pageant.[42]

Practical and politically savvy, Williams's advice would have put the Portland FTP in the enviable position of having already prepared the show Griffith would require when the lodge finally opened in late 1937 (though the Schlick script Williams described never materialized for the opening of Timberline Lodge). While 75,000 audience members traveling the 6,000 feet up the mountain to Timberline Lodge seems optimistic at best, particularly when the opening was delayed to coincide with the beginning of an Oregon winter, Williams's perception of audience interest in local pageants and his insight into pleasing Portland's civic leaders indicates that he was another shrewd administrator with the Portland FTP. Once established, this spirit of cooperation and engagement with local interests would characterize the Portland FTP's relationship with political and civic leaders, particularly with Griffith's demanding and hands-on style of leadership.

President Roosevelt dedicated Timberline Lodge and the Bonneville Dam on one leg of a journey to the West Coast in September 1937. As a part of the celebration, the FTP produced a series of dances that reflected regional themes and ideas, including *All the Weary People, The Indian Celebration Dance, Dance of the Flax-Scutching Machines, American Negro Interlude, Dance of the Sophisticates,* and *Dance of the W.P.A. Workers.* Little record remains of these dance pieces aside from photographic stills and newspaper reviews. The *Oregonian* printed a distinctly anti-Roosevelt editorial that described the FTP as "a WPA by-product." The description of the *Dance of the W.P.A. Workers* further conveyed the attitude of the unnamed critic toward the FTP, focusing on the comparison between the initial appearance of the "shameless men-about-town" who represented "outworn bourgeois and capitalist civilization," and the FTP actors in their "regulation Heil-Hitler brown shirts." The review closed with a reference to the conclusions "intelligent viewers" should reach regarding the passing of the "bankrupt bourgeois age" and the arrival of the "sterling WPA paradise" that was to come.[43] The FTP also produced *Bonneville Dam,* a piece described as simultaneously dance-drama, pageant, dance, musical, and living newspaper, and which focused on the nearby Bonneville Dam project. Like the movement-based pieces the FTP created for the opening of Timberline Lodge, only photographs of *Bonneville Dam* remain.

Griffith and Flanagan were both optimistic about a long-term relationship between Timberline Lodge and the FTP. Returning from a trip to New York where he saw several FTP plays, Griffith wrote a poem describing the amphitheatre at Timberline Lodge for Flanagan "in an attempt to give the readers an idea of the inspiring magnificence of the scene" (See Figure 6):

I built a theatre upon Olympus
Domed to the very heavens
Colored azure rose and silver
Figured with beams of sun and moon

I built a theatre of magnificence
Where buskined giants might declaim
Before a back drop of lofty Atlas
Majestic in its glistening mantle

I built a theatre for Apollo
Walled with Alpine fir and hemlock
A rainbow for proscenium arch
Ringed with bright stars for footlights

> I built a theatre fashioned from mountain peaks
> With foyer fountained with glacial cataracts
> And stage where man might dare to tread
> And feel the inspiration of the gods[44]

In his poem, Griffith clearly links the amphitheatre at Timberline Lodge with the majesty of the great outdoors, a fitting choice for a resort built to capitalize upon and glorify the tallest and most spectacular mountain in the state of Oregon. His references to the sun and moon as spotlights, walls of "Alpine fir and hemlock," stars serving as footlights, and the rainbow for the proscenium arch all draw attention to the connection between nature and the theatre. He also ties this outdoor amphitheatre to the heavens

Figure 6   Amphitheatre at Timberline Lodge, as seen from the audience's perspective. Timberline Lodge is visible in the far left side, and the Rocky Mountains provide the backdrop. After the amphitheatre opened, Griffith sent a poem to Flanagan, describing it as inspired by the Greek gods, "fashioned from mountain peaks" with "stars for footlights" and "a rainbow for proscenium arch." National Archives and Records Administration, Record Group 69, Work Projects Administration, 1922–1944, RG-69-PR, Oregon, Box 9, "Oregon."

and the pantheon of Greek gods, referencing Apollo, Atlas, and eventually, the "stage where man might dare to tread/And feel the inspiration of the gods." This connection to the gods suggests that he imagined the theatre could play a unique role in ennobling and uplifting its audience. Yet perhaps what is most interesting and touching about Griffith's poem is his repetition of the phrase "I built," which implies a deep sense of personal investment in Timberline Lodge and its theatre. While his vision may have differed from Flanagan's, Griffith also clearly envisioned theatre as central to American spiritual and cultural life. Griffith wanted a theatre company to perform in the amphitheatre, which he likened—both in his note to Flanagan and in his poem—to one of the huge outdoor theatres created in ancient Greece. In addition to the implication that the FTP followed in the footsteps of the first great Western theatre tradition, this comparison surely appealed to Flanagan in her quest for large audiences and a democratic theatre. Pleased with Griffith's new image of the Oregon FTP, Flanagan wrote, "Today when Mr. Griffith who once didn't even want a project, said 'Expand!—we'd like a whole new F.T. company so that one could tour and one could play'—I felt that you can change human nature."[45] Buoyed by Griffith's excitement, Flanagan raised her expectations for the project. She told Griffith that she would pursue an additional company and encouraged Whitcomb to persevere in locating and creating plays that would appeal to Portland audiences.

While the pieces performed at the opening of Timberline Lodge likely served as examples of the local relevance of the Portland FTP, Yasha Frank's *Timberline Tintypes* took that local resonance a step further. This musical production, dramatizing "highfalutin night-life in an early Oregon dance hall," linked local history with the successful exploitation of the various talents the FTP actors brought to the program.[46] Frank, most famous for the popular children's theatre adaptation of *Pinocchio*—the same *Pinocchio* that would serve as emblematic of the death of the FTP when the title character was placed in a coffin and carried in a funeral processional down the streets of New York City in 1939—created *Timberline Tintypes* specifically for the actors in the Portland FTP.[47] In considering the strengths of this production, it is important to recall the grievances about the actors on this unit; they hailed from vaudeville, circus, and other variety shows, lacked formal training, and found legitimate drama challenging or demeaning. Archival documents suggest that many of these players were past their performance primes and unable to execute their acts in entirety. With these limitations in mind, Frank chose the highlight of each individual performer's act and sculpted a loose narrative that would encompass all of them in a rollicking stage show. *Timberline Tintypes* opened at Timberline Lodge on August 12, 1938, then continued a two-week run in Portland.

Timberline Tintypes, described in the *Labor Newdealer* as a "monkey-glanded presentation of old-time beer-parlor variety acts with all their exaggerated histrionics,"[48] begins with the characters seated onstage in a traditional Oregon lodge enjoying stout drinks and hearty food, and good-naturedly attempting to top one another's tall tales, many of which focus on Paul Bunyan. The arrival of several arguing loggers and the ensuing wrestling match ends the tall tales talk and propels the evening forward into a series of acts including knife throwing, log bucking, juggling, imitations, a variety of songs, a scene from a melodrama, the cake-walk, the can-can, and even a trapeze act.[49] The show culminates in a square dance, which spills over into the audience and continues until the audience loses interest in the dance. Designed to highlight the best of each company member's talents, *Timberline Tintypes* recalls a bygone era in which vaudeville and variety show performers ruled the Portland stage. As Madge Wynne Crum elucidated in the *Timberline Tintypes* production bulletin, "'TIMBERLINE TINTYPES' proved to be popular theatre fare in that it created a nostalgia in the older members of the audience and afforded the younger ones the opportunity of hearing and seeing a type of entertainment now mostly passed into oblivion."[50]

So based is *Timberline Tintypes* on the bygone days of vaudeville that the written script often includes no more than the name of a number or act. The Woodsman "imitates Whipperwill," then the "Bobwhite (etc. etc. until Woodsman has finished repertoire)." The Porter simply "goes into his number," which has no name in the script, presumably because it was based on the choice of that particular actor. The Bum appears to give his rendition of the famous "Face on the Barroom Floor," a ballad in which an artist tries to explain his own ruin to the bartender, but falls down dead before he finishes;[51] the Bum in *Timberline Tintypes* drops dead as well, throwing the characters into turmoil and, not coincidentally, more vaudevillian acts. None of the songs denoted in the script contain any information other than the title. Salvation Nell sings the popular Christian hymn "Bringing in the Sheaves," Little Mary begs her father to come home in the famous temperance folksong "Father, Dear Father, Come Home With Me Now," and May Wheat, "the Rural Melba," croons "Bird in a Gilded Cage;" May's number culminates in a "punch finish" when a "pretty girl in a feather costume appears in a large gilded cage."[52] Each of these acts—whether musical, impersonation, or storytelling—represent standard vaudeville and variety act fare from the early twentieth century, and each appeared in this show expressly because an actor or actress in the Portland FTP excelled in its performance.

In addition to these well-known vaudeville acts, the company featured a comic/straight man team engaged in a rather lengthy discussion of one character's "rheumaticks" and the ideal alcohol-based remedy. Snodgrass, an elderly man with arthritis and poor hearing, gets the best of the waiter in an exchange of misinformation and misdirection that rivals Abbott and Costello's famous "Who's on first?" routine. When Snodgrass orders a scotch, the waiter suggests that rum and bitters would be the better remedy, so Snodgrass trades the scotch for the rum and neglects to pay for either:

> WAITER: Hold on! Ain't you forgot something?
> SNODGRASS: Let's see…got my hat and specs. Nope didn't forget nothing.
> WAITER: You forgot to pay for the rum and bitters.
> SNODGRASS: But I traded you the scotch for the rum and bitters.
> WAITER: But you didn't pay for the scotch.
> SNODGRASS: But I didn't drink the scotch.

The exchange continues, spiraling further into confusion with each line. Eventually, the pleasant old man leaves and the waiter stands "scratching his head and counting fingers, and finally throws up his hands" in defeat.[53]

In her direction, Margaret Barney emphasized the intimate nature of *Timberline Tintypes*, as well as the fast pace and positive energy required to make the show feasible on stage. Her Director's Report explained that Frank designed the show for the indoor stage at Timberline Lodge:

> It is a clubby, chuckling return to jokes, dances, songs and vaudeville of the end of the last century. This show lost a little in effectiveness when transferred even to so small a theatre as ours. The use of a tiny inner-stage on the main stage permitted rapid sequences of scenes, and that exhilaration of pace was an important factor in putting it over in theatre surroundings.[54]

In the Timberline Lodge production of the show, the stage was split into two sections: a small playing space located upstage center (complete with a curtain advertising "Asbestos") was distinct from rest of the set, which consisted of a lodge with a fireplace, a few tables, and a bar arranged on the left and right sides of the stage (See Figure 7).

Figure 7   This scene from *Timberline Tintypes*, "Father, Dear Father, Come Home With Me Now," features the musical appeal of Little Mary, begging her father to leave the bar and return to his family. Upstage, the image that appears to be a large picture of trees is actually the small stage upon which many of the play-within-a-play performances took place. NARA, E938, Box 491, "Timberline Tintypes Production Bulletin."

Center stage remained open for individual numbers that were not a part of the stage "performance" in the second half of the play. The first scene of the play occurs in the lodge area between the play characters, while the second scene focuses on a performance that takes place on the small stage for the loggers; once the second scene begins and the focus shifts to the performance-within-a-performance, quick skits, jokes, and acts from characters in the lodge ease the transitions between stage acts. Thus, between the cakewalk and the trapeze act, both of which occurred on the small stage, the lodge characters entertain the audience with a few skits involving tintype photography; this scene consciously evokes the play's title by creating tintype photographs of life in the Timberline Lodge area.[55] The production also used an onstage pianist and a small orchestra. It is important to remember that, while it was performed at Timberline Lodge, the audience experienced *Timberline Tintypes* while sitting in a lodge strikingly similar to the stage lodge set; they watched a group of actors playing characters who patronized the imagined lodge (and coincidentally performed brief sketches with knife throwing, wrestling, and log bucking), and then observed these characters playing spectators to an additional round of variety acts on the small stage. Moreover, since the play incorporated the (real) audience in the performance when the dance spilled out into the audience at the end, the production operated as a participatory comedy, even perhaps a play-within-a-play-within-a-play. This choice effectively made the audience a part of the production, drawing them into the fast-paced, "clubby" performance.

Reviews for *Timberline Tintypes* highlighted the fun and excitement of the show. The drama editor of the *Oregonian* proclaimed the show to be "colorful, noisy and talented" and teeming with "rip-roaring fun." His closing remarks noted the pleasing return to the "era when drama came thick and mustaches had curly ends."[56] According to the *Oregon Journal*, the production plainly confirmed the enduring stage adage that "tested recipes for stage fare prove the best entertainment."[57] The most lively review appeared in the *Labor Newdealer*, and described the show as "fun-poking, ranging from subtle satire to the more obvious hokum bordering on burlesque [...] What must have been the Worst of ham vaudeville in the last decades before the turn of the century, is transformed here into a darn swell Best of 1938."[58] These critical commentaries draw attention to the nostalgia-evoking fun of the show (and many of the men did, in fact, wear large, curly mustaches in the production). In its emphasis on the local culture, its attention to the talents that the individual performers brought to the FTP, and its capitalization on the resources available through Timberline Lodge, *Timberline Tintypes* proved an ideal production for the Portland FTP. This success further strengthened the foundations of the relationship between the Portland FTP, Griffith, and Timberline Lodge.

In fact, Timberline Lodge came to be a public rallying point for Flanagan as she considered the strengths of the different regions and determined where FTP money would be directed. Presumably due to the positive rapport the FTP had with Griffith in Oregon and the successes with productions such as *Yellow Harvest, Bonneville Dam,* and *Timberline Tintypes,* Flanagan's aspirations for a future, greatly expanded, FTP specifically discussed Timberline Lodge. In her 1938 "Design for the Federal Theatre's Season," printed in the *New York Times,* Flanagan used Timberline Lodge as an example of the FTP's success in creating locally relevant theatre:

This study of the local and regional aspects of American history and contemporary life as material for drama has reached the point where we are setting up in each region one large dramatic festival center. For the Northwest this center will be Timberline Lodge, built by the Works Progress Administration. [....] Now we are planning a Paul Bunyan festival, to be produced in conjunction with the opening of a museum of logging and lumberjack antiquities and to become the yearly center of a series of plays.[59]

From all appearances Timberline continued to be a success story for the FTP. In June of 1939, less than three weeks before Congress suspended FTP funding, Flanagan again cited Timberline as an FTP triumph in a *New York Times* article. The Paul Bunyan festival remained on the schedule for the summer and the article described Timberline Lodge as the "center for the Northwest," while Los Angeles would serve as the center for the Southwest.[60] Arrangements for the festival occupied the attention of many FTP employees and administrators for months before its anticipated summer performance. On the first of March, Flanagan joined the Paul Bunyan Celebration Committee for an extended discussion; others present at the meeting included Bess Whitcomb, Guy Williams, Thomas Laman (executive assistant, Federal Art Project), F. W. Goodrich (state director, Federal Music Project), T. J. Edmonds (state director, Federal Writers' Project), Aline Howell (assistant director, Women's and Professional Projects), and W. H. Marsh (administrative assistant in charge of public relations). Clearly, by this time the festival planning was sufficiently advanced to warrant the presence of the state directors of all four of the Federal One arts projects in the state of Oregon as well as Flanagan herself.

The meeting determined the feasibility of the festival and delineated responsibilities amongst the various projects. A single festival would occur, taking "the form of a rededication of the American tradition," and would run on weekends at Timberline Lodge for four to six weeks, depending on both the length of the season and the interest of the audience.[61] The theatrical portion of the celebration would consist of two plays, E. P. Conkle's *Prologue to Glory* and Dee Burke's *Paul Bunyan*, as well as the Myra Kinch dance troupe in *American Exodus*. Federal Music Project concerts would complement the theatrical program. Flanagan later explained that Whitcomb and Williams, "both ardent westerners," planned to supplement the festival at Timberline Lodge with wrestling matches, horseshoe throwing, and other special events throughout the state.[62]

Both Flanagan and Griffith had high expectations for the Paul Bunyan festival that summer. In a conversation with Griffith, Flanagan stated, "I want it to be a production that will say for the West dramatically what Timberline says for the West architecturally." Griffith replied:

> The Federal Theatre can do it. To tell you the truth I thought the company was hopeless at first, but now I go to everything they put on; I take all my friends, I'm amazed at the whole thing. After the Paul Bunyan festival we're going ahead building our civic center—and that's going to include a theatre to house the federal company, their dramas, children's plays, and living newspapers. The Paul Bunyan festival will celebrate this summer the coming of age of Portland's Federal Theatre.[63]

This festival was to be the crowning glory of the FTP's activities in the Pacific Northwest. It would unite four of the five arts projects in Federal One (excluding the Historical Records Survey), use the talents of the FTP actors, engage with an extensive FTP audience, and capitalize on local themes. It also provided the opportunity to commence a promising partnership with Griffith and the WPA. Unfortunately the Paul Bunyan Festival never opened; the FTP closed its doors on June 30, 1939, just a few short weeks before the festival was scheduled to take place.

CONCLUSIONS

The building of Timberline Lodge created an opening for the city of Portland and its FTP, particularly since Griffith ensured that the Lodge would contain a small indoor theatre in addition to the large outdoor amphitheatre. His attention to these specific inclusions demonstrated the rising importance with which Griffith regarded "his" theatre. *Timberline Tintypes* offered the vaudevillians in the Portland FTP the chance to showcase their specialties in an environment that supported their skills, and also marked a departure from the broad-based legitimate theatre that the national administration purportedly forced on the Portland players. With the Paul Bunyan Festival, the Portland FTP would have again embraced the talents of their actors and the interests of their community in an outdoor extravaganza that celebrated all of Portland's federal arts organizations.

These case studies of the Portland FTP—*Yellow Harvest, Timberline Tintypes,* and the planning of the Paul Bunyan Festival—offer a rich understanding of the breadth of the FTP as understood on its own terms. The Portland FTP was an example of a decentralized, yet cooperative unit. While it worked with companies in California and Washington, it retained its individual character and remained essentially distant from the political debates that infected many other FTP units. Though descriptions of some of the pageants presented at the Timberline Lodge dedication hint at an indictment of the capitalist system, the Oregon unit did not arouse the same level of controversy as other regional units. Perhaps the populations it played to were less politically sensitive, or perhaps the unit seemed so organic to the area that whatever politics it espoused seemed like part of a local discussion, rather than an external agenda being foisted on an unwelcoming population. Whatever the reasons for its local appeal, it is clear that many Oregonians failed to link *their* FTP with the *national* FTP that was targeted by Congress and the Dies Committee as an organization of communists and radicals requiring eradication. Burns Mantle, in a visit to the Portland FTP, noted his ongoing interest in the FTP as a whole. He commented on the Portland FTP's "constructive program," and remarked that "you appear to be completely detached."[64] This statement noted the separation between the national FTP and the Portland project, as well as the unique, local nature of the Portland FTP program. Even Nick Chaivoe, an alert, socially conscious FTP employee in Portland, had no idea that the FTP was under investigation or that other units were closed because of controversy: "We were in the hinterlands, after all. [...] We were completely insulated from what was going on in any other state. We just didn't hear about things in other states."[65] These statements clearly show the tension between the local and national levels within the FTP.

This insulation appears to have worked both for and against the Portland FTP. The comparable isolation of the Portland FTP offered both safety and autonomy in that the political controversies, Communist witch hunts, and scathing criticism leveled at the national organization slid from the veneer that surrounded the local relief theatre. In addition, the company was able to conduct its business with little interference from the FTP national administration. Because of this, the leaders of the city, state, and region were able to create a theatre that was locally relevant and appealed to large numbers of audience members. Thus, the Portland FTP integrated itself into the community by playing original productions at festivals, uniting efforts with the other arts projects and government organizations, capitalizing on a close relationship with Griffith and the WPA, and codifying relationships with civic organizations.

However, the insular nature of the Portland FTP also left it vulnerable to interference by state and local agencies that were often neutralized by the national FTP in other locations. Many of the disagreements and difficulties took place within the local unit and the state, and very few of these grievances were elevated beyond the regional level. Since interference by the national administration was not necessary in a system that worked well independently, this also left a lack of surviving documentation that is now a severe handicap to scholars attempting to explore the activities of the Portland FTP. Much of the correspondence that remains in the archives revolves around specific, large-scale situations like the Timberline Lodge dedication and the Paul Bunyan festival; these events required external efforts, either on a regional or national level. The day-to-day running of the Oregon units seems to have been handled in-house and thus lacks the kind of rigorous documentation that many of the other units received. Though the creation, loss, or intentional purging of these documents remains in question, the records of the Portland FTP that remain provide fascinating insights into a project that offered a timely, entertaining, and topical program to audiences that embraced it.

On those occasions when the national administration was involved, they realized the importance of the events in Portland. As I have suggested, Flanagan repeatedly referred to the Portland FTP's events as national success stories. Productions such as *Yellow Harvest* and *Timberline Tintypes* suggest that the Portland FTP served as a bridge between audiences and the federal government. The FTP's involvement in pivotal festivals and in the dedication of Timberline Lodge, as well as the hopes surrounding the unrealized Paul Bunyan festival demonstrate the vibrancy of the Portland FTP. Yet I suspect that the very success of the Portland FTP may be the reason that it is difficult to study today. When its administration worked well, it worked invisibly. Despite the paucity of information, the inclusion of these smaller FTP units remains a vitally important component in any study and evaluation of the FTP as a national entity. Perhaps more than any other unit nationwide, the Portland FTP may have been the epitome of Flanagan's stated goals, and as such, one of the great success stories of the FTP.

5. Theatre "In the Wilderness": The Federal Theatre Project Tours America ✥

Time and again these [FTP] units have plowed their way through ice and snow and sleet over mountain roads with precipices on one side and sheer drops on the other. They have been snowbound and icebound, but always the show has gone through.[1]

—Federal Theatre *magazine*

Although controversial productions of Federal Theatre Project units in major urban centers often garnered significantly more press than productions staged outside of major metropolitan areas, I would argue that productions like *The Swing Mikado* and Orson Welles's famous "*Voodoo*" *MacBeth* operated not in the mainstream but on the fringes of the FTP. This view resituates the well-documented scope of the FTP's dramatic activities. As Flanagan herself argued, "the activities of any one Federal Theatre in any one city must be seen as part of a pattern involving plays going on in many other cities."[2] So the 1936 nationwide, simultaneous opening of *It Can't Happen Here* in 17 cities and 21 theatres was part of the same federal organization that performed in prisons and mental institutions, and which pioneered a community drama training program, ran a circus in and around New York City nearly continually, and produced shows in German, Yiddish, Spanish, and a host of other languages. To truly appreciate the FTP's vision, purpose, and impact, scholarship must also embrace its activities beyond the boards of Broadway or the bright lights of the city.

This chapter diverges from the discussions of those that have come previously. Unlike previous chapters, which focused on FTP activities in specific locations—the Midwest, East, South, and West—this section shifts that examination to the many touring productions and companies within the FTP. These frequently ignored "middle children" of the FTP served the organization's mission in unique and important ways, and their omission from scholarly discourse leaves the overall picture of the FTP disturbingly incomplete. Indeed, as the case studies in this chapter will demonstrate, the FTP tours served far more extensive locations, played to diverse and new audiences, and offered a greater variety of performance than many units that were established in specific physical theatres.

The FTP brought drama to hundreds of rural locales across the United States. It infused small cities and country areas with tent theatres, traveling troupes, vaudeville, minstrel shows, and more, and brought theatre to the FTP's target audience. For the FTP, tours were a necessary element to the creation of a broad-based, national awareness of, and desire for, live theatre. In many ways the FTP's activities recalled the glory of the great touring circuits from the nineteenth and early twentieth centuries in the United States. Though the competition between the Theatrical Syndicate and the Shubert dynasty would virtually monopolize the legitimate American Theatre, and eventually coincide with the decline of "the road," tours had been a staple of American entertainment.[3] By the time the FTP emerged in 1935, large areas of the country had seen little or no live, professional theatre for a generation: "Interested factions agreed that 'the road' was dead; that people outside of the larger cities would not patronize plays with living actors."[4] In order to compensate, community theatre, stock companies, vaudeville troupes, and little theatres sprung up in many communities. Flanagan would capitalize on these local institutions outside of major cities in order to found and support FTP units throughout the country, but by the very nature of the relief program, the FTP could only begin operations where theatre professionals were already established in significant numbers. Touring productions would take the FTP considerably farther in reaching Flanagan's goal of locating new audiences in these largely underserved areas. By the FTP's seventh month of operations, most of the more than 400,000 people seeing Federal Theatre productions each week were "inhabitants of the smaller cities and towns of 'the road,' who were believed to have forsaken the theatre."[5] And yet ironically, since these performances are often the most difficult to research, they are the least likely to appear in scholarly analysis.

This chapter will bring my focus to two of the FTP's touring adventures. The first section will concentrate on the FTP companies that toured throughout Civilian Conservation Corps (CCC) camps performing Grace Hayward's *CCC Murder Mystery*. This appealing, participatory production sparked an astonishing response from those who saw it; in less than two years, the *CCC Murder Mystery* earned accolades from hundreds of CCC Commanders and Education Directors, and tens of thousands of CCC enrollees. The second half of this chapter examines the FTP's 1937 traveling troupe sent out to perform for the refugees of one of the most costly U.S. floods of all time. These performances fulfilled Flanagan's goals for a locally relevant, audience-centered national theatre in a way that was impossible for the big-city units to emulate. Through these case studies, I will explore the ways in which tours functioned within the larger infrastructure of the FTP, as well as examine the characteristics that bolstered the core values of Flanagan's FTP.

ON THE ROAD AGAIN: DEVELOPING PARTICIPATORY THEATRE IN THE CIVILIAN CONSERVATION CORPS CAMPS

Grace Hayward's *CCC Murder Mystery*—"a thrilling, entertaining, laugh-provoking mystery story, of, by, and for the boys of the CCC"[6]—was created specifically for the enrollees in Roosevelt's highly popular CCC camps. With an audience of almost exclusively young men, *CCC Murder Mystery* was a unique experiment in participatory theatre at an unprecedented level for the FTP, utilizing as many as 32 CCC boys in every performance. First staged by the FTP's newly created CCC Division at Camp Sp-8 in Peekskill, New York in May 1936, the play was so well received that it was quickly revised and the project expanded. Soon FTP units from Syracuse, Manchester, Boston, Philadelphia, and Portland (Maine) formed expressly to take the *CCC Murder Mystery* on the road. Traveling FTP companies performed the *CCC Murder Mystery* at hundreds of camps along the east and west coasts, and even strayed into the South and Midwest occasionally. The New York troupe alone performed *CCC Murder Mystery* at 51 different camps in New York, Pennsylvania, New Jersey, Maryland, and Virginia between September 10 and December 19, 1936.[7] CCC reports estimated total attendance along the Atlantic Seaboard at 46,000 officers and enrollees, with nearly 6,500 CCC boys playing active parts in the productions.[8]

Rife with laugh-out-loud comedy, spectacular tales, and tense courtroom drama, the *CCC Murder Mystery* is a convoluted mystery. At its core, the play hinges on creating the illusion of a real-life court trial. At the beginning of the play, a popular CCC boy is "arrested" and brought before a judge and jury of his peers on charges of arson and murder. The prosecutor alleges that the defendant lured his rival to a cabin in the woods, shot him, doused the body with gasoline, and finally blasted the evidence to bits using dynamite stolen from a local construction company. The drama unfolds as a stream of witnesses testifies, and the story eventually becomes clear. No murder has actually been committed. Instead the fictional trial reveals an elaborate plot to catch a member of an organized crime ring who has been masquerading as a butler and attempting to blackmail a local in order to steal his inheritance.

The *CCC Murder Mystery* serves as a distinctive case study of the creation and execution of two of Hallie Flanagan's primary goals for the FTP. Specialized, malleable, surprising, and terrifically entertaining for the CCC enrollees, the play could be adapted to fit a new geographic location with two days of preparation onsite prior to the FTP company's arrival. Moreover, through the hundreds of performances of this play, the FTP developed a new audience for the American theatre. By touring the country with this production, the FTP served a vital function for Roosevelt's so-called "Tree Army," boosting morale, inspiring creative activity in the CCC boys, and entertaining masses of high-energy young men. Thus the FTP's touring activity within the CCC intersected with other New Deal programs and promoted social usefulness, a feature that could have been pivotal in the ultimate endurance of the FTP. Because of these multiple facets, an interrogation of the CCC Division offers insights into the formulation of the FTP's identity and the possibilities of the FTP as a national "people's theatre."

Roosevelt founded the CCC during his notorious "First Hundred Days." One of two programs designed to deal with the disproportionate number of unemployed young men, the CCC would relocate young men to areas outside of cities, build up health and morale, and provide financial support for the families, while effecting conservation measures and increasing recreational opportunities throughout the nation.[9] The CCC commenced in March 1933, under the joint auspices of the U.S. Army and the U.S. Forestry Service, ultimately enrolling nearly 3 million young men in more than 4,000 camps nationwide. The majority of the enrollees were aged 17–20 and unmarried, and all members had to be strong enough to engage in hard physical labor. Boys could remain in the program for no longer than two years, and spots were difficult to obtain. In 1938, approximately halfway through its lifetime, the CCC admitted less than 20 percent of the applicants; even after the United States entered World War II and many young men joined in the fight abroad, only about two-thirds of the applicants gained admission. The boys and young men performed a variety of tasks ranging from planting trees and building bridges to fire prevention, wildlife and soil conservation, and the making of recreation facilities.[10] In the process, the boys gained physical strength, work experience, and maturity, and the government sent $22–$25 of their $30 monthly wages home to their families. All in all, the federal government funneled more than 3 billion dollars into the CCC, much of which went directly toward salaries and conservation efforts. By the time the nation's war requirements forced the CCC to disband in 1942, it had "constructively altered the landscape of the United States," transforming more than 118 million acres.[11] The CCC garnered extraordinary public support; a 1936 poll found that 82 percent of the population favored the continuation of the CCC, and a second poll completed in 1939 ranked the CCC as the second greatest accomplishment of the New Deal programs, placed only behind the Federal Deposit Insurance Corporation (FDIC).[12]

It is likely that the popularity of the program stemmed from its dual abilities to create and conserve natural resources and to occupy otherwise unemployed young men with socially useful tasks. Conveniently, this effectively removed them from the oversaturated, able-bodied workforce, thus freeing up jobs for older men with familial responsibilities. While successful in many ways, this left the leaders of the various camps with large groups of strong, spirited young men, isolated far from their homes, families, and sweethearts. Since the camps themselves were often located in the same wilderness in which the enrollees would work, camp staff was frequently tasked with creating opportunities for the hard-working young men to relax at the end of the day. Many camps offered education options and job training, and sports, singing, and other social activities often took place in the evenings and over the weekends. Even so, the gathering of so many young men in such remote locations often led to restlessness, boredom, and minor criminal activities; diversions were a requirement. Theatrical entertainments proved to be quite popular, particularly when they were light, fast-paced, and funny.

Though many are now unaware of it, a minor division of the Federal Emergency Relief Administration's (FERA) Public Works Division preceded the FTP's CCC Division. Initially started with a grant in 1934, FERA increased support to $300,000 the following year so as to send 20 different touring groups consisting of 300 actors, stagehands, technicians, and designers to entertain at CCC camps in six Eastern states.[13] Yet these activities were rife with difficulties. Actors complained bitterly about the traveling and working conditions. The companies often trekked long distances in army vehicles that lacked heat, endured difficult audiences, and slept either in the mess hall or in unfinished storage buildings. One actor described shivering himself to sleep while watching snowflakes descend upon him through holes in the ceiling and walls.[14] When the FTP absorbed the FERA units in 1935, Flanagan faced multiple issues. First, the quality of FERA's productions was suspect; FERA's guidelines for theatrical production and professionalism were not as stringent as those of the FTP. Second, touring the CCC camps would require astonishing administrative hurdles for the decentralized FTP. Since the CCC camps were spread across the country's wilderness, the vast majority of these camps were located in areas with little or no FTP activity; they would require ongoing travel across state lines, an activity that would test the creative mettle of many regional FTP leaders.

Flanagan chose to continue FERA's work in the CCC camps but demanded high quality, relevant performances: "Three hundred thousand boys in C.C.C. camps throughout the United States want dramatic entertainment...they do not want from us pallid productions of the classics or lukewarm imitations of Broadway. The camps deserve and should have the best that we can send out."[15] She went on to ask that the FTP imitate the fun, participatory style of the CCC semi-official newspaper, *Happy Days,* in the energy of its productions. At its core, this request mirrored Flanagan's ideas for many FTP activities; she frequently advised her administrators to seek out the aesthetic strategies that already worked in specific locales, and then emulate them in style, content, and approach. In the case of the CCC, *Happy Days* solicited extensive participation from its readers, requesting poems, gossip, stories, inventions, and anecdotes. Flanagan's appeal for a theatrical piece modeled after *Happy Days* would set the stage for a distinctive experiment in participatory theatre.

Flanagan appointed Major Earl L. House as national coordinator of the FTP's newly created CCC Division in March of 1936. Uniquely suited to heading this division, House boasted more than ten years of stage experience and was one of the first Army reserve officers called up to command the CCC when it was newly formed in 1933.[16] Prior to House's appointment, an interim group of FTP vaudeville players toured CCC camps in California. Supervisor Norman Feusier, in reporting on the activities of his traveling group of players to House that May, complained that his troupe suffered many of the same problems that the FERA performers experienced. The stage furnishings were poor. Transportation was uncomfortable in the best of times and distressingly hazardous through the winter months. Yet the morale of the company and their reception in the camps were good. Feusier praised his company, stating that they adhered to the show business axiom "The Show Must Go On" to such a degree that they readily assisted "in pushing the trucks out of the mud during the rainy season." His communication concluded by expressing the need for better performance facilities, living quarters, and transportation options for his "worthy performers."[17]

House would prove to be a quick and decisive administrator of these traveling companies. In consultation with Flanagan, he united the three major divisions of CCC entertainment—the Touring Companies, the Resident Drama Division, and the Motion Picture Division—into a single umbrella organization that worked regionally rather than individually on a state level. With centers in New York, Chicago, and Los Angeles, state boundaries effectively disappeared for the FTP's CCC Division, allowing groups to travel efficiently throughout their regions.[18] House also commissioned designers to create stages that could be quickly and easily transported on the road, replaced the army vehicles with much more comfortable trucks sporting "Federal Theatre Project" painted on their exteriors, and required the CCC camps to feed and house the touring companies.

Yet it was not until later in 1936, when the so-called "Theatre of the Wilderness" began productions of Grace Hayward's *CCC Murder Mystery*, that the FTP's CCC Division really began to bear fruit in exciting and unexpected ways. In fact, the play was so successful that House shifted the mission of the CCC Division to mirror the strategies used in the play. As announced in a 1936 press release, House discontinued activities that extolled the objective of "mass entertainment" in favor of a program in which "the boys themselves take an active part, and from which they can benefit both in experience and knowledge." House noted the *CCC Murder Mystery* as the success story that spurred this crucial change.[19]

Though written by Broadway playwright Grace Hayward, the *CCC Murder Mystery* was clearly not intended for a Broadway audience. As the *Syracuse Post-Standard* reviewer explained: "no Broadway audience would appreciate it. It is simply and solely for the boys in such camps—and they love it."[20] *CCC Murder Mystery* used a cast of 12 FTP actors and could be performed on a stage, in a mess hall or recreation room, or even outdoors.[21] The show required extensive travel because it depended on surprise; the idea of the "trial" would lose its urgency (and charm) if the boys in the audience realized that it was an imaginary trial replayed by actors every night. Ultimately, the playwright even suggested that the camps hand out "court passes" to the boys to prevent hecklers visiting from other camps from revealing the play's secrets in the midst of the performance. Sitting in the audience of a production of *CCC Murder Mystery* one summer night, Flanagan noted the spontaneity and "reality" of the performance:

> It was very warm and the small hall was crowded with boys, sitting on the floor, on tables, on windowsills. I wondered how any actors could hold this high-spirited, restless audience. Suddenly an automobile drove up, a man jumped out and, displaying a sheriff's badge, drew the commander aside for a whispered consultation. Everyone grew silent. The sheriff pounded on the table, "Men, I'm sorry to break in on your meeting this way but on account of the fact that so many witnesses in this case are C.C.C. workers, and that the camp is so far from the county courthouse, His Honor has decided to hold court right here."[22]

With this highly unusual prologue, which directly and unexpectedly involved one the CCC camp enrollees, the *CCC Murder Mystery* began.

The *CCC Murder Mystery* plot is wildly implausible, chaotic, and full of surprising twists; ultimately it relies on the tried and true "babies switched at birth" plot device. In fact, while arson, kidnapping, and fraud form integral points, the murder of which the defendant is accused never occurred; the burnt-out skeleton found in the remains of a house near to the camp actually belonged to a dog that had been hit by a car, shot, left in the woods, moved into the house, dressed in a CCC uniform, doused with gasoline, and dynamited by a gangster who was masquerading as a butler and hoping to blackmail one of the switched-at-birth babies into turning over his inheritance. In an even greater twist, the audience of CCC enrollees learns this information when the townsperson who supposedly burned to death in the fire appears in the courtroom to testify that he had been kidnapped by the gangster-turned-butler and escaped. While this certainly tests the limits of the willing suspension of disbelief—and raises doubts about the forensic science practiced in small towns in the 1930s—searching for viability misses the point of the production. *CCC Murder Mystery* seeks to enthrall and pleasantly confound the rowdy and easily distracted audience of young men in the CCC camps.

The *CCC Murder Mystery's* participatory nature distinguishes its dramaturgical thrust. In addition to the role of the accused, the CCC boys also played jury, witnesses, and audience. In the weeks before the performance, the FTP set the stage for the performance in two ways. First, the information forwarded to the camp education supervisors described the facilities and set pieces required for the production, requested the loan of an empty revolver, and asked that a notice be posted in a prominent location: "A Court Session will be held on (date) at this Camp in the Recreation Hall. The occasion being the trial of a Camp Member for the Murder of James Fenton, who lived in a cottage near the camp. All are eligible to attend."[23] Specific information about the date, location, and accused would be adjusted in each camp. Secondly, the FTP asked the camp leaders to cast boys that best fit the 33 specific parts designed to be played by enrollees. The outline sent ahead provided character sketches, lines, and cues, as well as brief stage directions and warnings to "speak loudly and distinctly" and pay careful attention during the performance.[24] Two days prior to the troupe's arrival, a dramatic coach appeared to rehearse each of the enrollees employed for the production individually. All were sworn to secrecy—the details of the show and participants were to remain cloaked in mystery—and the directions cautioned the camp leadership to keep the script locked away so none of the boys would happen upon it and ruin the surprise. As the playscript's introduction explained:

> You are invited to participate in an entertainment, given by the Federal Theatre Project, in the _____ Hall of your Camp, on _____.
>
> This amusement is present in the form of a trial—a trial of one of your buddies who is accused of arson and murder. We know most of you boys like him and will enjoy helping to clear him. [...] Some of the boys, residents of the camp, will be supoenaed [*sic*] as witnesses, jurors, etc. You have been selected as one of them.
>
> [...]
>
> A famous jurist has said: "The witness is the most important personage at a trial. What he says or how he acts makes or ruins a case. Lawyers may talk and Judges may rule, but the witness supplies the ammunition on which largely determines the conclusion."[25]

This summons served as an opening for the boys to become unofficial, secret members of the FTP for the evening. It united the boys by referring to one of their "buddies who was accused of arson and murder" by outsiders and observed that most of the witnesses liked the accused and would probably want to help clear him of the charges. The concluding note, stating that "the witness is the most important personage at a trial," emphasized the vital role that the CCC boys would play in this "amusement." It was not a stretch to suspect that the majority of the CCC boys handpicked to play active roles in *CCC Murder Mystery* would enjoy the opportunity to play clandestine, but vitally important, heroes in the ensuing hilarity.

The CCC participants used their own names and personalities, and directors encouraged the boys to extemporize in their own words so long as they answered the questions correctly. The script described characters as "a little bashful," "best comedian," "big and not afraid to have some fun," "the famous fighter of the camp," "handsome," "a great lover," "having oiled hair," and even "Chocolate bar" (meaning half nuts).[26] This strategy promoted the individualization of the show at each camp since the CCC boys played so many of the roles. Each boy could make the role his own, inserting bits of local color and "'cracks' involving local enrollees."[27] Along with the ability to take on dramatic roles—a first foray into theatre and performing for many of the CCC boys who participated—CCC Company Commanders and Education Directors commented most frequently on the way enrollees blossomed when given a solid push to perform in front of their peers. These officers saw this performance as the first step toward a solidified interest in drama in the camps and often cited the creation of drama groups following participation in the performance in their praise. Commanding Officer Charles Cormack testified that the "men who did take parts in the CCC Murder Mystery [*sic*] were so surprised by their own acting ability that they immediately formed a dramatic club."[28] Education Director Robert Fara concurred: "Its value in entertainment was due to the fact that the members participated and provided the entertainment for the others at their own expense. It will in all probability be the nucleus of a dramatic club in the camp and disregarding entertainment, this in itself will be of great value."[29]

Hayward wrote *CCC Murder Mystery* strategically, so that FTP actors could set the tone and pace at the beginning, intervene when necessary to excite or calm the audience, and provide essential plot details. The cast of characters includes two actors, Jenkins and Toby, who dress in CCC uniforms and move throughout the audience. Toby regularly instigates audience commentary. He heckles the other actors, shouts for joy when evidence against his colleague is thrown out, and leads applause and laughter. As Hayward explains in the introductory information: "The Attorneys, Judge and Bailiff must be capable of leading [the CCC boys] through their parts so that they are not conscious of this effect."[30] The Bailiff, Judge, and Attorneys regularly sport lines that would likely be interpreted in any real court as blatant attempts to lead the witness, so if one of the CCC boys forgets a line integral to the evidence, he can be prompted in a way that bears little departure from the rest of the dialogue. Most of the roles the boys play are comedic, and many of the lines have fail-safes embedded in the script; laugh lines can be saved by one of two comic FTP players, who can repeat or adapt any line that the CCC amateurs forget or mishandle.

For example, when one of the witnesses calls Mugs, the comic female lead, a "Dumb Dora,"[31] she cries:

> MUGS: I ain't either no Dumb Dora. And don't speak to me no more, I don't know you from Adam!
> SMITH: You ought to. I got more clothes on.[32]

The retort is supposed to be spoken by the CCC boy on the witness stand, but the script specifically states that the CCC boy played by an FTP actor, Jenkins, should cover the line should the real-life CCC boy forget it. Numerous other lines in the text bear similar suggestions for Jenkins, Mugs, or one of the other characters, implying that the remaining lines could either be missed or covered by the most logical actor. Each performance also includes a court stenographer—usually played by the camp's Education Director—who knows all of the performers by name, has a copy of the script in front of him, and can be called on at any point to repeat an important line. All in all, the strategy appears to have worked well for the FTP; several of the written comments sent to House were from Education Directors who remarked with surprise about the actors' collective ability to help the CCC boys successfully navigate the text.

In addition to the mechanical strategies in place to help the amateur CCC actors remember their lines and incite laughter, the dialogue itself draws from the vaudeville patter that was an audience favorite during the early twentieth century. Quick exchanges pepper the play, setting the tone for a fast-paced, cheeky, courtroom comedy. The first witness—one of the only witnesses played by a member of the FTP company—illustrates this as the bailiff swears him in:

> BAILIFF: Do you swear to tell the truth, the whole truth and nothing but the truth, so help you God?
> JENKINS: What did he say?
> JUDGE: The bailiff is asking you if you swear.
> JENKINS: <u>No</u>. No, sir, I never swear.
> TOBY: The hell he don't.
> JUDGE: He means, if you swear to tell the truth.
> JENKINS: Oh.
> BAILIFF: Do you swear to tell the truth, the whole truth and nothing but the truth, so help you God?
> JENKINS: *(Laughs)* Sure.
> BAILIFF: Then raise your right hand and swear.

JENKINS: I can't. I'm left handed.
BAILIFF: Well, swear anyway.
JENKINS: *(Holds up his right hand and says solemnly)* Damn it.[33]

In this exchange, completed before the first witness even takes the stand, Jenkins verbally spars with the Bailiff and Judge. He responds cheerfully, never seeming to take pleasure in discomfiting either figure of authority but accomplishing that feat nevertheless. This sassy "CCC boy" sets the stage for a series of amusing interactions between the remaining witnesses—the real CCC boys—and the authority figures in the play, providing an opportunity for the boys to challenge authority to humorous effect and without fear of repercussions. For example, during the Defense Attorney's questioning he attempts to determine what, exactly, Jenkins observed on the night of the alleged crime:

DEF. ATTORNEY: On the night of the fire, did you or did you not hear the alarm?
JENKINS: Well, you see—it was like this—
DEF. ATTORNEY: Answer yes or no.
JENKINS: Yes or no.
DEF. ATTORNEY: You mean you didn't?
JENKINS: No.
DEF. ATTORNEY: Oh, you mean you did?
JENKINS: Yes.[34]

Wordplay that hinges on the comic effect of misinterpretation is common in the *CCC Murder Mystery*. Throughout the play, the CCC boys constantly "misunderstand" the questions posed by officers of the court, but they emerge from these verbal scuffles the victors and earn loads of laughs from their audience. In another exchange, a CCC witness politely responds to the District Attorney's interrogation:

JACOB: Will you please tell the gentleman—(Pointing to the Judge) that I don't want to answer that question?
D.A.: Don't call the court "gentleman"; say "your Honor."
JACOB: *(Rises and bows to the Judge)* I'm sorry. I apologize for calling Your Honor a gentleman.[35]

In this exchange, the CCC witness again refrains from any appearance of impropriety; in fact, he graciously apologizes for referring to the Judge as a gentleman. The Judge simply laughs at the exchange and forgives the witness easily, thus donning the guise of an affable ally to the CCC boys. In this way, the Judge, District Attorney, and Defense Attorney all became fodder for the amusement of the boys, effectively providing the enrollees with the opportunity to get the better of their "authorities" in an innocuous way (See Figure 8).

Even as these authority figures drop their heads into their hands in frustration, they provide the framework through which the FTP actors exert control over the performance. In the same way that the Judge, Bailiff, and Attorneys sculpt lines to help the CCC boys when they fall victim to stage fright, these characters also have the ability to halt the action of the play at any point. The Judge regularly intercedes after the comic moments peak, pounding his gavel and commanding, "Order in the court. Another interruption of this kind and I'll clear the courtroom! Proceed."[36] Just as a real

Figure 8 In this *CCC Murder Mystery* scene, a CCC boy has a good laugh on the stand. The Defense Attorney (left) also enjoys the moment, while the District Attorney (right) and Judge perform frustration and reign in the amusement. NARA 69-TC, Box 46, "CCC Murder Mystery."

courtroom judge may bring the courtroom's testimony and arguments to a standstill, the Judge in *CCC Murder Mystery* can refocus the action at any point. Similarly, both Attorneys pace the patter as the straight men for the CCC boy comedians and have the authority to quickly dismiss witnesses that struggle with or derail the performance. The Bailiff serves as physical intimidation; by virtue of his position, he can move throughout the performance space and into the audience, intimidating hecklers, encouraging comic participation, or even throwing out particularly unruly audience members. Though the play often seems to slip from the performers' fingers and verge on chaos, I suggest that this constructed lack of control was actually an effective strategy to cede a layer of power to the CCC boys, thus providing a much-needed psychological release for camp enrollees. In reality, these performative authority figures could quickly wrest control back to the frame of the performance without jeopardizing the world of the play, making the "courtroom" paradigm with its many rules and authority figures the ideal vehicle for realizing this participatory comedy.

Grace Hayward's positive portrayals of the CCC and the young men who were selected to participate in it are appealing elements of *CCC Murder Mystery* for the show's target audience. The play frequently highlights the boys' trickster side, which allows them to gain the upper hand on the witness stand, eliciting an almost carnivalesque atmosphere. In one scene, a surprise witness emerges from the audience, claiming to know something vitally important about the crime. The District Attorney (D. A.), the least likable (and most liberally lampooned) character in the play, objects. The stage directions state that he turns to the audience in dismay and cries, "These CCC boys seem to be primed for 'most anything. Heaven only knows what he is liable to say."[37] The Judge quickly overrules the unpopular D. A.'s objections in favor of gaining more evidence so as to uncover the truth. Coming from the detested D. A., this complaint seems more like a compliment than degradation. The CCC boys are capable young men— "primed for 'most anything'"—as they successfully demonstrate each time they humiliate the D. A. In a later scene, the D. A. interrogates the accused CCC worker's girlfriend, a wide-eyed, helpless young lady who breaks down into tears when the D. A. impugns her honor. The CCC boys rally to her defense, demanding that the D. A. "lay off her." In fact, the stage directions describe several of the boys marching to the front of the courtroom to confront the D. A., protesting loudly to the Judge all the while:

> BUD: I've stood just as much as I can from this guy. He's been pulling a line about us boys, and he better lay off. We ain't a lot of sissies.

JENKINS: The government don't pick that kind.
TOBY: You bet they don't, Buddie. *(Bud, pulling up his trousers, getting ready to fight, starts toward D.A.)*[38]

In this exchange, the CCC boys show their affinity for finding the truth, protecting the honor of a lady, and securing their own reputations. As Bud describes it, the boys have patiently listened to the D. A. maligning their characters, accusing their friend of murder and arson, and failing to find the truth. In light of this attack, the boys in the audience are more than willing to settle matters with a physical altercation; they are not "a lot of sissies" who fail to intervene when they witness an attack on an innocent young woman. In fact, none of the CCC boys would stand idly by in the face of these sorts of insults and affronts, as the government doesn't accept this type of "unmanly" behavior into the highly selective ranks of the CCC. Yet they are willing to listen to reason. When the Judge responds to their threat of violence, he compliments the young lady, endorses the loyalty and bravery of the CCC enrollees, and compares the lawyers to children who require leniency. Finally, he promises to ensure justice. Here a recognized authority figure praises the boys' response and effectively elevates them into the role of long-suffering parents who must endure the juvenile taunts and poor manners of the D. A. The boys quickly agree that justice is the priority and return to their seats. Exchanges of this type portray the CCC boys in a positive light, interpreting the easily aroused protective instinct (or defensiveness) of proud young men in a government relief program as a positive trait and highlighting their loyalty, courage, and strength of character.

Its adaptability, positive portrayal of its target audience, and laugh out loud comedy made the *CCC Murder Mystery* wildly popular with the CCC boys; it even traveled to high schools and prisons in the guise of the *High School Murder Mystery* and the *Prison Murder Mystery*. Each time the show met a new audience, it was transformed; the traveling troupe changed the title, adapted the costumes to fit the new environment, and chose representatives from among the audiences who would play their carefully defined roles—further reshaping the play each night. As a reviewer in the *Syracuse American* wrote: "No matter whether it's a baseball game or theatrical performance, it is admittedly more fun if you are in it yourself." The critic went on to claim that the "novel" play was certain to be performed in every CCC camp in the country.[39] While the play did not, in fact, tour every CCC camp in the country, it did play to hundreds of camps and met great acclaim. Rave reviews and fan mail touting *CCC Murder Mystery* poured in to both House and Flanagan. As Broadway director Charles Hopkins explained in his enthusiastic appraisal of the New York touring company:

> I can heartily recommend the booking of this play in every CCC in the country, as well as in prisons, training camps and any other institutions providing audiences of young men between the ages of approximately seventeen and twenty-eight.
>
> This murder mystery comedy is an entertainment concocted to appeal to a definite audience, and in the writing, casting (in the main) and staging, it hits the nail squarely on the head.
>
> As you know in so many cases in the theatre, there isn't any hammer and there isn't any nail.[40]

Just as important as the positive reviews given by critics and theatre professionals were the approbations received from the CCC's target audience. House received thousands of letters praising *CCC Murder Mystery* from CCC officials and enrollees all over the country. Fifty-five pages of the 87-page report entitled *The Federal Theatre Project of the Works Progress Administration and the CCC* consists of short quotes and commentary pertaining specifically to performances of the *CCC Murder Mystery*. For example, Leo Guibault, a first Lieutenant at a CCC camp in Connecticut, wrote: "This is an excellent play with interesting rapid fire comedy, commanding the immediate attention of the audience and holding the interest of the twenty-five men who took part in the play itself, which was well managed and excellently presented."[41] Similarly, in a letter to Grace Hayward, Martin Primoschic, Commanding Officer of the CCC camp in Manahawkin, New Jersey, declared: "After the widespread success of your play, I feel that my words are but as the echo of the beat on the drum of approbation, yet I shall reiterate that it was (in the vernacular) a 'wow.' "[42]

While the *CCC Murder Mystery* may not have appealed to a Broadway audience, the ways in which the play adapted to and included its audience—as well as the many positive letters, reviews, and requests for more plays like this one—illustrate its effectiveness. For the FTP as a whole, this play is an example of drama created by and for the FTP, and which successfully navigated the often overwhelmingly complex negotiations between states and regions. Hundreds of actors took part in the touring productions, and the show was based solidly in the needs of its target audience, not pandering to, but working with the CCC enrollees. In addition, it required minimal funding to tour—royalties were only $5 per performance, and with the $15 fee that each camp paid for a performance (in addition to some travel costs, which often came out of the mess hall budget), it cost the government approximately $100 a week to have the entire company perform five to six times.[43]

More important than a single production, the FTP had a captive audience of young men, desperate for diversion, and ideal for recruiting as future audience members. According to a study completed by House, approximately 40 percent of the CCC enrollees had never seen live theatre prior to the FTP shows at the camps.[44] The success of touring productions like *CCC Murder Mystery* thrust the CCC boys into the performing arts. As Moren would argue in the report documenting the impact of the CCC Division, it urged the boys to "develop their own theatre, and has encouraged them in self-entertainment—one of the most acute problems of the CCC administration."[45] One driven CCC resident drama director described his first experience sharing theatre with the "sullen" enrollees of his assigned CCC camp who appeared utterly uninterested in his pitch for the theatre:

> I was furious at myself as I looked at them, for thinking that they would know or care anything about the theatre, and as soon as I finished, I said, rather tartly: 'The talk is over now and none of you need to stay unless you would be interested in forming a theatre group here'. I sat down. No one moved. I thought they had not understood, so I said again: 'That is all for tonight; you may all go now—unless there are a few of you who would like to start a dramatic club.' Again no one moved, but a tall boy in the back of the room, one of the most sullen-looking said: 'Well, I guess if it has anything to do with the theatre, we'd all like to join the club'.[46]

In such ways, the FTP's CCC Division not only took theatre to isolated pockets of people who needed it, but also supplied them with the means and motivation to begin their own creative endeavors during their leisure time. The National CCC Script Service, a program that provided selected manuscripts of short plays and entertainments offered the means; with 16,000 scripts sent out, more than half of the 2002 CCC camps in operation in mid-1937 took advantage of this service.[47] Motivation would come in the form of the nationwide CCC Playwriting Contest, sponsored by the FTP in 1936. In order to help the entrants create better plays, the FTP also offered a "Short Outline of the Technique of Playwriting," available free to any person who requested a copy. The contest garnered more than 400 submissions from writers in 48 states.[48]

In point of fact, the CCC Division of the Federal Theatre Project would prove to be extraordinarily active. The New Productions Department designed the portable and collapsible stages that would be used by both the CCC Division and numerous other FTP units for road shows. The companies performed many different pieces in addition to the *CCC Murder Mystery*, often focusing on vaudeville, minstrelsy, variety acts, and short one-act dramas. In Indiana, for example, the touring company was particularly energetic, boasting of having played at least once at every camp in the state in every calendar year of its existence. A Louisiana minstrel troupe toured its home state and Arkansas in army trucks; at one point, this company played to an estimated audience of 35,000 CCC boys and local community members in an outdoor amphitheatre in a state park. In Missouri, an FTP troupe traveled into camps deep in the Ozark mountains, locating thousands of audience members who had never before seen live theatre.[49] Though the FTP always prioritized the CCC camps in these entertainments, they invited local community members whenever possible. In light of this level of activity, the ability to reach a vast new audience, and the hundreds of relief workers employed, it is surprising that Flanagan chose to discontinue the CCC Division of the FTP when the sweeping funding cuts came through in the summer of 1937. In spite of this, some states chose to continue offering theatrical amusements to their CCC camps but coordinated these performances through the state WPA rather than the FTP.[50]

The *CCC Murder Mystery* stands as a unique production in the FTP repertoire. By tailoring this show to the interests of the CCC boys, the FTP gave the *CCC Murder Mystery* the wide appeal of a national hit; by leaving so much of the dialogue and acting in the hands of the CCC boys themselves, the performances relied on the locale, creating one of the few pieces that was simultaneously local in purpose and yet national in its scope. The *CCC Murder Mystery*, like many of the performances given at CCC camps throughout the country, was not necessarily groundbreaking in theatrical aesthetics. However, just as attempting to apply a veneer of logic to *CCC Murder Mystery* misses the point of the production, so too does judging the value of the CCC Division based on their contributions to traditional theatre aesthetics. Describing a performance at a CCC camp in Missouri, Flanagan articulated this distinction:

> Only one who has seen such a troupe in action and watched the audiences at these performances should have the temerity to say whether or not such work is useful and needed as a part of a theatre in this country. Certainly such performances and such audiences are the antithesis of our usual conception of the theatre—metropolitan productions attended by the privileged and affluent few.[51]

These performances, for these audiences, would never play on prominent Broadway stages. However, this case study encourages the reassessment of the FTP as a socially influential national theatre that reached hundreds of thousands of CCC boys and nearby community members, thereby returning the magic of theatre to communities that had seen little or no living theatre for decades. The FTP's flood tour would continue this trend by forwarding the FTP as an organization that responded to the vast social needs of the country.

A NATION IN NEED: DISASTER RELIEF AND THE FEDERAL THEATRE PROJECT[52]

In January of 1937, the United States experienced one of the most costly disasters in its history. Though the year began innocently with a bit of a chill and a mild excess of rain, the end of the month would see the Ohio River, the mighty Mississippi River, and many of their tributaries at some of the highest flood levels ever recorded. Flood waters poured into cities and towns in Pennsylvania, Ohio, Virginia, West Virginia, Kentucky, Indiana, Illinois, Missouri, Tennessee, Arkansas, Mississippi and Louisiana. Between January 18 and February 5, 385 people were killed, one million became homeless, and property losses exceeded $500 million (approximately $6.5 billion today).[53]

Although one might expect to see the federal government send substantial aid in such a situation, one might not expect that government-sponsored aid to come in the form of theatre. Yet the FTP served as one means of addressing this national catastrophe. At the invitation of the American Red Cross (ARC), Major House and Herbert Stratton Price (director of the Georgia Experiment) organized an expedition into the regions of the flood zone. Price departed with a traveling company of FTP actors and a single CCC Division truck in mid-February 1937, producing performances in what were then called "concentration camps"[54] throughout Tennessee, Arkansas, Illinois, Indiana, and Ohio. Like the tours of the CCC Division and the efforts of the Georgia Experiment, theatre scholars have largely ignored this sort of community-based relief activity within the FTP. Yet, as I have argued, they are a vital part of National Director Hallie Flanagan's goals for the FTP on both a regional and national scale. The discussion that follows will place the Great Flood of 1937 within contemporaneous disasters, outline the activities of the flood tour, and resituate these endeavors inside the FTP as a whole. First, however, it is necessary to understand the circumstances and aftermath of the Great Flood of 1937.

When considering environmental catastrophes of the Great Depression, the Dust Bowl tends to receive the majority of attention. Covering approximately

97 million acres of land in Colorado, Kansas, Texas, Oklahoma and New Mexico, historians generally agree that the Dust Bowl was caused by the combination of drought and years of poor soil treatment. By "Black Sunday," April 14, 1935, the frequent dust storms culminated in the most devastating "black blizzard" seen in the 1930s. Winds reached more than 60 miles per hour that day; victims described the dust as feeling like "a shovelful of fine sand flung against the face. [...N]o light in the world can penetrate that swirling murk."[55] While the enormity and lengthy duration of the Dust Bowl certainly deserves careful consideration, other detrimental natural disasters occurred across the U.S. as well. Earthquakes rattled Californians in Long Beach (1933), the Great New England Hurricane struck (1938), and a series of deadly tornadoes swept through central Illinois (1938), to name only a few of the many environmental disasters that plagued the United States during the Great Depression.[56] And yet, the Dust Bowl—and the possibility that it could continue to spread—made rain a desirable commodity. As Avis Carlson famously explained in *New Republic*, "We have been taught that until it rains and rains all along that mighty strip of drought-baked prairie running from Canada to the Gulf and reaching to the feet of the Rockies, our own showers are but moments when we almost swim back to consciousness."[57] Indeed, the country desperately needed rain. Unfortunately, the rains of 1937 not only failed to alleviate the drought but also created an entirely different problem for another quadrant of the country—floods.

The Great Flood of 1937 followed hard on the heels of another devastating and deadly flood. Less than a year earlier, heavy spring rains and melting snows merged into a devastating flood that saturated the eastern states. Within one week, flood waters poured into cities and towns along the Connecticut River and its tributaries; Pittsburgh, Springfield (Massachusetts), Binghamton (New York), and many others cities and towns from Maine to the Midwest saw unprecedented waters. Damages throughout the twelve affected states reached over half a billion dollars.[58] Determined to prevent another such calamity, the government stepped into action; the Flood Control Act of 1936 gave the federal government the authority to institute multistate collaborations in the fight against Mother Nature.

Though it seemed impossible that a natural disaster could cause more devastation than the flood of 1936, the Great Flood of 1937 did just that.[59] Due to the collisions between a stalled cold front and a series of moist tropical air masses, more than 165 billion tons of rain fell on the Ohio River Valley in January 1937.[60] Admiral Grayson, national chairman of the American Red Cross (ARC), described the raging floods as "the greatest emergency the country has faced since the World War."[61] In Cincinnati, for example, the flood of 1936 reached just over 60 feet; in 1937, the water was nearly 20 feet higher, earning it the dubious status of the highest flood-waters on record. It caused ten gasoline tanks to explode and destroyed the homes of about 20 percent of the local population (an estimated 100,000 people).[62] Large parts of Cincinnati burned while floodwaters prevented firefighters from reaching the flames. A *Time* magazine reporter depicted a landscape that had once been a city and was now "a shoreless yellow sea studded here and there with tree tops and half submerged buildings. To people crouching on house roofs, it was an immeasurable amount of ugly yellow water surging higher and higher."[63] The ARC described the events as an "inferno of water" that "only a Dante could describe in verse, or a Wagner in music, the overwhelming character of the flood at its worst and the amount of human misery it caused."[64] As a result, more than one million refugees fled from the 12,721 square miles affected and arrived destitute in the camps of the ARC.[65]

For the FTP, the Great Flood of 1937 and the "human misery it caused" provided an opportunity to demonstrate the FTP's role as a provider of emotional and moral support. This national disaster would strain an already overburdened economy, putting the infrastructure of disaster relief to a gruesome test. If the FTP could capitalize on the strength, unity, and resources it had as a federally funded relief organization while serving the needs of hundreds of thousands of displaced refugees, it could pave the way for a reconsideration of the FTP as a socially useful organization that was "good" for the country. Thus, the flood tour offered an opportunity for positive publicity for the FTP as a whole, while serving as a successful example of Flanagan's goal of a sweeping federation of theatres. Here was a production team, composed of members from a variety of locations and backgrounds, creating a series of music and vaudeville skits for a widespread audience of varying classes, races, and ages. These traveling FTP troupes performed primarily in concentration camps—liminal locations that housed thousands of refugees from both urban and rural environments.

For weeks, preparation for the mobile unit that was to tour the flood zone was the primary topic of conversation for FTP administrators touting the benefits of a national theatre. E. E. McCleish, acting deputy director, explained their purpose as complementary to the rescue efforts of the ARC:

> The concentration camps give such shelter, as the Red Cross in the flood emergency can set up, to many thousands who have lost homes and belongings in the flood waters. The Red Cross considers it highly important in rehabilitating

these families to build up and maintain morale; one of the greatest difficulties in the refugee work is lifting the spirit of the homeless.[66]

References to morale abound in the literature of the ARC, particularly when disasters require the long-term care of refugees, as in the case of the 1937 flood. To help with the rebuilding of morale, the ARC assigned recreational directors to coordinate activities for both children and adults housed at concentration camps. For the Great Flood of 1937, the ARC provided recreation and educational programming for more than 25,000 refugees in Tennessee and Kentucky, and pursued further possibilities with outside organizations.[67] These activities ranged from organizing sports and games to continuing classes for school-aged children; entertainment was also in great demand. The ARC report noted:

> The refugees were in a state of mental and physical shock. Unless this condi-
> tion were changed the adjustment to temporary hardship would be even more
> difficult and the recovery of pre-disaster morale would be greatly delayed. It
> was seen that programs on both active and passive recreation would do more to
> help the flood victims reestablish themselves physically and mentally than any
> other measure that might be undertaken.[68]

The FTP flood tour was one of many activities that addressed this need for recreational programs and was welcomed enthusiastically by ARC officials. Hence the two organizations formed a symbiotic relationship: the FTP offered a prepackaged program of entertainment, and the ARC's need for morale enhancement helped to legitimize the work of a national theatre hoping to establish itself as socially useful.

One challenge of conducting research on this particular Federal Theatre activity is that the records of a theatre troupe traveling and performing in the disheveled territories of a major disaster area tend to be somewhat haphazard when they remain at all. Helpfully, the troupe's leader, Herbert Stratton Price, supplied several first-hand accounts of the activities to both Flanagan and Pierre de Rohan, editor of *Federal Theatre* magazine. However there remains little in the way of more traditional historiographical evidence. Most local newspapers were closed due to flooding and coverage from outside of the flood zone focused on damage estimates, refugees, and the horror stories that inevitably accompany national disasters. Moreover, the normally exhaustive FTP administration was necessarily meager in this case since the company was traveling through disaster areas, so Price's reports constitute some of the only records of this adventure. While this leads to necessary questions about Price's reliability, it is important to note that a variety of memos, letters, and other administrative materials generally corroborate his reports. Other verification in the form of the CCC Division's role in the project remains in the 1937 report documenting the FTP/CCC relationship; it discussed the flood tour for two pages, and included the name of CCC Supervising Playwright Stan Stanley, one of the few individuals mentioned by Price in his onsite reports.[69] Finally, though many of the performances are documented based on first-hand accounts, no extant scripts remain; thus, this examination will focus on bringing these important activities to light in order to gain a better picture of the complete FTP during its brief existence.

When the ARC approached the FTP in search of morale-building assistance for the flood refugees, Flanagan broached the question to Herbert Stratton Price and Major House. For all the reasons that Price was ideally suited to the Georgia Experiment, so too was he a logical choice for spearheading the flood tour. As demonstrated by his work coordinating the sweeping CCC Division, House was an expert coordinator who had the personnel, administration, and equipment to set a tour into motion quickly and efficiently. At the "urgent request of the WPA and the American Red Cross," the FTP would swing into action. As Moren explained in his report, "At no time during the history of the CCC Division did this motorized equipment assume greater importance than when the Federal Theatre was confronted with the problem of providing recreational relief to the victims of the flooded area of the Mississippi valley."[70] The flood tour company was comprised of 12 FTP employees from the NYC offices and CCC Division—all volunteers—and planned to be on the road from three weeks to two months, depending on the duration of the flood and the needs of the refugee camps.

Price created the plans for the tour, most likely in close consultation with House: "As I see it, Clearing Houses [information and activity centers] have been set up on the outskirts and highlands of some of the larger cities in the stricken area of the Southland."[71] He targeted a series of refugee camps on the banks of the Ohio River from Cincinnati to Cairo, Illinois, with stops in Paducah, Kentucky, Coffee County, Tennessee, and throughout Memphis. In many of these places, the ARC had evacuated refugees from their home states into out-of-state regions less severely affected by the flood. Price suggested that the FTP flood tour perform in moderately sized camps of 500–5,000 refugees, avoiding the larger locations because they often had a more extensive ARC infrastructure in place.

Price planned to proceed to Memphis, Tennessee to set up a centralized point of communications once he had cleared "matters of importance" related to the Georgia Experiment.[72] This proposal experienced the fastest approval and the fewest bureaucratic hindrances I have seen in my extensive research on the FTP. Price sent his suggestions to Flanagan on February 5th. Flanagan forwarded the request to Ellen Woodward, Assistant Administrator of Women's and Professional Projects and the person in charge of all four of the WPA's Arts Projects. Woodward spoke to Aubrey Williams, who was second-in-command to Harry Hopkins, head of FERA, the parent organization of the WPA. In a Herculean defeat of red tape, Woodward received approval from Williams for the flood tour and authorized Flanagan to proceed on the *same day* that Price submitted his plan to Flanagan. As these approvals processed, others cleared the way for House and Price to meet in person to discuss the ideas so as to ensure that travel complications, cast choices, and myriad other minor issues were quickly solved.[73] This expediency on the part of FTP, WPA and FERA administrators emphasizes not only the magnitude of the 1937 flood but also implies that all involved had a sharp sense of the dire circumstances stemming from the catastrophe.

While Price worked on the strategy and concept of the flood tour, House and the CCC Division would create the programming. Already in rehearsal, a new musical revue modeled after the participatory *CCC Murder Mystery* would be transformed virtually overnight to appeal to the flood refugees. The proposal for the revue noted that the lead actor would be the CCC Division's Stan Stanley, a comedian with a special "flair" for working with the audience in participatory theatre, and that six others would accompany him. The show would include peppy songs, a scene in a hospital room, and a "comedy boxing bout," all tied together with Stanley's comic patter.[74] In ten days, the writers added new roles and comic "business," rehearsed, and then sent the show out for preview performances in Central Valley, New York. Three days later, the company departed for the flood zone with this new production and other light-hearted vaudeville fare.[75]

This flood tour would not be the only FTP activity though. Just as Price planned upwards of 72 performances for the two months the company would potentially be traveling in the flood zone, other FTP companies worked the situation as well. In Cincinnati, for example, the local FTP unit traveled voluntarily:

Over flooded roads 70 to 90 miles a day, setting up their makeshift scenery in any hall or school available in the flooded towns... [they] played by candlelight and lantern light to the cheers of mothers and fathers and children whose minds have been lifted from their worries.[76]

That the Cincinnati unit was willing to travel through these regions with little notice (and no additional "hazard" pay) indicates the lengths to which the employees of the FTP were willing to go in order to aid others during this national disaster. In the two-week period covered by one report, the Cincinnati unit played 40 engagements to a reported audience of 14,660 refugees. The report, quoted in *Federal Theatre,* painted a heart-breaking picture: "Mr. Strahoning, amusing the crowds with his antics as a clown, had lost everything; only the roof of his house was visible above the muddy water. [Mr. Strahoning's] partner had not seen his wife for a week; his home was under 20 feet of water."[77] Though this *Federal Theatre* magazine article says that the Cincinnati units were not alone in their efforts, specific evidence of these flood relief activities no longer exists.

In documenting the flood tour activities of the NYC employees, Price peppered his reports with pithy puns—the company's portable stage truck "acted up"—but his accounts also vividly described the flood victims and the conditions of the concentration camps they visited, which were segregated by race, gender, and class. The first performance was of a vaudeville review titled *The Stooge*. It took place at a camp in Knoxville, Tennessee, on February 20, 1937, where the ARC turned an old shirt factory into an assembly hall, dining room, headquarters, and refuge for approximately 750 African Americans. White refugees stayed in an adjacent building. These African American refugees had been evacuated from the considerably more rural environment of Paducah, Kentucky. According to Price: "they were not allowed to leave the building unless under escort by special permission. The local authorities were afraid the refugees might wander off and get lost, as this was for the majority, the first contact they had ever had with city life." He wrote of the only bit of cheer in the camp coming from three pet canaries singing from their cages in a dark corner of the women's sleeping quarters, and noted a sign that read "ONE ACCIDENT MIGHT TAKE ALL THE JOY OUT OF LIFE FOR YOU AND YOUR FAMILY," an ironic remnant from the building's days as a shirt factory.[78]

The racial segregation experienced in the Knoxville concentration camps was not unusual and speaks to an anxiety that surrounded the liminal communities created by the flood. Floods and other natural disasters may have been considered great equalizers in human misery, but this leveling did not necessarily carry over into the composition of refugee camps. The concern that African American refugees from small towns would "wander off and get lost" in the big city leads one to wonder about the underlying reasons informing this determination. Were authorities really worried about the welfare of the African American refugees or were they bothered by the idea of hundreds of recently relocated African Americans wandering through the city of Knoxville? Moreover, what would be the consequences if these African Americans decided that they preferred Knoxville to their own communities in rural Paducah? Scholars have described the Depression-era conditions in rural southern communities as "atrocious" for African Americans, noting that blacks were required to work so hard that culture and pleasure often seemed less important in the face of mere survival.[79] That said, my intent here is not to interrogate the reasons behind the segregated camps or their interactions with the community at large but to consider the FTP reaction (or lack thereof) to the situation. Price noted that African Americans were housed in different camps and implied that these camps enjoyed less in the way of comforts than did those housing white refugees. Yet he did not seem to feel that any kind of public comment or reaction on the racial segregation (and condescension) was warranted. In light of the well-known and lauded FTP initiatives dealing specifically with African Americans, it is troubling that, on the whole, the FTP seems to have turned an institutional blind eye to this instance of racial prejudice.

Price's report also specified class distinctions in the FTP audiences, though he again refrained from commenting on or critiquing their situations. In spite of his silence regarding these segregated circumstances, the FTP flood tour endeavored to bring entertainment to people housed in all the camps, regardless of class or race; like the touring productions of the *CCC Murder Mystery*, the flood tour often invited local community members as well. The FTP company touring the flood areas built a stage out of loaned lumber and performed for more than 900 refugees in Knoxville. On the second morning in Knoxville, they performed for another group of "underprivileged men, women and children" in a small local mill; that Price distinguished between the refugees and the "underprivileged" is remarkable. He enacts this type of notation throughout his reports, carefully observing the times that the company played to impoverished people and again when the destitute were also flood victims. On another occasion, the flood tour played to "so called 'poor whites' from Ark[ansas];" Price explained that these people were "sometimes known as 'river-bottom' folk" but went into no further detail to show why this distinction was relevant to his report.[80]

The flood tour's travels and Price's chronicles continued in this vein. As Price described in his reports—and as the letters of support from ARC recreation directors corroborated—dirty, crowded, despairing flood refugees glimpsed a glimmer of hope when the company performed. Price's traveling company played in CCC barracks, on their truck, in the community sleeping quarters, and in factories, schools, and the great outdoors (See Figure 9). In Tullahoma, Tennessee, they performed on two tabletops with the audience perched on beds, tables, and even in the crossbeams of the roof to see the show. In Forrest City, Arkansas, the company played outside (in February) and, while the audience did not seem to mind the cold, damp air, the pianist, cellist, and violinist had to "run around between numbers to stay warm."[81] They "played in vacant stores,- on improvised out of door stages,- in churches, and on platforms

Figure 9 This FTP company from Portland, Maine, was about to embark on a tour of local CCC Camps with their production of the *CCC Murder Mystery*. Though there is no evidence linking this company to the flood tour, the carryall trucks in the background serve as an example of the vehicles used by the FTP's CCC Division. Major Earl House, Director of the CCC Division, is in the center wearing the light beige coat. Library of Congress, Box 1190, "CCC Project—Maine."

made of table tops," with the headlights of automobiles as their only illumination.[82] The travel was grueling and often involved lengthy struggles to remove the truck from huge tracks of knee-deep mud or detours of up to one hundred miles when the floodwaters had washed out roads or bridges. Like the *CCC Murder Mystery,* the company regularly used audience members in the performances, bringing them on stage and having them participate in the varied skits and numbers. In addition, each performance ended with a "community sing" in which some member of the refugee group—often a minister or spiritual leader—would lead the audience and actors in a rousing chorus of "Goin' Home."[83] At times the community sing would go on for half an hour or more after the performance officially ended.[84]

The audience response to the traveling troupe was largely positive. An area director of the Recreational Refuge Program expressed her thanks in a letter, writing: "the audience was delighted and sat in wide-eyed wonder thruout [*sic*] the performance. Of course, in many cases it was the first time they had seen a 'real show' and all of them agreed that it was a big treat."[85] Another director of the Division of Recreation Projects wrote to Flanagan that "the Supervisor of one of the Nashville parks, where the Troupe played to a group of about two hundred children, telephoned the following day to express her appreciation of the fine spirit of the Unit who entered so whole heartedly in the spirit of the occasion, playing and singing with the playground children a half hour after the closing performance."[86] These positive responses reaffirm the importance of the traveling troupes of players. As the ARC hoped, the FTP flood tour offered a momentary respite for thousands of refugees during a time of unprecedented despair.

Clearly Price, House, and the company felt that their work was worth the hardships they endured, as did the FTP administrators who touted the tour. For Price though, there was one additional sacrifice. The time and energy of touring would ultimately pull Price away from his efforts to set up more permanent rural FTP efforts in Georgia. He had worked for more than a year to convince the national administration that the Georgia Experiment would satisfy a local need, employ theatre artists, and help to secure the FTP's position in Georgia and the South. The Georgia Experiment began in early January 1937, with each project beginning on a staggered basis so as to enable Price to personally supervise each opening, make introductions for key personnel, and assist in overcoming early challenges. The flood tour began only a few weeks into this coordinated process and overlapped with the foundational weeks for several of the community drama leaders. In the face of this national emergency, Price put the Georgia

Experiment aside in favor of the flood tour; he was virtually unreachable during this crucial period, unable to add anything but the most cursory assistance to the five people charged with spearheading the project during their 90-day window of opportunity. The Georgia Experiment offered the very real potential of becoming a localized, national theatre for the rural areas of the South, but the flood tour trumped this effort, robbing the Georgia Experiment of potential resources and energy, and eclipsing it in the FTP's rhetoric. Thus in spite of the short-term gains of the flood tour in the national perception of the FTP, the long-term losses included a worthwhile project that had the potential to change the proverbial face of the FTP and theatre in the South.

It is also important to note that the Flood of 1937 came at a crucial time for the FTP nationally. Having finally found its feet, determined where theatre people were eligible for relief, and deployed companies throughout the country, the FTP was finally beginning to raise its standards. The national administration was no longer satisfied by a unit simply overcoming bureaucratic red tape and practical difficulties to open a show. As McCleish explained: "The press comment generally throughout the country on Federal Theatre as an enterprise is losing its superficial acerbity of criticism and shows signs of editorial acceptance of the project as a cultural development worthy of support."[87] In this light, the FTP flood tour's activities were an opportunity to capitalize on this critical shift, showing that the FTP could be more than entertainment: it could minister to the emotional wounds of the country—in a very public, service-oriented way.

Ironically, this transition in critical perception highlights the attitude that likely relegated to obscurity the work of the CCC Division, the flood tour, and many other touring and rural companies on the FTP payroll. As the scathing critiques gradually softened, the individuals that made up the FTP began thinking of the organization in more professional, highbrow terms, and the FTP leadership focused less on lowbrow forms such as vaudeville and traveling tent shows. Instead, the Living Newspapers, splashy big-city musicals, and controversial pieces such as *The Cradle Will Rock*—comparatively large-scale, commercial pieces produced in urban locales—received the majority of the Project's attention. These pieces reinforced the interpretation of the FTP as an artistic force in the nation, particularly in New York City, Chicago, and Los Angeles. Yet if one recalls Flanagan's visionary intentions for the FTP, vaudeville and other popular entertainments that played to rural audiences deserve critical investigation precisely because their actions are vital to understanding a more complete picture and driving ethos of this one and only foray into composing an American national theatre.

To this point, the tent shows, rural enterprises, and traveling companies of the FTP have been largely ignored by scholars.[88] This trend began within the FTP as Flanagan and other FTP administrators highlighted the most visible successes of the organization, and it has continued in contemporary scholarship. In light of the FTP's role as a national theatre—fundamentally and repeatedly defined by its relationship to the working class in both urban and rural settings—this is a lamentable omission that has colored the ways in which scholars perceive the FTP as a whole. Efforts such as the *CCC Murder Mystery* and the 1937 flood tour demonstrate the FTP's activity simultaneously at its best and worst. In both cases, the administration was able to coordinate its efforts quickly and efficiently, use the united resources of the national project, and meet a very real need of the American people. The *CCC Murder Mystery* also demonstrated the versatility of the FTP in a way that used the national and regional resources of a major federal organization to create appealing, adaptable entertainment for the boys in the CCC. In the case of the CCC Division, though, the FTP failed to market its efforts to the public in a meaningful way that provided evidence of its usefulness. Perhaps this was due to the fact that this show was not created for Broadway consumption and seemed irrelevant to an American public outside of the CCC camps. Few people knew about these efforts, so when the national administration was faced with the task of severing a large percentage of the organization, the CCC Division became a target. In addition to its lack of notoriety, the structure and audience expectations for the CCC Division did not easily lend themselves to content that would align with the progressive artistic agenda of the FTP. In the case of the flood tour, the FTP failed to address concerns of race or class, or to tailor the production to the specific needs of the local populations it addressed in a significant way. In this case though, the needs of the local population may have become secondary to the psychological and emotional needs of the liminal community of refugees. Thus the flood tour itself provided a meaningful and essential service to a large part of the country. The lack of scholarly and critical attention has confined the work of the CCC Division and the flood tour to obscurity, thus hiding these lowbrow, rural, and vitally important efforts in plain sight.

Epilogue: An American Audience for the "People's Theatre" ∾

We have played, I think I am safe in saying, the widest variety of American audiences that any theatre has ever played.[1]

—*Hallie Flanagan*

In 1999, Tim Robbins created and directed the Hollywood version of *The Cradle Will Rock*. Boasting a well-known cast of actors, including Vanessa Redgrave, Susan Sarandon, Cherry Jones, John Turturro, Bill Murray, John Cusack, Joan Cusack, and Hank Azaria, the film documented one of the most oft told and exciting stories of American theatre history—the build up to the production that would become one of the clearest demonstrations of censorship in the United States, lead to the resignations of John Houseman and Orson Welles, and rock the foundations of the FTP. The legendary tale involves armed security guards blocking off a theatre, a determined cast resisting the powerful combined forces of their own unions and the U.S. government, a crowd—intent on seeing this dangerous production—marching along the streets of New York City, and even a piano on a rented truck circling the block for hours in the hopes that a theatre would become available for the show. *The Cradle Will Rock* is frequently held up as a pivotal moment in the history of American theatre, and serves as an illustration of the many reasons that theatre practitioners should remain wary of government involvement in the creation of theatre; moreover, it is frequently pinpointed as the catalyst that brought about the downfall of the FTP.

I enjoyed the film immensely; in fact, it was one of the reasons I began studying the FTP, and I still show portions of it to my classes today. Yet as Barry Witham has documented, the archival evidence surrounding the production of the infamous "runaway" opera does not, in point of fact, support this romanticized chronicle. Witham systematically debunks the major components of the mythological account, ultimately arguing that *The Cradle Will Rock* needs to be contextualized within the larger picture of the FTP and that events may have been manipulated by a young Orson Welles about to break with the FTP. Ultimately, Witham cautions those who would repeat the story to refine it based on the evidence. Written seven years before the production of the Hollywood film, the article brings a delightful twist of irony to the film's tagline, "Art is never dangerous—unless it tells the truth."[2]

The mythology of *The Cradle Will Rock*—probably the most famous FTP production in the aftermath of Robbins's film—provides a metaphorical bridge into my study of the FTP in this volume. This powerful, pro-labor musical debuted in 1937, the same summer that had seen a proliferation of strikes and unionization, including Chicago's Memorial Day Massacre, the defeat of U.S. Steel, and the attacks on the so-called "little steel" companies. Using the steel strikes as a metaphor for all of the worker rebellions across the nation, *The Cradle Will Rock* accused those who chose to withdraw from the strikes of ideological prostitution and called on all workers to unite against the capitalist forces that would crush them. Like *Waiting for Lefty*, Clifford Odets's masterpiece of agitational propaganda, *The Cradle Will Rock* was dangerously relevant to the workers. Though it played to a comparatively small number of audience members, and never actually opened for the FTP, this production has become a symbol of the national organization as the epitome of successful failures. For my purposes, Robbins's film offers an ideal example of the disconnect between the archival evidence and the mythology of the event, as well as the choice to highlight this New York City production at the expense of others. While symbols and icons are useful in creating sweeping pictures of a moment, they also require nuance and contextualization in order to become part of a rich, developed history. In the case of the FTP, scholars have done an enviable job of studying its emblematic moments; in my study, I have pushed beyond those representative and highly visible examples in the hope of uncovering some of the many accounts that have, to this point, remained untold.

The case studies included here span the United States. Ranging from *Altars of Steel*, the production deemed as "dangerous as *Uncle Tom's Cabin*" in Atlanta, to *Spirochete*, the show that served on the front lines in the national war against syphilis, these productions demonstrate the many and varied functions of the FTP.[3] Just as importantly, undertakings such as the flood tour, the Georgia Experiment, and the many versions of the *CCC Murder Mystery* show the ways in which the FTP located millions of new audience members and reintroduced theatre back into the lives of the people of the United States. By focusing on these activities, my study examines the tensions, triumphs, and disappointments that emerged from this nation's only national theatre in a way that respects the breadth of that organization. In so doing, I have attempted to highlight the FTP's efforts to stage the "people" of the United States and, in so doing, appeal to a demographic not typically associated with theatregoing. Smaller FTP units throughout the country sought out these audiences—seeking the stories, conflicts, and important moments of their lives—and then created appealing, locally relevant productions. In this way, the FTP gave a voice to the millions of poor and working-class Americans, reimagining the American theatre as an entity that served a wider spectrum of audiences and confronting limitations of race, class, gender, ethnicity, and religion. This is not to say that the FTP integrated the nation as a whole into the theatre it produced, or that it always succeeded in its presentation of demanding subject matter. Certainly its content often targeted members of the working class and excluded individuals with particularly conservative politics. Though the FTP repeatedly demonstrated that it *could* succeed on Broadway's terms, it instead sought to provide an alternative to Broadway. At its best, the FTP—and the theatre it created—became a medium for the transmission of daily news, entertainment, and important social issues that captured the cultural essence of the United States in the 1930s.

This journey throughout the North, South, Midwest, East, and West demonstrates that an emphasis on New York City and major urban centers is not only misleading but also excises the heart and soul from the FTP. By refocusing scholarship on specific case studies in different regions of the country, I have attempted to reveal the depth and local appeal of the FTP, and to suggest that its scope, geography, and accomplishments were far more wide-ranging than has been previously understood. Despite the richness of this inquiry, it also highlights the challenges of providing a truly nuanced view of this important moment in American theatre history. These difficulties also show that unless scholars continue documenting and exploring the full range of contributions to the FTP, it would be all too easy to be left with a monolithic, urban view of the FTP. The latter half of this book, which discusses the Georgia Experiment, Portland FTP, CCC Division, and the flood tour, examines some of the many FTP activities that have, to this point, gone largely unexplored. Unfortunately, due to the scarcity of relevant archival material, there is much that remains unknown about these projects, as well as many of the other small FTP units throughout the country. While the previous chapters provide the details I have located in my visits to the many archives holding FTP materials, I would now like to take the opportunity to lift the proverbial curtain to reveal the obstacles inherent in reading history from such a scanty archive. I do so in the hope that being as transparent as possible will allow subsequent histories to fill the gaps that this study identifies, and because I anticipate this volume to be the first step in a journey that will continue to bring the FTP's lesser-known adventures into the scholarly conversation.

The primary challenge the researcher faces in approaching the smaller units of the FTP is a surprising lack of archival materials, given the extent to which the FTP has been documented as a whole. It is true that the major FTP collections at the National Archives and the Library of Congress contain well over a million documents related to the production and administration of various projects throughout the country and that many local archives, historical societies, and public libraries also contain FTP ephemera related to local projects. In addition, Lorraine Brown spearheaded an extensive oral history initiative through George Mason University's Special Collections and Archives; this collection now contains more than 400 oral histories as well as associated donated memorabilia. However, while it is common to find entire boxes devoted to specific productions in urban centers, it is rare to find extensive portions of any of the major FTP archives dedicated to the smaller units. Instead, the scholar must pick through the archives and the finding aids with a specific idea of people and productions directly relevant to the unit in question. It is difficult to navigate hundreds of thousands of documents when little secondary information is available and the search itself is for the primary documents that will begin to tell the story. In this case, one may not know what one is seeking until one has already found it, and rigorous researchers (rightly) tend to look askance at a reliance on chance as a methodology. At times though, archival serendipity can lead to glorious discoveries.

In my own research, my discovery of the identity of Thomas Hall-Rogers, the pseudonym of the playwright of *Altars of Steel*, became one of these moments of serendipity. Convinced by Susan Duffy's compelling circumstantial evidence for the playwright being John Temple Graves II, I decided to try to document the link. I noted the similarities between the two names—both three parts with the associative link between the central components of "Hall" and "Temple"—and determined that a trip to explore Graves's personal papers in the Birmingham Public Library's archival collection was required. Everyone I spoke with seemed similarly convinced of the parallels and thought that the match between Graves and Hall-Rogers would eventually prove to be correct. We were all wrong. Disappointed by my archival findings, or lack thereof, I pursued other avenues of research at the library. This onsite visit revealed several uncatalogued items, including a clippings file that supplied articles that would ultimately provide the foundation of my argument regarding *Altars of Steel*. I returned to the National Archives, convinced that contemporary scholars would never know the identity—real or false—of the mysterious Thomas Hall-Rogers. Yet armed with the new data I had gathered in Birmingham, I recognized connections I had previously dismissed—links that ultimately allowed me to identify the writer as Josiah Bancroft, document his role in southern theatre, trace his background, and make sense of his fear of discovery.

In short, my trip to the Birmingham Public Library, although it failed to link John Temple Graves II to *Altars of Steel*, provided the information required to make vitally important connections between seemingly disparate data in the major FTP holdings. This small, local archive became the key to unraveling a mystery that would otherwise have persisted. While this was certainly a moment of archival serendipity, it also brings into sharp relief the importance of attending to these small archives throughout the country. Often the information they contain relates directly to the more localized activities of the FTP and proves invaluable in their rigorous documentation.

Because the archival evidence extant for many of the small, regional units of the FTP is scarce, it is often far more difficult to determine what happened in these projects. Their histories are inevitably less able to fit into a precise model, do not necessarily flow as a smooth, coherent narrative, and resist preconceived agendas; the availability of documents dictates the direction the scholarship can take. Moreover, as demonstrated by the movement and vaudeville-based pieces frequently produced in Oregon and by the CCC Division, certain physicality-based-production activities defy analysis when few pictures remain and scripts and assorted ephemera fail to clearly render these events. The gaps in documentation—negative spaces in the archives—force the scholar to make extrapolations and suppositions about events, personalities, and motivations. Additionally, as is often the case in archival research, the researcher's best efforts can be frustrated by inconsistencies in the data that does exist. What is one to do, for example, when the only two extant pieces of evidence documenting an event contradict one another? Unfortunately, these difficulties have resulted in the omission of the activities of the smaller and rural units from the scholarly discussion regardless of their contributions. Worse, the organization of the FTP archives themselves—typically focused on geographic locations, influential individuals, and specific productions—causes serious problems when the scholar is attempting to locate the activities of traveling companies that performed miscellaneous, often unnamed vaudeville skits, and which included few major personalities. By its very nature, the present state of the archive limits the possibilities of researching these activities.

I must note that it is not my intention here to accuse the archives of bias; records must be organized somehow and, in my experience, the major FTP archives have done an admirable job of maintaining them. In fact, much of the organization in place at the major archives mirrors that of the FTP itself. In a hasty end to the era of federally funded theatre, Hallie Flanagan requested and obtained one month on the government payroll to collect and organize the FTP's records in July 1939, immediately after the project closed. During this brief period, Flanagan's primary concern was taking care of the many administrative details that accompanied the closing of a national theatre operating in 20 states with more than 8,000 employees, millions of dollars in equipment, dozens of theatre leases, and outstanding royalties. A grant from the Rockefeller Foundation in 1940 allowed Flanagan to begin the archiving process in the following year, and gave her the time to write *Arena*, her memoir of the FTP and still the definitive work that outlines its goals, activities, and scope.[4]

Thus, the form of the organization of these records emerged directly from its national director, suggesting that Flanagan prioritized specific types of performance, often grounded in a given locale. These choices imply a hierarchy of value within the structure of the FTP, minimizing the importance placed not only on the traveling companies and rural performance but also on multistate activities outside of the prominent nationwide openings and well-known living newspapers. The fact that neither the CCC Division, nor activities such as the flood tour or Georgia Experiment survived the cuts in the summer of 1937 seems to indicate that the FTP administration perceived these activities as of lesser importance or sustainability than those of the high-profile urban units.

In light of Flanagan's assertions that the FTP would specifically seek out previously unknown audiences in areas of the country that had been untouched by theatre, this implication is troubling. But I would suggest that this apparent incongruity between stated FTP ideology and practice may have been cultivated by the need to establish the vitality of the FTP in a way that was intelligible to those who provided funding or other support for the organization, particularly critics, congresspersons, and other political bureaucrats. Since these potential supporters were more numerous in urban areas, it would be logical to shape the archive in a way that would appeal to the less theatrically sophisticated eyes of politicians or other outside reviewers. It is possible, then, that this organizational structure may not be a realistic indication as to what was valued by Flanagan or the FTP; instead, the archive could be attempting to conform to the expectations (real or imagined) of these outsiders. When seen in this light, Flanagan's lack of emphasis on these lowbrow forms may actually be an indication of the degree of her political savvy rather than a reflection of a bias against particular forms of performance.

Funded as a relief organization, the FTP was—first and foremost—designed to employ theatre professionals on relief; it accomplished this goal every time a production opened, an actor appeared for a rehearsal, or a playwright set pen to paper. Yet Flanagan envisioned more. She imagined the FTP as a "federation of theatres" that would locate new audiences and create and produce locally relevant drama across the nation. In many ways, these goals came to fruition as well. FTP units in New York City may have attracted more than 12 million audience members, but the other 18 million audience members came to theatres in Atlanta, Chicago, Los Angeles, Seattle, Manchester, Hartford, Little Rock, Tulsa, Portland, and dozens of other cities and towns.[5]

Still more listened to FTP productions on the radio; between 1936 and 1939, the FTP produced an average of 2,000 radio programs each year and played to an estimated audience of ten million a week.[6] Though the importance of the many innovative and stirring productions in major urban centers—*The "Voodoo" MacBeth, The Cradle Will Rock,* and *One-Third of a Nation,* to name only a few—cannot be denied, it is equally vital to round out this view with studies of the multifaceted activities that occurred in other areas. This work has certainly already begun with studies such as Barry Witham's examination of the Seattle FTP, but much remains. The examples proffered in this volume provide insights into the strengths, weaknesses, and breadth of the FTP, raising these regional efforts to the prominent historical position they have earned.

My overriding concern with this project has been to recover these important regional activities with an eye toward resituating the FTP itself as a part of a significant cultural moment. The 1930s saw exhilarating changes in the theatre. It was a decade in which the American people would have the opportunity to reimagine their theatre as a form of art that could entertain, provoke, and excite change; it was an era in which theatre rediscovered an audience that was lost when "the road" died. For the FTP, this audience came to see productions of *Spirochete, Altars of Steel,* and *Created Equal* in Chicago, Atlanta, and Boston. They also attended tent shows in rural Illinois, the circus in Central Park, pageants and festivals on the slopes of Oregon's Mt. Hood, *CCC Murder Mystery* trials in the wilderness, and vaudeville skits as they huddled in refugee camps. I hope to place these events side by side with the FTP's most famous productions as emblematic of the United States's only national theatre. The Federal Theatre Project—in all its tremendous breadth—was indicative of this pivotal cultural moment in which American theatre transformed itself into a popular, democratic form that truly staged the people.

Notes ᴏᴠ

INTRODUCTION: THE "PEOPLE'S THEATRE": CREATING AN AUDIENCE OF MILLIONS

1. "200,000 New Words Credited to U.S.," *New York Times*, November 10, 1936, 23.
2. Hallie Flanagan, *Arena* (New York: Duell, Sloan and Pearce, 1940), 134.
3. Charles H. Meredith, "America Sings," *Federal Theatre* 1, no. 6 (1936): 12.
4. Mark Franko, *The Work of Dance: Labor, Movement, and Identity in the 1930s* (Middleton, CT: Wesleyan University Press, 2002), 22–3.
5. For more on Hallie Flanagan, see Flanagan, *Arena*; Jane de Hart Mathews, *The Federal Theatre, 1935–1939: Plays, Relief, and Politics* (Princeton, NJ: Princeton University Press, 1967); and Joanne Bentley, *Hallie Flanagan: A Life in the American Theatre* (New York: Alfred A. Knopf, 1988).
6. The Historical Records Survey would join the ranks of Federal One under the jurisdiction of the Federal Writers' Project in November 1935; it became an independent member of Federal One in October 1936. William F. McDonald, *Federal Relief Administration and the Arts* (Columbus: Ohio State University Press, 1969), 214.
7. Flanagan, *Arena*, 23.
8. House Committee on Patents. *Department of Science, Art and Literature: Hearings before the Committee on Patents.* Transcript, 75th Congress, 3rd sess., 1938 (Washington, DC: Government Printing Office, 1938), 93.
9. Burgess Meredith first compared the cost of the FTP to the cost of building a battleship in December 1937 in *Equity*. At that time, FTP expenditures approximated 22 million dollars, or about one-half the price of a battleship. Flanagan, *Arena*, 434–6.
10. Quoted in John O'Connor and Lorraine Brown, *Free, Adult, Uncensored: The Living History of the Federal Theatre Project* (Washington, DC: New Republic Books, 1978), 2.
11. Barry Witham documents Edwin O'Connor's attempts to establish a showboat FTP unit in Seattle, a project scuttled by Don Abel, director of the Washington state WPA. The WPA district director in southern California, Colonel Connolly, bluntly stated that he defined a good theatre project as "anything that ke[pt] out of the papers," a theory that he exercised repeatedly

at the expense of the FTP in his region. Ole Ness, regional director of the West, explained to a baffled Flanagan that the Oregon WPA had withdrawn use of its typewriters. Barry Witham, *The Federal Theatre Project: A Case Study* (New York: Cambridge University Press, 2003), 7–20; Flanagan, *Arena*, 273–5; Ole Ness to Hallie Flanagan, "Weekly Report," October 21, 1938, NARA, E856, Box 100, "Region V—1938 & 1939," 2.

12. In New York City a number of Broadway Theatre managers negotiated a strict agreement with the FTP regarding theatre locations, effectively banning it from the Broadway Theatre area (between 42nd and 52nd streets). The FTP violated this "gentlemen's agreement" on numerous occasions, which earned the rancor of the managers as well as angry letters of protest and petitions. Flanagan, *Arena*, 40.

13. Ibid., 42–44.

14. Hallie Flanagan, "Excerpts from National Director's Report, January, 1939," *Federal Theatre*, NARA, E920, Box 357, "The Prompter," 1.

15. Flanagan, *Arena*, 372.

16. For an informative discussion of the FTP as a "People's Theatre," see Loren Kruger's *The National Stage: Theatre and Cultural Legitimation in England, France, and America* (Chicago: University of Chicago Press, 1992), 152–8; David Weissman, "Uncle Sam as a Showman," *Los Angeles Times*, April 18, 1937, I11.

17. John Cambridge, "Federal Theatre Draws the Fire of Some Defenders of Commercial Drama," *Sunday Worker*, May 29, 1938, 12.

18. Dana Rush, "Audience Survey Report: *It Can't Happen Here*, Blackstone Theatre, Chicago," NARA, E907, Box 254, *It Can't Happen Here*—Chicago.

19. "Pinocchio Dies in New York as Federal Theatre Drops Curtain," *Life,* July 17, 1939, 20; John O'Connor, "The Federal Theatre Project's Search for an Audience," in *Theatre for Working-Class Audiences in the United States, 1830–1980,* edited by Bruce A. McConachie and Daniel Friedman (Westport, CT: Greenwood Press, 1985), 171–172.

20. Hallie Flanagan, "Congress Takes the Stage," *New York Times*, August 20, 1939, sec. 9, 1.

21. Natalie Zemon Davis, *Society and Culture in Early Modern France* (Stanford, CA: Stanford University Press, 1965), xvi; L. P. Hartley, *The Go-Between* (London: H. Hamilton, 1953), 1.

22. Robert Darnton, *The Great Cat Massacre and Other Episodes in French Cultural History* (New York: Basic Books, 1999), 6.

23. Ibid., 6.

24. From *the Salem News*, quoted in Flanagan, *Arena*, 228.

25. Flanagan, *Arena*, 226–7.

26. Ibid., 88.

27. Hallie Flanagan, "The People's Theatre Grows Stronger," *Federal Theatre* I, no. 6 (May 1936): 6.

1 DANGER, DISEASE, AND DESPOTISM: BALANCING ON THE TIGHTROPE OF CHICAGO

1. Flanagan, *Arena*, 134.
2. Harry Minturn was the third and final director of the Chicago FTP. Quoted in Flanagan, *Arena*, 134.
3. Many of the newspapers, including the *Chicago American*, the *Chicago Herald-Examiner*, and the *Chicago Daily News* contained varying degrees of anti–New Deal sentiment, while the *Chicago Daily Tribune*, the *Chicago Times*, and the African American *Defender* supported Roosevelt's programs. The *Chicago American* and the *Chicago Herald-Examiner*, both owned by William Randolph Hearst, were "friendly but [...] governed by [anti–New Deal] policy." On May 6, 1938, the *Chicago Daily News*, a staunchly anti–New Deal paper, ran a front-page story titled "Plain Intolerable Intimidation," in which it referred to Roosevelt as "power-drunk" and compared his administration to the Nazi regime. In contrast, the *Defender*, one of the most widely circulated African American papers of the time, typically supported efforts of the FTP's Negro Units. The democratic *Chicago Daily Tribune* was pro–New Deal and often supported the efforts of the WPA and FTP. "Meeting in Chicago Minutes: Publicity and Promotional Activities, Great Northern Theatre, Blackstone Theatre and Negro Theatre," May 2, 1936, NARA, E839, Box 15, Midwestern Region; "Plain Intolerable Intimidation," *Chicago Daily News*, May 6, 1938, 1.
4. "Meeting in Chicago Minutes," May 2, 1936, NARA, E839, Box 15, Midwestern Region, 4.
5. George Kondolf, interview by Lorraine Brown, Rumson, New Jersey, tape recording, WPA Oral Histories Collection, Special Collections and Archives, George Mason University, February 21, 1976, 4.
6. "Farm Politics of Two Decades Told in Drama," *Chicago Daily Tribune*, July 10, 1938, 24.
7. John McGee was an integral member of the FTP national administration and a close friend of Hallie Flanagan. The story surrounding *The Swing Mikado* was fraught with turmoil and documented closely. The report cited here was labeled "Personal and Confidential" and only declassified by the National Archives in 1999. "Narrative Report of Events Leading to Dismissal of John McGee as Regional and State Director of the Federal Theatre Project," NARA, E839, Box 15, "Mikado"—Rpt. RE: Dismissal of John McGee & "Mikado"—Investigations.
8. Melvin G. Holli, *The American Mayor: The Best & the Worst Big-City Leaders* (University Park, PA: Pennsylvania State University Press, 1999), 12–13.
9. Quoted in Curt Johnson and R. Craig Sautter, "Wicked City Chicago: From Kenna to Capone," *December Magazine* (special issue) 37, no. 1 (1994): 223.
10. Ibid., 325, 330.
11. Roger Biles, *Big City Boss in Depression and War: Mayor Edward J. Kelly of Chicago* (DeKalb, IL: Northern University Press, 1984), 4–5.

12. Holli, *The American Mayor: The Best & the Worst Big-City Leaders*, 12–13; Curt Johnson and R. Craig Sautter, "Wicked City Chicago: From Kenna to Capone," 269; "Citizens Demand $14,000,000 Cut in State Taxes," *Chicago Daily Tribune*, December 12, 1926, 5; "'Cut Your Tax' Card Stirs Up State Inquiry," *Chicago Daily Tribune*, September 6, 1928, 1; Broadus Mitchell, *Depression Decade* (New York: Rinehart and Co., 1947), 105; Biles, *Big City Boss*, 21–23; George Schottenhamel, "How Big Bill Thompson Won Control of Chicago," *Journal of Illinois State Historical Society* 45, 1 (Spring 1952): 46.

13. Biles, *Big City Boss*, 31–32; Roger Biles, "Edward J. Kelly: New Deal Machine Builder," in *The Mayors: The Chicago Political Tradition*, rev. ed., ed. Paul M. Green and Melvin G. Holli (Carbondale: Southern Illinois University Press, 1995), 113–115, 120.

14. Quoted in Hallie Flanagan, "Visit with Mayor Kelly of Chicago...," undated, NARA, E839, Box 15, Midwestern Region, 1–3.

15. "Mayor Starts Decency Test of All Plays," *Chicago Daily Tribune*, October 23, 1935, 13.

16. *Model Tenement*, much like *One Third of a Nation*, dealt with the nation's housing problems by presenting both sides—tenant and landlord—sympathetically, ultimately supporting Roosevelt's federal housing projects. The content was particularly relevant to Chicago because of the number of people displaced from their homes by the Great Depression.

17. Meyer Levin, whose *Model Tenement* would fall prey to the Chicago censors, described Kondolf as a "troubleshooter" who "tried to please everyone." Meyer Levin, interview by Ellen Vanas, Herzlia, Israel, index of tape recording (no transcription available), WPA Oral Histories Collection, Special Collections and Archives, George Mason University, January 4, 1978, 3; "Meeting in Chicago Minutes," 4.

18. George Kondolf, to Hallie Flanagan, May 18, 1936, NARA, E839, Box 13, George Kondolf.

19. Meyer Levin was the president of the Free Speech Association of the Midwest and on the editorial board of *Esquire* magazine. *Esquire* offered to finance a lawsuit against the WPA if evidence that the WPA stopped *Model Tenement* came to light. Flanagan's investigations into the matter were inconclusive. Hallie Flanagan, "Visit with Mayor Kelly of Chicago...," undated, NARA, E839, Box 15, Midwestern Region, 1–3.

20. Ibid., 2–3.

21. "Halts Opening of WPA Show Over Morals," *Chicago Daily Tribune*, October 10, 1936, 1.

22. Quoted in Flanagan, *Arena*, 200.

23. "WPA Puts Off Play's Opening a Second Time," *Chicago Daily Tribune*, October 15, 1936, 10.

24. Sid Kuller, Ray Golden, and Phil Charig, *O Say Can You Sing*, NARA, E914, Box 309, 74–78. Hereafter, Kuller, Golden, and Charig, *O Say Can You Sing*, Original Version.

25. Because none of these scripts were dated, I based my determinations on a comparison between the scripts, the production bulletin, and the program. It is interesting to note that this production—geared so very much toward the city of Chicago—was translated into Spanish for production in Tampa. Even more curious, Hedley Gordon Graham, director of the Chicago version, also directed the well-received Tampa version in spite of his inability to speak Spanish. The FTP hired translators for rehearsals.

26. A *Chicago Daily Tribune* article put the price tag of *O Say Can You Sing* at only $55,042 as of January 1937 (including salaries). John McGee, "The Brutal Dope on Chicago," to Hallie Flanagan, November 10, 1936, NARA, E839, Box 14, John McGee, 2; "Spend Million on WPA Theater Units," January 3, 1937, *Chicago Daily Tribune*, NARA, E981, Box 25, Chicago; *O Say Can You Sing* Production Bulletin, LOC, Box 1048, 1; Flanagan, *Arena*, 140.

27. Kondolf Interview, 3.

28. *O Say Can You Sing* Production Bulletin, Box 1048; "Federal Flier," *Time*, December 21, 1936, http://www.time.com/time/magazine/article/0,9171,757227,00.html.

29. Flanagan, *Arena*, 138.

30. Kuller, Golden, and Charig, "*O Say Can You Sing*," Original Version, 1–7.

31. Within the context of the census, white ethnics consist of foreign-born and second-generation immigrants, typically from Czechoslovakia, Germany, Hungary, Italy, Lithuania, Poland, Russia, Sweden, Yugoslavia, the Netherlands, or Norway. For a breakdown of the percentages of each ethnic group listed, see Appendix 1; John M. Allswang, *A House for All Peoples: Ethnic Politics in Chicago, 1890–1936* (Lexington: University Press of Kentucky, 1971), 19; U.S. Bureau of the Census, *Fifteenth Census of the United States: 1930, Volume 1, Population, Number and Distribution of Inhabitants* (Washington, DC: Government Printing Office, 1931), 23.

32. Dominic A. Pacyga, "Chicago's Ethnic Neighborhoods: The Myth of Stability and the Reality of Chicago," in *Ethnic Chicago: A Multicultural Portrait*, 4th ed., ed. Melvin G. Holli and Peter d'A Jones (Grand Rapids, MI: William B. Eerdmans Publishing Co., 1995), 613–614; Allswang, *A House for All Peoples*, 42–46.

33. Richard C. Lindberg, *To Serve and Collect: Chicago Politics and Police Corruption from the Lager Beer Riot to the Summerdale Scandal* (New York: Praeger Publishers, 1991), 260.

34. Kuller, Golden, and Charig, *O Say Can You Sing*, LOC, Box 725, 2. Hereafter, Kuller, Golden, and Charig, *O Say Can You Sing*, Produced Version.

35. Kuller, Golden, and Charig, *O Say Can You Sing*, Produced Version, Optional Scenes, 3.

36. Quoted in Biles, *Big City Boss*, 31.

37. Kuller, Golden, and Charig, *O Say Can You Sing*, Produced Version, 17.

38. All ellipses are quoted directly from the script. Ibid., 21.

39. Ibid., 18.

40. Ibid., 83.

41. Ibid., 38–9.

42. John M. Allswang, *The New Deal and American Politics: A Study in Political Change* (New York: John Wiley & Sons, 1978), 86.

43. Kuller, Golden, and Charig, *O Say Can You Sing*, Original Version, 27–31.

44. Widely seen by many immigrants as "a way of establishing the hegemony of traditional American values, and traditional Americans, over new values and new people," nearly 90 percent of Chicago's immigrant populations voted against Prohibition. In four opinion referenda regarding Prohibition occurring between 1919 and 1930, 73–83 percent of Chicagoans voted against Prohibition, with immigrant populations voting against the measure in even greater numbers. Allswang, *The New Deal and American Politics*, 4.

45. Kuller, Golden, and Charig, *O Say Can You Sing*, Produced Version, Optional Scenes, 14–18.

46. Kuller, Golden, and Charig, *O Say Can You Sing*, Produced Version, 76.

47. As a playreader, Sundgaard read and reported on two plays each day. However, Glaspell had plans for Sundgaard; in order to allow him more time for playwriting, she began giving him "bad plays" to read so as to "keep [his] burdens as light as possible." Sundgaard was a self-professed "expert on bad plays," noting that he could complete his daily quota in the morning and have the rest of the day to write, research, or explore Chicago theatre. Arnold Sundgaard, interview by John O'Connor, Boston, Massachusetts, tape recording, WPA Oral Histories Collection, Special Collections and Archives, George Mason University, September 5, 1976, 4–5.

48. It is interesting to note that *Spirochete* (the play itself, rather than the topic) became the subject of a pitched battle between the national administration and the rights of writers on the FTP. In the case of *Spirochete* (written almost entirely on Sundgaard's own time), Glaspell was a strong advocate for Sundgaard's rights; she wrote several letters of support, elicited the assistance of the Dramatists Guild, and threatened to leave her position as head of the Midwestern Play Bureau. She and Sundgaard ultimately prevailed, but the process irreparably tarnished her relationship with the FTP, and she left the project not long after the resolution. Ironically, the victory ultimately cost Sundgaard his job with the FTP; the royalties that he earned for the numerous FTP productions of *Spirochete* made his income (briefly) high enough that he was no longer eligible for relief.

49. Gold, "*Spirochete*," *Variety*, May 4, 1938, 56.

50. Arnold Sundgaard, *Spirochete*, in *Federal Theatre Plays*, ed. Pierre de Rohan (New York: Random House, 1938), 8–14. Unless otherwise noted, further references to *Spirochete* will use this text.

51. R. A. Vonderlehr, "Are We Checking the Great Plague?" *Survey Graphic* (April 1, 1940); Thomas Parran, "Public Health Control of Syphilis," *Annals of Internal Medicine* 10 (July 1936): 65; Allan M. Brandt, *No Magic Bullet: A*

Social History of Venereal Disease in the United States since 1880 (New York: Oxford University Press, 1987), 129.

52. Articles focusing on the dangers and treatments of syphilis appeared in medical journals and popular magazines nationwide, including the *Illinois Medical Journal, Ladies Home Journal, Survey Graphic,* and *Reader's Digest.* Parran's book, *Shadow on the Land,* joined half a dozen others including Morris Fishbein's *Syphilis: The Next Great Plague To Go,* S. William Becker's *Ten Million Americans Have It,* S. Funkhouser's *The Great American Taboo,* and Winfield Scott Pugh's *Lingering Death.* "Great Pox," *Time,* October 26, 1936 accessed January 10, 2010, http://www.time.com/time/magazine/article/0,9171,788606-2,00.html; Brandt, *No Magic Bullet,* 131.

53. Virginia Gardner, "Jam Marriage Bureau to Beat Test Deadline," *Chicago Daily Tribune,* July 1, 1937, 1; "Cupid's Busiest Day," *Chicago Daily Tribune,* June 30, 1937, 11; "Crown Point Weddings Held Valid in Illinois: Health Law Evasions are Legal, Says Kerner," *Chicago Daily Tribune,* September 29, 1937, 3; "A Compulsory Test for Syphilis Before Marriage?" *Reader's Digest* 31, No. 187 (November 1937), 129–130.

54. "Fight On Syphilis Put Up To Doctors," *New York Times,* July 26, 1937, 21.

55. The free blood tests proved so popular that the state changed from the Wassermann to the Kahn method because it could be completed more quickly. Developed in 1906, the Wassermann Test had an incubation period of two days with a 95 percent successful diagnosis rate. The cheaper Kahn Test, evolved from the Wassermann Test, showed results in two hours but with less reliable accuracy. Most authorities used the Wasserman test as a confirmation for samples that received a positive from the Kahn Test. "New Tests Supplant Wassermann in City," *New York Times,* January 4, 1947, 30; "Chicago Speeds Blood Tests," *New York Times,* August 2, 1937, 21; "Adopt Kahn Test For Use in City's War on Syphilis," *Chicago Daily Tribune,* September 3, 1937, 13; "Polls Chicagoans on Syphilis Tests," *New York Times,* July 25, 1937, 10.

56. "*Tribune* Staf [*sic*] Asked to Take Syphilis Tests," *Chicago Daily Tribune,* March 15, 1938, 5.

57. "War on Syphilis in 2,800 Illinois Factories Urged," *Chicago Daily Tribune,* June 26, 1938, 6; "Safeguard Jobs in Syphilis War, Physicians Urge," *Chicago Daily Tribune,* June 9, 1938, 14; "Concerns Hiring 15,000 Support Syphilis Tests," *Chicago Daily Tribune,* March 17, 1938, 5.

58. Harry Minturn to Hallie Flanagan, March 1, 1938, NARA, E839, Box 26, "*Spirochete.*"

59. Hallie Flanagan to Harry Minturn, February 24, 1938, NARA, E839, Box 13, Living Newspaper—Syphilis (Chicago), 2; Douglas McDermott, "The Living Newspaper as a Dramatic Form," PhD dissertation, University of Iowa, 1963, 20–1.

60. Arnold Sundgaard, letter to anonymous recipient [probably Hallie Flanagan], 1938, NARA, E839, Box 13, *Spirochete.*

61. Arnold Sundgaard, "Susan Glaspell and the Federal Theatre Project Revisited," *Journal of American Drama and Theatre* 9 (Winter 1997): 9.

62. Mercury—in the form of an ointment, pill, or steam—was one of the primary treatments for syphilis for centuries, though its effectiveness remains unclear. Administered weekly for a year or longer, the correct combination of arsenic and chloride could cure 60–80 percent of those who had been infected for a lengthy period, and 80–90 percent of recent syphilitics. Penicillin would replace these methods in the 1940s. Sundgaard, "Susan Glaspell and the Federal Theatre Project Revisited," 9.

63. Florence S. Kerr to Hallie Flanagan, March 12, 1938, NARA, E839, Box 13, "Living Newspaper—Syphilis (Chicago)."

64. Charles Collins, "Syphilis Story Well Told in a Good Drama," *Chicago Daily Tribune*, April 30, 1938, 15.

65. "*Spirochete*," *Time*, May 9, 1938, http://www.time.com/time/magazine/article/0,9171,759611,00.html

66. Emmet G. Lavery to Hallie Flanagan, 1938, NARA, E839, Box 13, "*Spirochete*."

67. Hallie Flanagan, "Introduction," in *Federal Theatre Plays*, ed. Pierre De Rohan (New York: Random House, 1938), xii.

68. John O'Connor, "*Spirochete* and the War on Syphilis," *The Drama Review* 21, no. 1 (March 1977), 92–93; Flanagan, *Arena*, 172, 250–1, 301, 309.

69. Sundgaard, "Susan Glaspell and the Federal Theatre Project Revisited," 9.

70. Sundgaard, *Spirochete*, 14.

71. When *Spirochete* premiered in Philadelphia, the Knights of Columbus strenuously objected to the idea that Columbus was responsible for the spread of syphilis throughout Europe and the new world. Sundgaard refused to change the scene. Finally, someone suggested that the play simply refer to an "unnamed sea captain" who sailed to the Americas in 1492. Surprisingly, the Knights of Columbus and Sundgaard both agreed. The name of Columbus was removed and the "unnamed sea captain" that took his place became an inside joke that nearly everyone in the audience understood. Flanagan, *Arena*, 251.

72. Sundgaard, *Spirochete*, 26.

73. Ibid., 22–5.

74. Ibid., 62.

75. Ibid., 73–4.

76. Ibid., 83.

77. Ibid., 102.

78. Ibid., 85.

79. Ibid., 84–87.

80. Ibid., 88–90.

81. Ibid., 90.

2 DEMYTHOLOGIZING AMERICA: PAST AND PRESENT COLLIDE IN BOSTON

1. In spite of the impression this quote gives, Boston had a number of theatres regularly producing work prior to the arrival of the FTP. Philip Hale, "The Theatre," *Boston Herald,* November 23, 1930, Harvard Theatre Collection, Boston—Copley Theatre, clippings file.
2. Joanne Bentley, *Hallie Flanagan,* 229.
3. Flanagan, *Arena,* 229–30.
4. Quoted in Flanagan, *Arena,* 225.
5. Bentley, *Hallie Flanagan,* 216–7.
6. Flanagan, *Arena,* 223–4.
7. Quoted in Paul S. Boyer, *Purity in Print: The Vice-Society Movement and Book Censorship in America* (New York: Charles Scribner's Sons, 1968), 180.
8. Ibid., 198–201; John H. Houchin, *Censorship of the American Theatre in the Twentieth Century* (Cambridge: Cambridge University Press, 2003), 111–2.
9. Flanagan, *Arena,* 224.
10. Blanding Sloan to Hallie Flanagan, TD, June 9, 1938, NARA, E839, Box 5, "*Created Equal #2.*"
11. *Proceedings of the City Council of Boston,* April 13, 1931, 162; Susan Traverso, *Welfare Politics in Boston, 1910–1940* (Amherst: University of Massachusetts Press, 2003), 94–5.
12. Charles H. Trout, *Boston, The Great Depression, and the New Deal* (New York: Oxford University Press, 1977), 87.
13. Quoted in Flanagan, *Arena,* 227.
14. "Union Pickets W.P.A. Office," *Boston Sunday Globe,* January 10, 1937, 14.
15. "Remodeled Copley Nearing Completion," *Boston Globe,* September 26, 1937, Harvard Theatre Collection, "Boston   Copley Theatre (1)," clippings file.
16. Philip Hale, "As the World Wags," undated, Harvard Theatre Collection, "Boston—Copley Theatre (1)," clippings file.
17. Flanagan, *Arena,* 228.
18. From the *Salem News,* quoted in Flanagan, *Arena,* 228.
19. Flanagan, *Arena,* 228.
20. Robert V. Johnston, "Report by Publicity Man on Promotion Work For Production 'Created Equal,'" NARA, E839, Box 5, "*Created Equal #2.*"
21. "Radio Talk," Jon B. Mack, Boston, NARA, E839, Box 5, "*Created Equal #1.*"
22. John Hunter Booth to Jon B. Mack, TL, 21 January 1938, NARA, E839, Box 5, "*Created Equal #1.*"
23. Flanagan, *Arena,* 254–5.
24. The third version of *Created Equal,* available at NARA, is a marked copy of the abbreviated radio version. This production was the third in the "Federal

Theatre of the Air" Series, and was broadcast on Station WEVD, New York, December 22, 1938, from 10:00–10:45 p.m. EST.

25. John Hunter Booth, *Created Equal* (Revised Edition), GMU, introductory material. Hereafter, Booth, *Created Equal*, Revised Edition.

26. "Radio Talk," Jon B. Mack, Boston, NARA, E839, Box 5, "*Created Equal* #1."

27. John Hunter Booth, *Created Equal*, NARA, E914, Box 277, "Created Equal," 2. Hereafter, Booth *Created Equal*, Original Edition; Booth, *Created Equal*, Revised Edition, 1–2.

28. Booth, *Created Equal*, Revised Edition, 1.

29. Ibid., 3.

30. Jack Tager, *Boston Riots: Three Centuries of Social Violence* (Boston, MA: Northeastern University Press, 2001), 170.

31. John. H. Booth, "Created Equal Production Bulletin, Boston, Mass.," NARA, E937, Box 441, "Created Equal," 4.

32. It is interesting to note the complex historical implications of choosing Phillip Schuyler as representative of the American ideal because a historical figure by the same name lived during the colonial era. The real Phillip Schuyler was an English gentleman and soldier who came to the colonies, was elected to the First Continental Congress, served as a Major General in the Continental Army, and remained active in politics until his death in 1804. His daughter Elizabeth married Alexander Hamilton in 1780 thereby offering Hamilton access to powerful political circles. The irony of the character of Phillip Schuyler—young gentleman-turned-frontiersman—turning to Hamilton (his historical son-in-law) for assistance is powerful. Though it is hard to believe that Booth could have so thoroughly researched colonial history for the play and missed this connection, no evidence remains to document his intent. For more information on Hamilton's relationship with the real Phillip Schuyler, see John C. Miller, *Alexander Hamilton: Portrait in Paradox* (New York: Harper & Brothers, 1959), 62–80.

33. Booth, *Created Equal*, Revised Edition, 57–8.

34. *Created Equal* includes a number of specific grammatical choices, all of which have been retained throughout this chapter in quotes from the text. John Hunter Booth, scene attached to letter, Blanding Sloan to Emmett Lavery, TL, 26 May 1938, NARA, E839, Box 5, "*Created Equal* #2."

35. Ibid.

36. Constance K. Burns and Ronald P. Formisano, eds., *Boston, 1700–1980: The Evolution of Urban Politics* (Westport, CT: Greenwood Press, 1984), 135.

37. Quoted in Trout, *Boston, The Great Depression, and the New Deal*, 81–4.

38. Booth, *Created Equal*, Original Edition, 15–6.

39. Booth, *Created Equal*, Revised Edition, 13.

40. Booth, *Created Equal*, Original Edition, 41.

41. Ibid., 58–9

42. Booth, *Created Equal*, Revised Edition, 82.

43. Booth, *Created Equal*, Original Edition, 87.

44. Booth, *Created Equal,* Revised Edition, 89.
45. Booth, *Created Equal,* Original Edition, 76–7.
46. Ibid., 131–2.
47. Ibid., 133.
48. Booth, *Created Equal,* Revised Edition, 121.
49. Ibid., 123–4.
50. Ibid., 124.
51. Ibid., 124–127.
52. Mordaunt Hall, "Federal Theatre Presents Cavalcade of U.S. History," *Boston Transcript,* June 14, 1938; and Elinor Hughes, "'Created Equal' is presented at the Shubert-Copley Theatre," *Boston Herald,* June 14, 1938, NARA, E937, Box 441, "*Created Equal* Production Bulletin, Boston."
53. "Summer Plans Set for WPA Theatre," *New York Times,* June 11, 1939, 47.
54. *Lucy Stone* Production Bulletin, LOC, Box 1034, 2.
55. Gen. 3:16 (English Revised Version).
56. Converse Tyler, "Lucy Stone Playreader Report," LOC, Box 247.
57. Mrs. Guy W. Stantial (Emma?) to Hallie Flanagan, April 30, 1939, NARA, E840, Box 40, "Lucy Stone."
58. Emmet Lavery to Jon B. Mack, March 7, 1939, LOC, Box 1034, "Lucy Stone—Correspondence & Research," 1.
59. Barbara Stuhler, *For the Public Record: A Documentary History of the League of Women Voters* (Westport, CT: Greenwood Press, 2000), 2–28.
60. Alice Stone Blackwell, "Introduction," in Maud Wood Park, *Lucy Stone: A Chronicle Play,* National American Suffrage Association Collection, Rare Book and Special Collections Division, Library of Congress, 3.
61. Flanagan, *Arena,* 230.
62. Finch expressed grave concerns over his lack of credit in letters to Russak. Finch argued that he had spent an extraordinary amount of time on the revisions—much of which was unpaid—expressly because he believed his name would be publicly associated with the play. Robert Finch to Ben Russak, April 29, 1939, LOC, Box 1034, "Lucy Stone—Correspondence & Research."
63. Robert Finch to Ben Russak, April 29, 1939, LOC, Box 1034, "Lucy Stone—Correspondence & Research"; Robert Finch to Ben Russak, received March 13, 1939, LOC, Box 1034, "Lucy Stone—Correspondence & Research."
64. Many different versions of *Lucy Stone* are available at NARA, LOC, and GMU. In my analysis of the FTP production text, I am using the script described as the "2nd Revised Boston Version," dated June 16, 1939, which is the latest version available. Maud Wood Park, *Lucy Stone,* revised by Robert Finch, LOC, Box 701, 6. Hereafter, Park, *Lucy Stone,* revised by Finch.
65. Maud Wood Park, *Lucy Stone: A Chronicle Play* based on *Lucy Stone, Pioneer,* by Alice Stone Blackwell (Boston: Walter H. Baker Co., 1938), National American Suffrage Association Collection, Rare Book and Special Collections Division, Library of Congress, 75. Hereafter, Park, *Lucy Stone,* Original Edition.

66. Ibid., 79.

67. Park, *Lucy Stone,* revised by Finch, 52–57.

68. Ibid., 71–2.

69. Ibid., 76.

70. Park, *Lucy Stone,* Original Edition, 86–7.

71. Ibid., 93.

72. Ibid., 96.

73. Park, *Lucy Stone,* revised by Finch, 69.

74. Ibid., 84.

75. "Woman Candidate to Open Her Campaign," *Boston Herald,* December 5, 1921, 16.

76. "Most of Council Candidates Unknown," *Boston Herald,* December 5, 1921, 3; "Mrs. Chipman opens her campaign," *Boston Globe,* December 7, 1921, 8; "Boston Women Making Their Political Bow—Is It a Debut or a Fight?" *Boston Globe,* December 4, 1921, 2.

77. Quoted in Sarah Deutsch, *Women, Space, and Power in Boston, 1870–1940* (New York: Oxford University Press, 2000), 255.

78. "Is Fifth Woman to Seek Council Post," *Boston Globe,* October 26, 1931, 5.

79. Deutsch, *Women, Space, and Power in Boston,* 259.

80. *Lucy Stone* Production Bulletin, LOC, Box 1034, 3–4.

81. Elinor Hughes, "Lucy Stone," *Boston Herald,* May 10, 1939, Harvard Theatre Collection, "Lucy Stone," clippings file.

82. Elliot Norton, "Play on the Record of Lucy Stone," *Boston Post,* May 10, 1939, LOC, *Lucy Stone* Production Bulletin, Box 1034, 13.

83. Edwin F. Melvin, "'Lucy Stone' in Premiere at Copley Theater," *Christian Science Monitor,* May 10, 1939, Harvard Theatre Collection, "Lucy Stone," clippings file.

84. Flanagan, *Arena,* 230; "B.U. Women to Sponsor 'Lucy Stone' Premiere," *Christian Science Monitor,* April 25, 1939, 9.

85. "Lucy Stone Benefit Performance Friday," Harvard Theatre Collection, "Boston—Copley Theatre (1)," clippings file.

3　"THE GREAT AMERICAN THEATRICAL DESERT": FEDERAL THEATRE IN THE SOUTH

1. Foreword to *A Brief History of the Federal Theatre in the South,* New York Public Library for the Performing Arts, Billy Rose Theatre Collection, Hallie Flanagan Papers, Series V—Scrapbooks, "Federal Theatre in the South Scrapbook," Box 35.

2. Josef Lentz, interview by John O'Connor, New Orleans, LA, WPA Oral Histories Collection, Special Collections & Archives, George Mason University Libraries, April 7, 1977, 21.

3. McGee, *A Brief History of the Federal Theatre in the South.*

4. Ibid.
5. Flanagan, *Arena*, 81.
6. Ibid., 81.
7. McGee, Foreword to *A Brief History of the Federal Theatre in the South*.
8. Flanagan, *Arena*, 88.
9. Though the recent discovery of additional archival documents has altered part of my *Altars of Steel* analysis, much of this section is from "Yankee Consternation in the Deep South: Worshipping at the *Altars of Steel*," by Elizabeth Osborne, published in *Theatre Symposium: Tours of the South*, © 2005 by the University of Alabama Press.
10. Glenn Feldman, *Politics, Society and the Klan in Alabama, 1915–1949* (Tuscaloosa: University of Alabama Press, 1999), 219.
11. Ibid., 219–20; Robin D. G. Kelley, *Hammer and Hoe: Alabama Communists During the Great Depression* (Chapel Hill: University of North Carolina Press, 1990), 14.
12. Neal R. Pierce, *The Deep South States of America: People, Politics, and Power in the Seven Deep South States* (New York: Norton, 1974), 282.
13. David M. Kennedy, *Freedom from Fear: The American People in Depression and War, 1929–1945* (New York: Oxford University Press, 1999), 303.
14. William Warren Rogers, Robert David Ward, Leah Rawls Atkins, and Wayne Flint, *Alabama: The History of a Deep South State* (Tuscaloosa: University of Alabama Press, 1994), 480–5.
15. Walter Galenson, *The CIO Challenge to the AFL: A History of the American Labor Movement, 1935–1941* (Cambridge, MA: Harvard University Press, 1960), 92; Kenneth Warren, *Big Steel: The First Century of the United States Steel Corporation, 1901–2001* (Pittsburgh: University of Pittsburgh Press, 2001), 164–6.
16. Feldman, *Politics, Society, and the Klan in Alabama*, 243.
17. Ibid., 274.
18. "Negroes Beware" Poster, 1933, Birmingham Alabama, Guy Benton Johnson Papers #3826, Southern Historical Collection, The Wilson Library, University of North Carolina at Chapel Hill, Research Projects 1922–1977 and undated, Ku Klux Klan Study, Folder 1005.
19. Feldman, *Politics, Society and the Klan in Alabama*, 243–246.
20. Henry P. Guzda, "United Steelworkers of America: 26th Convention," *Monthly Labor Review* 115, no. 12 (1992), 46–7; Maeva Marcus, *Truman and the Steel Seizure Case: The Limits of Presidential Power* (Durham, NC: Duke University Press, 1994), 51; Warren, *Big Steel: The First Century of the United States Steel Corporation*, 164–6; Kelley, *Hammer and Hoe*, 223–227; Feldman, *Politics, Society and the Klan in Alabama*, 243–246.
21. Thomas Hall-Rogers, *Altars of Steel*, LOC, Box 578, "Altars of Steel," 1.
22. Ralph T. Jones, "*Altars of Steel* Highly Praised as Best Drama Ever Presented Here," *Atlanta Constitution*, April 2, 1937, 11; Tarleton Collier, "Behind the Headlines," *Atlanta Georgian*, April 6, 1937, 3; Mildred Seydell, "*Altars*

of Steel Aids Communism with Tax Money," *Atlanta Georgian*, April 4, 1937, 4D; Flanagan, *Arena*, 89. For a detailed discussion of the newspaper coverage of *Altars of Steel* in Atlanta, see Susan Duffy, *American Labor on Stage: Dramatic Interpretations of the Steel and Textile Industries in the 1930s* (Westport, CT: Greenwood Press, 1996), 96–101; John Russell Poole, *The Federal Theatre Project in Georgia and Alabama: An Historical Analysis of Government Theatre in the Deep South* (PhD Diss., University of Georgia, Athens, 1995), 80–88; McGee, *A Brief History of the Federal Theatre in the South*, 12.

23. Jane de Hart Mathews, *The Federal Theatre, 1935–1939: Plays, Relief, and Politics* (Princeton, NJ: Princeton University Press, 1967), 181.

24. "Problem Play Author's Name is Kept Secret," *Philadelphia Inquirer*, April 18, 1937, in McGee, *A Brief History of the Federal Theatre in the South*, 17.

25. Quoted in John McGee, *Federal Theatre of the South: A Supplement to the Federal Theatre National Bulletin*, Quarterly Bulletin 1, no. 2 (October 1936), NARA, E920, Box 357.

26. McGee, *Federal Theatre of the South*; Duffy, *American Labor on Stage*, 83–85.

27. U.S. Census Bureau, *15th Census of the United States: 1930 Population Schedule*, Precinct 9, Jefferson County, Alabama, sheet 9B, accessed March 16, 2010, http://search.ancestry.com/iexec?htx=View&r=an&dbid=6224& iid=ALT626_23-0562&fn=Josiah+W&ln=Bancroft&st=r&ssrc=&pid=119 663711; John McGee to J. W. Bancroft, September 24, 1936, NARA, E850, Box 62, "Correspondence #2;" John McGee to J. W. Bancroft, September 9, 1936, NARA, E850, Box 62, "AL—Correspondence # 1."

28. For further discussion of TCI's role in creating Fairfield, see Marlene Hunt Rikard, "An Experiment in Welfare Capitalism: The Health Care Services of the Tennessee Coal, Iron and Railroad Company" (PhD diss., University of Alabama, 1983), 132-6

29. Judith Stein, *Running Steel, Running America: Race, Economic Policy and the Decline of Liberalism* (Chapel Hill: University of North Carolina Press, 1998), 41.

30. John McGee to Mary Weber, January 14, 1936, NARA, E850, Box 62, "AL—Correspondence #1."

31. The only other correspondence addressed directly to Bancroft that I have located is a telegram to Bancroft, which noted an "excellent," unnamed script. John McGee to J. W. Bancroft, September 24, 1936, NARA, E850, Box 62, "Correspondence #2;" John McGee to J. W. Bancroft, September 9, 1936, NARA, E850, Box 62, "AL—Correspondence # 1."

32. John McGee to Frances Nimmo Green, November 11, 1936, NARA, E850, Box 62, "AL—Southern Play Bureau."

33. John McGee to Frances Nimmo Green, November 3, 1936, NARA, E850, Box 62, "AL—Southern Play Bureau."

34. Louis Solomon, a playreader for the FTP's Play Policy Board in New York, commented that *Altars of Steel* showed an "improbable simplification of a complex problem [and was] too naïve to merit consideration." John Rimassa, another playreader, also rejected the play, writing that it was "very bad! [...] The conclusion rammed at the audience is: benevolent corporations with assets up to $25,000,000 make for a happy humanity while very large corporations spell disaster for mankind." Playwright John Wexley's report was most damning though, "My most serious criticism of the play is [...] that it is hardly a play;" he then proceeded to rip apart the structure, theme, characters, and plot, and suggested that FTP audiences would find the play "very uninteresting" and "ludicrously unreal." Letter, John Wexley to Hiram Motherwell, 27 March 1937, LOC, Box 138, *Altars of Steel*; Louis Solomon, "Playreader Report: *Altars of Steel*," LOC, Box 138, *Altars of Steel*; John Rimassa, "Playreader Report: *Altars of Steel*," LOC, Box 138, *Altars of Steel*.

35. Lentz noted that the Atlanta FTP shared its theatre space with a boxing ring every Friday night; this required that design elements be carefully chosen so they could be packed and moved each week. Lentz, interview, 4–5, 13.

36. Verner Haldene, "Production Bulletin for three-month period beginning January 1, 1937," December 29, 1936, NARA, E850, Box 62, "Southern Play Bureau."

37. Just as *Altars of Steel* slipped through the numerous rejections of the various playreaders, Hallie Flanagan was in the process of instituting a new policy for play approval. During the fall of 1936, buoyed by Harry Hopkins's promise to support any FTP play that had her personal approval, Flanagan insisted that all production plans be made at least three months in advance and pass through the Play Policy Board. While this procedure was still in the process of being implemented when *Altars of Steel* began rehearsals, it is clear that the intended January production was subject to this system, as is evidenced by Verner Haldene's proposal for the first quarter of 1937, in which he places the opening of *Altars of Steel* in late January. Mathews, *The Federal Theatre*, 96–7; Poole, *The Federal Theatre Project in Georgia and Alabama*, 56–59; Haldene, "Production Bulletin for three-month period beginning January 1, 1937."

38. Memorandum, John McGee to Hallie Flanagan, March 16, 1937, NARA, E839, Box 25, Southern Trip, 2–3.

39. Poole, *The Federal Theatre Project in Georgia and Alabama*, 51.

40. The Birmingham audience submitted only 22 surveys, which serve as the basis for this report. Dana Rush, "Audience Survey Report for *It Can't Happen Here*," November 23, 1936, NARA, E907, National Play Bureau Audience Survey Reports, Box 254.

41. "Federal Unit Drops Curtain," *Birmingham Post*, November 25, 1936, Birmingham Public Library, Birmingham Federal Theatre, clippings file.

42. Verner Haldene, "Production Bulletin for three-month period beginning January 1, 1937."

43. John McGee to Frances Nimmo Green, November 11, 1936, NARA, E850, Box 62, "AL—Southern Play Bureau."

44. John McGee to Harriett B. Adams, November 5, 1936, NARA, E850, Box 62, "AL—Correspondence #2."

45. John McGee to Josef Lentz, December 15, 1936, NARA, E850, Box 62, "AL—Correspondence #2."

46. Hedley Gordon Graham, interview by Lorraine Brown, New York City, New York, tape recording, WPA Oral Histories Collection, Special Collections and Archives, George Mason University Libraries, February 27, 1977, 1.

47. Hall-Rogers, *Altars of Steel*, 88.

48. Rogers et. al., *Alabama: The History of a Deep South State*, 470; Marjorie Longenecker White, *The Birmingham District: An Industrial History and Guide* (Birmingham, AL: Birmingham Historical Society at the Birmingham Publishing Company, 1981), 65; "Oysters, Junk, Perfume, Steel," *Time*, June 3, 1935, accessed February 9, 2008, http://www.time.com/time/magazine/article/0,9171,883430-1,00.html; Henry M. McKiven, Jr., *Iron and Steel: Class, Race, and Community in Birmingham, Alabama, 1875–1920* (Chapel Hill: University of North Carolina Press, 1995); Sanford M. Jacoby, *Employing Bureaucracy: Managers, Unions, and the Transformation of Work in the 20th Century* (Mahwah, NJ: Lawrence Erlbaum Associates, 2004), 169.

49. See White, *The Birmingham District*, 91–97; Rogers, et al., *Alabama: The History of a Deep South State*, 284–286; Warren, *Big Steel: The First Century of the United States Steel Corporation*, 77–83; Ethel Armes, *The Story of Coal and Iron in Alabama* (Birmingham, AL: Chamber of Commerce, 1910); Joseph Bishop Bucklin, *Theodore Roosevelt and His Time Shown in His Own Letters*, Vol. 2 (New York: Charles Scribner's Sons, 1920), 54–63.

50. T. R. Roosevelt to Attorney General Bonaparte, November 4, 1907, quoted in *Bulletin of the American Iron and Steel Institute* 43, no. 2 (February 1, 1909): 1.

51. Hall-Rogers, *Altars of Steel*, 28–31.

52. Rikard, "An Experiment in Welfare Capitalism: The Health Care Services of the Tennessee Coal, Iron and Railroad Company," 274–5.

53. Hall-Rogers, *Altars of Steel*, 8.

54. Ibid., 15.

55. Dennis G. Jerz, *Technology in American Drama, 1920–1950: Soul and Society in the Age of the Machine* (Westport, CT: Greenwood Press, 2003), 88.

56. By 1917, officials at TCI concluded that they could increase productivity (and decrease labor unrest) from the workers if they provided better work conditions. John Eagan, chairman of the American Cast Iron Pipe Company, revealed his "Golden Rule" approach to big business in 1921. McKiven, Jr., *Iron and Steel*, 115–7.

57. Hall-Rogers, *Altars of Steel*, 15.

58. Kelley, *Hammer and Hoe*, 130–1.

59. Several different versions of the play exist, each of which is structured slightly differently and features a different ending. In the version on file at NARA, Worth's son is killed at the end of the play as his father tries to diffuse the angry mob of workers. The version discussed in this chapter was produced for Atlanta and Miami audiences.

60. Much of this portion is from "Storytelling, Chiggers, and the Bible Belt: The Georgia Experiment as the Public Face of the Federal Theatre Project," by Elizabeth Osborne, published in *Theatre History Studies*, © 2011 by the University of Alabama Press.

61. Quoted in Flanagan, *Arena,* 92.

62. Ibid., 92.

63. Ibid., 91.

64. Herbert S. Price, "Federal Theatre Community Drama Program in Georgia," NARA, E952, Box 523, "Price File—Rome."

65. Four of the five drama consultants were a part of the community drama training program in New York City at the time of their assignment, earning $95.44 monthly. Mary Dirnberger, the representative assigned to Savannah, was working in North Carolina at the time of this assignment, and continued on that salary at $125 monthly while working in Georgia. Herbert Price to Ellen S. Woodward, undated memorandum, NARA, E952, Box 523, "Price File—Community Drama, General."

66. Herbert S. Price, "Federal Theatre Community Drama Program in Georgia (Rome to be included)," NARA, E952, Box 523, "Herbert S. Price, Correspondence."

67. Gay B. Shepperson to Herbert Price, January 26, 1937, NARA, E952, Box 523, "Price File—Community Drama, General."

68. *Georgia: A Guide to its Towns and Countryside,* compiled and written by Workers of the Writers' Program of the Work Progress Administration in the State of Georgia, American Guide Series (Athens: University of Georgia Press, 1940), 443.

69. Each of the five drama consultants was to have been preapproved for travel expenses and a per diem of three dollars per day for the first 21 days in the field. However, subsequent communications between the drama consultants and various FTP administrators document that this process was not a smooth one and that most of the drama consultants were forced to place their belongings in storage, live in cheap hotels or with new acquaintances, and self-fund their work-related travels for the majority of their time in Georgia. Herbert Price to Madalyn O'Shea, December 1, 1936, NARA, E952, Box 523, "Price File—Community Drama, General."

70. Edward J. Hayes to Charlotte Holt, received March 23, 1937, NARA, E952, Box 523, "Price File—Rome, Georgia."

71. R. H. Elliott to Herbert Price, March 1, 1937, NARA, E952, Box 523, "Price File—Rome, GA."

72. "Federal Theatre Director Arrives Here February 22," *Rome News-Tribune*, February 14, 1937, 12.

73. "Details of Federal Theatre To Be Given," *Rome-News Tribune*, February 17, 1937, 2; "Federal Theatre Director Comes To Begin Duties," *Rome News-Tribune*, February 24, 1937, 2; "Federal Theatre Begins In Rome With 'The Fool,'" *Rome News-Tribune*, February 26, 1937, 10; "Cast Announced for 'The Fool,' Federal Drama," *Rome News-Tribune, March 21, 1937, 11.

74. Edward J. Hayes to Charlotte Holt, Received March 23, 1937, NARA, E952, Box 523, "Price File—Rome, GA."

75. "Religious Plays To Be Presented By Drama Players," *Rome News-Tribune*, April 20, 1937, 2.

76. These verses focus on the meeting of Mary, future mother of Jesus Christ, and Elisabeth, future mother of John the Baptist, during Elisabeth's pregnancy.

77. "Rome Drama Unit to Present Play Sunday Afternoon," *Rome News-Tribune,* March 26, 1937, 2.

78. Edward J. Hayes to Charlotte Holt, received March 23, 1937, NARA, E952, Box 523, "Price File—Rome, GA."

79. "Cast Announced For 'The Fool,' Federal Drama," *Rome News-Tribune*, March 21, 1937, 11.

80. Edward J. Hayes to Herbert S. Price, April 6, 1937, NARA, E952, Box 523, "Price File—Rome, GA."

81. The records of the *Marietta Journal* are unfortunately incomplete, particularly between January and March of 1937, and as such, fail to chronicle the search for a community drama consultant or the efforts of Hayes to work within the Marietta community. "Theatre Group to Present Play May 21–22," *Marietta Journal*, May 7, 1937, 3.

82. Eugene Bergmann and his wife attended the spaghetti dinner to celebrate the opening of *The Hired Husband*. Ibid.; "Theatre Guild Gives Spaghetti Supper For Cast," *Marietta Journal*, May 24, 1937, 3.

83. D. G. Nichols to Gay Shepperson, November 17, 1936, NARA, E952, Box 523, "Price File—Community Drama, General."

84. "Church Programs in the City Today," *New York Times*, July 1, 1934, p. N6.

85. "Obituary," *New York Times,* September 4, 1935, 19; "Rev. Mother Blandine," *New York Times,* May 20, 1937, 21.

86. It is important to note that these data are, according to the cautionary note on the census, "seriously incomplete"; hampered by lack of funds and cooperation from churches, the survey results in "significant undercounts for many denominations throughout the South," noting particularly the strangely low numbers of the Southern Baptist Convention and the Methodist Episcopal Church, South. Thus, the referenced percentages are likely at least somewhat lower than a historically accurate count would have been. In calculating these percentages, I excluded all individuals under the age of 14 because the numbers provided by the Census of Religious Bodies considered only those individuals

who were of age and official members of the church. The 1930 U.S. Census calculated the total population of Floyd County, Georgia at 48,667, and the population of individuals aged 14 or over at 33,146. I have also combined the many different branches of the Baptist and Methodist churches into a single percentage for the sake of clarity. For the complete, detailed results of this survey, see Department of Commerce and Labor, Bureau of the Census, *United States Census of Religious Bodies, County File, 1936*, Association of Religion Data Archives, accessed March 12, 2010, http://www.thearda.com/Archive/Files/Downloads/1936CENSCT_DL.asp; U.S. Census Bureau, *Census of Population and Housing*, Population—Georgia, Table 13, Composition of the Population, By County, 1930, accessed March 12, 2010, http://www.census.gov/prod/www/abs/decennial/1930.html.

87. Price immigrated to the United States in 1920 at the age of 18. At the onset of the Depression, he began work in community entertainments and recreation, serving as the entertainment coordinator at a Civilian Conservation Corps camp before joining the FTP in 1935. Like John Houseman (an immigrant from Romania), Price experienced a series of firings and hirings by the FTP in 1937 because he was not a full citizen of the United States; Flanagan and numerous others repeatedly requested special consideration for Price because of his expertise in the area of community drama. Herbert Stratton Price, "Personal History Statement," November 20, 1935, NARA, E840, Box 39, "Price, Herbert Stratton—Personnel;" Herbert Price to Hallie Flanagan, "The Georgia Experiment in Community Drama," April 5, 1937, NARA, E839, Box 5, "Community Drama—Herbert Price;" "Herbert Stratton Price," July 17, 1920, Statue of Liberty-Ellis Island Foundation, Inc., Original Ship Manifest, *The Celtic*, 1093-4, accessed February 10, 2007, http://www.ellisisland.org/search/shipManifest.asp?MID=0280573159016406 2144&FNM=HERBERT&LNM=PRICE&PLNM=PRICE&CGD=M&bS YR=1901&bEYR=1903&first_kind=1&last_kind=0&RF=2&pID=1038370 20095&lookup=103837020095&show=%5C%5C192%2E168%2E4%2E227 %5Cimages%5CT715%2D2800%5CT715%2D28001094%2ETIF&origFN =%5C%5C192%2E168%2E4%2E227%5CIMAGES%5CT715%2D2800%5 CT715%2D28001093%2ETIF.

88. Herbert Price to Hallie Flanagan, "The Georgia Experiment in Community Drama," April 5, 1937, NARA, E839, Box 5, "Community Drama—Herbert Price."

89. Herbert Price to Dorothy Braley, undated memo, NARA, E839, Box 5, "Community Drama—Herbert Price."

90. Charlotte Holt to Mary McFarland, April 29, 1937, NARA, E839, Box 5, "Community Drama—Herbert Price."

91. Herbert Price to Hallie Flanagan, May 4, 1938, NARA, E839, Box 5, "Community Drama—Herbert Price."

92. Herbert Price to Hallie Flanagan, July 15, 1938, NARA, E839, Box 5, "Community Drama—Herbert Price," 4.

93. *Federal One* was produced by the Institute for the Federal Theatre Project at George Mason University. The article Price responded to was a brief excerpt of the story told by Flanagan in *Arena* and was printed following the "Curator's Column" in the October 1976 volume (1, no. 4, page 16) of *Federal One*.

94. Herbert Price to Lorraine Brown and Laraine Carroll, July 31, 1980, WPA Oral Histories Collection, Special Collections & Archives, George Mason University Libraries, "Price, Herbert."

95. Thomas Postlewait, "The Criteria for Evidence: Anecdotes in Shakespearean Biography, 1709–2000," in *Theorizing Practice, Redefining Theatre History*, ed. W. B. Worthen and Peter Holland (New York: Palgrave Macmillan, 2003), 65.

96. *A Brief History of the Federal Theatre in the South* includes a section that outlines the productions of each city as an overview; one of the features is a short statement about the audience reaction to the show. In the Atlanta section, the majority of the productions are described as "excellent," "fair," or "very good." *Altars of Steel* is the only production that stands out in this regard; its audience reaction is labeled "very interesting." Writing in *The Leader*, critic Dudley Glass similarly wrote, "Whether 'Altars of Steel,' given its first performance anywhere at the Atlanta Theatre Thursday night, is a great drama, I don't know. [...] I've never seen anything like it. This can be said with conviction: It is intensely interesting." *A Brief History of the Federal Theatre in the South*, 2, 10.

4 THE FADING FRONTIER: EXCAVATING THE PORTLAND FEDERAL THEATRE PROJECT

1. An early version of this chapter appeared in "Disappearing Frontiers and the National Stage: Placing the Portland Federal Theatre Project," by Elizabeth Osborne, published in *Theatre History Studies*, © 2009 by the University of Alabama Press; Flanagan, *Arena*, 272.

2. See Barry Witham's *The Federal Theatre Project: A Case Study* for an excellent, in-depth study of FTP activities in Seattle, Washington.

3. Flanagan, *Arena*, 271–73.

4. Ibid., 301.

5. NARA contains correspondence regarding project proposals and early funding problems between late 1935 and early 1936, a few documents from late 1937 centering on a local political conflict, some information from the spring of 1939 on a proposed radio show and the Paul Bunyan festival, one Audience Survey Report and a few regional reports that briefly mention the Portland FTP. The LOC collection includes several production books with varying degrees of information, as well as scraps of publicity information, playreader reports, and a script of E. P. Conkle's *Paul Bunyan and the Blue Ox* (the script proposed for the Paul Bunyan festival). George Mason University possesses one oral history and brief notes from another untaped interview. It is also worth noting that many of the Portland FTP productions centered on dance

and movement, a characteristic that makes these scripts less telling than dramas or musicals. While it is certainly possible that more information regarding the Portland FTP is available, it is not easily located in the archival collections connected to the FTP, nor do contemporary histories cite other personal or private archives where additional sources might be located. The most helpful secondary source was written by Karen Wickre, one of the staff members involved in the organization of what is now the Library of Congress's collection when it was on loan to George Mason University; *An Informal History of Oregon's WPA Federal Theatre Project* is an unpublished document that describes many of Portland's productions.

6. The numbers of employees in each branch during 1936 and 1939, respectively, were as follows: Maine (36 to 46), Colorado (26 to 44), Oregon (34 to 53), and Louisiana (50 to 114). The figures for the fifth state, Georgia (0 to 13), are misleading because the FTP did not begin in Georgia until January 1937, when all Birmingham FTP personnel were transferred (along with *Altars of Steel*) to Atlanta. Flanagan, *Arena*, 434–35.

7. Workers of the Writers' Program of the Works Projects Administration, *Oregon: End of the Trail* (Portland: Binfords & Mort, 1940; reprint, Portland: Binfords & Mort, 1972), 122–23.

8. Nick Chaivoe, interview by Shirley Tanzer, Portland, Oregon, transcript, WPA Oral Histories Collection, Special Collections and Archives, George Mason University, January 18, 1978, 44.

9. Guy Williams to R. G. Dieck, January 6, 1936, NARA, E850, Box 69, "OR—Project Proposals #1;" Flanagan, *Arena*, 297; Glenn Hughes to R. G. Dieck, December 9, 1935, NARA, E850, Box 69, "OR—Project Proposals #1."

10. Alice Henson Ernst, *Trouping in the Oregon Country: A History of Frontier Theatre* (Portland: Oregon Historical Society, 1961), 175; Chaivoe, interview, 43.

11. Guy Williams to Hallie Flanagan, January 15, 1936, NARA, E850, Box 69, "OR—Project Proposals #1."

12. Mathews, *The Federal Theatre: Plays, Relief, and Politics*, 155.

13. Chaivoe, interview, 49.

14. E. J. Griffith to Evan Roberts, April 20, 1939, NARA, E839, Box 17, "Oregon."

15. "Dumb acts" referred to scenes or bits without sound. These popular vaudeville pieces were typically performed at the very beginnings and endings of shows and allowed noisy audiences to enter and exit the theatre while enjoying a bit of entertainment. These scenes also allowed non-English-speaking immigrant populations to attend and enjoy the theatre.

16. Lester Lorenzo Schilling, Jr., "The History of the Theatre in Portland, Oregon, 1846–1959" (PhD diss., University of Wisconsin, 1961), 454.

17. "*Taming of the Shrew* Production Bulletin," LOC, Box 1079, "Taming of the Shrew," 8, 15.

18. Schilling, "The History of the Theatre in Portland, Oregon, 1846–1959," 454–5.
19. Hallie Flanagan to Bess Whitcomb, March 6, 1939, NARA, E839, Box 29, "Western Region #1."
20. Bess Whitcomb to Hallie Flanagan, November 17, 1937, NARA, E839, Box 29, "Western Region #1;" Bess Whitcomb to Ole Ness, December 1, 1937, NARA, E839, Box 29, "Western Region #1."
21. Margery Hoffman Smith, interview by Lewis Ferbrache, April 10, 1964, San Francisco, California, transcript, Archives of American Art, Smithsonian Institution, accessed August 3, 2010, http://www.aaa.si.edu/collections/oral-histories/transcripts/smith64apr.htm.
22. Ole Ness to Hallie Flanagan, "Weekly Report for 12 March 1938," NARA, E856, Box 100, "Region V—1938 & 1939," 3.
23. Ole Ness to Hallie Flanagan, "Weekly Report," undated, probably January 1938, NARA, E856, Box 100, "Region V—1938 & 1939," 3.
24. Miller sent his letter to Mary McFarland; she sent an extended quotation from the letter to the named recipients, which is the source of this quote. Mary McFarland to Mr. O'Brien and Mr. Krimont, May 21, 1936, NARA, E850, Box 69, "OR—Project Proposals."
25. Ole Ness to Hallie Flanagan, "Weekly Report," June 2, 1938, NARA, E856, Box 100, "Region V—1938 & 1939," 1–2.
26. Ernst, *Trouping in the Oregon Country,* 171–7.
27. "Oregon Creates Its Own Plays," *Federal Theatre* 2, no. 3 (1937): 11.
28. Steve Wyatt, "The Flax Industry of Lane County," *The Lane County Historical Society* 35, no. 2 (Summer 1990), 28; Donald W. Fishler, "Fiber Flax in Oregon," *Economic Botany* 3, no. 4 (Oct–Dec. 1949), 395–7; "Oregon Creates Its Own Plays," 11.
29. *Yellow Harvest* is inexplicably catalogued with the CCC scripts at NARA (and unavailable anywhere else). To the best of my knowledge, this production was not linked to the CCC, and was performed only during the flax festival on Mt. Angel. Frederick Schlick, *Yellow Harvest*, NARA, E917, Box 355, "Yellow Harvest," 8.
30. Steve M. Wyatt, "Flax and Linen: An Uncertain Oregon Industry," *Oregon Historical Quarterly* (1994): 159–60; Charles Sumner Hoffman, Jr., "Oregon Low-Lands Suitable for Flax," *Economic Geography* 12, no. 2 (April 1936): 164–6.
31. Wyatt, "Flax and Linen," 157–8.
32. "New Flax Plant Dedicated Today," *Oregonian*, September 5, 1936, 1; Stims Vernon, "City Celebrates Advent of Flax," *Oregonian*, September 6, 1936, 10. Harry Hopkins's presence, though unremarked in *the Oregonian*, is documented in a picture of festival attendees published in Wyatt, "Flax and Linen," 166.
33. Schlick, *Yellow Harvest,*1.

34. The script of *Yellow Harvest* contains many dashes, ellipses, misspellings, and otherwise ungrammatical punctuation. I have replicated all of these stylistic choices in my quotations of the text. Schlick, *Yellow Harvest*, 2.

35. Ibid., 8.

36. Ibid., 21–2.

37. Ibid., 22.

38. "Oregon's Record to Date," *Federal Theatre* 2, no. 5 (1937): 26.

39. Ole Ness to Hallie Flanagan, "Report—Portland, San Francisco, Denver," June 2, 1938, NARA, E856, Box 100, "Region V—1938 & 1939," 1.

40. Hoffman Smith, interview.

41. Griffith's report estimated local contributions of $28,620, placing the total cost of the project at $275,513. When President Roosevelt decided to dedicate the building in 1937, last-minute rush funding poured in to the project; apparently there is no record of exactly how much money arrived and how it was spent, so the final cost of Timberline Lodge is unavailable. The resulting investigation came to no conclusions. Jean Burwell Weir, "Timberline Lodge: A WPA Experiment in Architecture and Crafts, Volume One," (PhD diss., University of Michigan, 1977), 37, 68–71, 292.

42. Guy Williams to Hallie Flanagan, January 15, 1936, NARA, E850, Box 69, "OR—Project Proposals #1."

43. "Dance of the Sophisticates," *Oregonian*, October 4, 1937, 10.

44. Poem attached to letter from E. J. Griffith to Hallie Flanagan, December 4, 1937, NARA, E839, Box 29, "Western Region #2."

45. Hallie Flanagan to Philip Davis, probably February 1939, Hallie Flanagan Papers, *T-Mss 1964–002, Billy Rose Theatre Collection, The New York Public Library for the Performing Arts, Series I: General Files, Sub-Series 2, Personal Papers, Box 4, "Excerpts from Flanagan's letters (1935–39)."

46. "*Timberline Tintypes* Production Book," LOC, Box 1081, "Timberline Tintypes," program.

47. Frank's hugely successful marionette adaptation of *Pinocchio* played in Los Angeles, Portland, Boston, and many other cities nationwide. It was this production of *Pinocchio*, in fact, that played on Broadway in one of the last performances of the FTP. Instead of the traditional ending in which Pinocchio transforms into a real boy, Frank rewrote the ending so that shots offstage interrupted Pinocchio's change. A voice announced "Pinocchio is dead," and proceeded to list the names of all of the Congressmen who voted against the FTP appropriations. The cast collected around the body of Pinocchio onstage, mourning his demise. *Life* magazine photographed the event, and the dead Pinocchio became the symbol for the death of the FTP. Lowell Swortzell, ed., *Six Plays for Young People from the Federal Theatre Project* (New York: Greenwood Press, 1986), 3; "Pinocchio Dies in New York as Federal Theatre Drops Curtain," *Life* (July 17, 1930): 20.

48. C. A. S., "Timberline Show Scheduled," *Labor Newdealer*, August 25, 1938, 2.

49. Log bucking is the process of cutting a felled tree into smaller pieces. Historically, it was a popular competitive sport in which a pair of loggers would race to complete the cutting first and colleagues would wager on the outcome.

50. "*Timberline Tintypes* Production Book," LOC, Box 1081, "Timberline Tintypes," 25.

51. Hugh Antoine D'Arcy's "The Face on the Barroom Floor" provided the basis for a short 1914 Charlie Chaplin film by the same name. The "face" is one that the storyteller, a former painter, attempts to draw on the floor of the bar to show the sailors with whom he is drinking the beauty of his lost love. In both the ballad and the film (and *Timberline Tintypes*), the storyteller dies before completing his drawing.

52. Yasha Frank, *Timberline Tintypes*, NARA, E914, Box 332, "Timberline Tintypes."

53. Frank, *Timberline Tintypes*, 11–13.

54. The program states that Margaret Barney directed *Timberline Tintypes*, and credits Yasha Frank with the arrangement of the piece. The Director's Report is unsigned. Though Karen Wickre attributes the report to Frank in her *Informal History of Oregon's WPA Federal Theatre Project*, the tenor of the writing and the fact that Barney is listed as director suggest that Barney wrote this report for the production book. "Director's Report," "*Timberline Tintypes* Production Book," LOC, Box 1081, "Timberline Tintypes," 7.

55. Created in the mid-nineteenth century, tintype photographs were produced on a metallic sheet. This cheap and simple form of photography remained popular in many rural locales through the early twentieth century, and would have been another way to evoke the nostalgia that *Timberline Tintypes* so consciously created in performance.

56. Herbert L. Larson, "WPA Players Score Big Hit," *Oregonian,* August 15, 1938, 4.

57. "'Tintypes' Pleased First Night Crowd at WPA Theatre," *Oregon Journal,* April 25, 1938, 16.

58. C. A. S., "Timberline Show Scheduled," 2.

59. Hallie Flanagan, "Design for the Federal Theatre's Season," *New York Times,* September 4, 1938, 99.

60. "Summer Plans Set for WPA Theatre," *New York Times,* June 11, 1939, 47.

61. "Minutes of Meeting of Paul Bunyan Celebration Committee," recorded by Bernadine Whitfield, March 1, 1939, NARA, E839, Box 17, "Oregon."

62. Flanagan, *Arena*, 302.

63. Ibid., 302.

64. "Noted Critic Pays Brief Visit While on Lecture Tour," *Oregon Journal,* March 16, 1939, 21.

65. Chaivoe went on to earn a law degree from Northwestern University and practiced law in Portland into the 1990s. Chaivoe, interview, 61.

5 THEATRE "IN THE WILDERNESS": THE FEDERAL THEATRE PROJECT TOURS AMERICA

1. "*CCC Murder Mystery* in 189 Camps," *Federal Theatre* 2, no. 5 (1937), 18.
2. Flanagan, *Arena*, 78.
3. John Frick, "A Changing Theatre: New York and Beyond," in *The Cambridge History of American Theatre, Volume II: 1870–1945*, ed. Don B. Wilmeth and Christopher Bigsby (New York: Cambridge University Press, 1999), 217–8.
4. "Federal Theatre: Seventh Month," *Federal Theatre* 1, no. 5 (April 1936): 5.
5. Ibid., 5.
6. Quoted in McDonald, *Federal Relief Administration and the Arts*, 559.
7. B.A. Holway, "*CCC Murder Mystery* Bookings, March 4th to December 31, 1936," January 15, 1937, NARA, E839, Box 4, "CCC."
8. Accurate as of June 15, 1937, these figures include performances throughout New York, New Jersey, Pennsylvania, Delaware, Maryland, Virginia, Vermont, New Hampshire, Massachusetts, and Maine. "*CCC Murder Mystery* in 189 Camps," *Federal Theatre* 2, no. 5 (1937), 18; Niles G. Moren, *The Federal Theatre Project of the Works Progress Administration and the CCC*, NARA, E873, Box 127, "CCC Division—Niles G. Moren, June 1937," 6.
9. The Depression devastated the young adult workforce. Nearly 40 percent of Americans under the age of 25 were unemployed or underemployed at the time the 1940 census was completed. Mitchell, *Depression Decade*, 328; John C. Paige, *The Civilian Conservation Corps and the National Park Service, 1933–1942: An Administrative History* (Washington [?]: National Park Service, Department of the Interior, 1985), accessed May 8, 2010, http://www.nps.gov/history/history/online_books/ccc/ccc5.htm.
10. President Roosevelt's efforts to preserve national resources are frequently noted as an early step in conservation in the United States, particularly via the CCC. Mitchell, *Depression Decade,* 328–30; Guy-Harold Smith, *Conservation of Natural Resources* (New York: John Wiley & Sons, 1950), 19; Henry Jarrett, *Perspectives on Conservation: Essays on America's Natural Resources* (Baltimore: Johns Hopkins University Press, 1958), 14.
11. The CCC's achievements included planting more than 2 billion trees, developing 800 state parks, constructing 46,000 bridges and 13,000 miles of hiking trails, eliminating 400,000 predatory animals, and much more. CCC director Robert Fechner's *Annual Report of the Director of the Civilian Conservation Corps: Fiscal Year Ended June 30, 1939* is quoted in Neil M. Maher, "A New Deal Body Politic: Landscape, Labor, and the Civilian Conservation Corps," *Environmental History* 7, no. 3 (July 2002), 437.
12. Hadley Cantril and Mildred Strunk, eds., *Public Opinion, 1935–1946* (Princeton, NJ: Princeton University Press, 1951), 111, 405.
13. Free shows for schools and other institutions originally began with a grant through the Civil Works Administration. The program eventually

transferred over to the Public Works Division of New York's Emergency Relief Administration, and then to FERA. According to *Variety,* the CCC programs were so popular that they were virtually assured automatic extensions until more permanent relief measures could be taken. Mathews, *The Federal Theatre,* 5–6; Jack Pulaski, "The Year in Legit," *Variety,* January 1, 1935, 134; "CCC Free Drama Units Continue; More Shows, Talent May Be Added," *Variety,* January 22, 1935, 53; "$5,000,000 Relief Program, Equity Files Bid in Wash.," *Variety,* February 27, 1935, 59; Witham, *Federal Theatre Project: A Case Study,* 37.

14. Susan Quinn, *Furious Improvisation: How the WPA and a Cast of Thousands Made High Art out of Desperate Times* (New York: Walker Publishing, 2008), 85.

15. Quoted in Flanagan, *Arena,* 242.

16. Moren, *The Federal Theatre Project of the Works Progress Administration and the CCC,* 2; "Special Feature Release for New York City," July 24, 1936, NARA, E873, Box 126, "CCC Press Releases," 3.

17. Norman R. Feusier to Earl House, May 25, 1936, NARA, E873, Box 127, "Bookings."

18. "Special Feature Release for New York City," July 24, 1936, NARA, E873, Box 126, "CCC Press Releases," 5–6.

19. "Special Release, New York State Papers," December 18, 1936, LOC, Box 989, "CCC Murder Mystery Publicity."

20. "Novel Play Utilizes Audience, Makes Big Hit with CCC Boys," *Syracuse Post-Standard,* September 11, 1936, NARA, E873, Box 124, "Bookings."

21. At House's request, Hayward later revised the script to reduce the number of actors from 12 to eight. This would allow the touring companies to travel with only one automobile, rather than the two required to transport the cast of 12. This version of the script appears to have gone into production in the late spring or early summer of 1937. All references to the script in this analysis are from the 12-actor version, which is more readily available and appears to have been produced more frequently.

22. Flanagan, *Arena,* 242.

23. Grace Hayward, *CCC Murder Mystery,* NARA, E917, Box 354, "CCC Murder Mystery," iv.

24. Grace Hayward, "Part Designated in the Script as Arthur Adams," LOC, Box 862, "CCC Murder Mystery Fragments."

25. Hayward, *CCC Murder Mystery,* xi.

26. Ibid., ix–x.

27. Myron B. Farwell to Arthur Roberts, September 19, 1936, NARA, E839, Box 4, "CCC."

28. Charles M. Cormack to Federal Theatre Project offices in Syracuse, February 17, 1936, NARA, E839, Box 4, "CCC."

29. Robert H. Fava, quoted in Niles Moren, *The Federal Theatre Project of the Works Progress Administration and the CCC,* NARA, E873, Box 127, "Report—'Federal Theatre Project and the Civilian Conservation Corps,'" 26.

30. Hayward, *CCC Murder Mystery*, vii.
31. Based on the well-liked comic strip of the same name and subtitled "She's not as dumb as she looks," "Dumb Dora" was slang for a sweet, silly, addle-headed woman during the 1920s and 1930s. Gracie Allen played a particularly popular version of the "Dumb Dora" character in her vaudeville act with George Burns; Allen's version of the "Dumb Dora" character was one of her trademark roles, which she created for television, radio, and film.
32. Hayward, *CCC Murder Mystery*, 32.
33. I have omitted the majority of the stage directions in this quote. Emphasis is from the script. Ibid., 9.
34. Ibid., 17.
35. Ibid., 25.
36. Emphasis from the script. Ibid., 19.
37. Ibid., 53.
38. Ibid., 58.
39. "Thrills of the CCC," *Syracuse American*, September 20, 1936, NARA, E839, Box 4 "CCC."
40. Charles Hopkins to Hallie Flanagan, September 17, 1936, NARA, E839, Box 4, "CCC." 1.
41. Moren, *The Federal Theatre Project of the Works Progress Administration and the CCC*, 24.
42. Lieutenant Martin A. Primoschic to Grace Hayward, January 6, 1937, NARA, E839, Box 4, "CCC."
43. Moren, *The Federal Theatre Project of the Works Progress Administration and the CCC*, 19.
44. "Special Feature Release for New York City," July 24, 1936, NARA, E873, Box 126, "CCC Press Releases," 4.
45. Moren, *The Federal Theatre Project of the Works Progress Administration and the CCC*, 1.
46. Quoted in Hallie Flanagan, "Men at Work: Southeast," *Federal Theatre* 1, no. 5 (April 1936): 12.
47. Moren, *The Federal Theatre Project of the Works Progress Administration and the CCC*, 5.
48. The winning play, P. Washington Porter's *Return to Life*, earned a small cash prize, a six-week intensive workshop with a Broadway playwright in New York City, and a production in Holyoke, Massachusetts. Bernard Winstock and George Gill's musical *CCC* took second place. Flanagan, *Arena*, 233; Moren, *The Federal Theatre Project of the Works Progress Administration and the CCC*, 4; "CCC Playwrights Welcomed Here," *New York Times*, April 3, 1937, 21.
49. Minstrel shows were some of the most popular entertainments in CCC camps nationwide. In addition to the FTP troupes that toured with various minstrel shows, minstrelsy scripts distributed to camps often came with specific directions on how to recreate the humor and add local flavor. Moren, *The Federal Theatre Project of the Works Progress Administration and the CCC*, 8–10.

50. Flanagan, *Arena*, 420–1; McDonald, *Federal Relief Administration and the Arts*, 560.

51. Flanagan, *Arena*, 174.

52. Much of this section was originally published in my article, "A Nation in Need: Disaster Relief and the Federal Theatre Project," *Journal of American Drama and Theatre* 22.2 (Spring 2008). Copyright © 2008 Martin E. Segal Theatre Center. Reproduced by permission.

53. "Flood of '97: Infamous Floods," *Cincinnati Enquirer*, Commemorative Special Section, "Rivers Unleashed," accessed July 20, 2007, http://www.enquirer.com/flood_of_97/history5.html.

54. In the mid-1930s "concentration camp" was not yet a term loaded with the horrors of World War II. Instead, it was the term of choice for locations that harbored refugees.

55. Avis D. Carlson, "Dust," *New Republic*, May 1, 1935, 332–3; R. Douglas Hurt, *The Dust Bowl: An Agricultural and Social History* (Chicago: Nelson-Hall, Inc., 1984), 2–3; Sean Dennis Cashman, *America in the Twenties and Thirties: The Olympian Age of Franklin Delano Roosevelt* (New York: New York University Press, 1989), 176.

56. R. L. Duffus, "When Wind and Water Strike at Man," *New York Times*, February 7, 1937, 125; "10 Die, Loss Heavy as Rains Lash East," *New York Times*, September 21, 1938, 27; Warren Moscow, "Floods Add Peril to New England," *New York Times*, September 23, 1938, 22; "Tornadoes Kill 27, Injure Hundreds; 5 States Stricken," *New York Times*, March 31, 1938, 1; "Long Beach Gripped in Terror of Shock," *New York Times*, March 11, 1933, 1.

57. Carlson, "Dust," 332–3.

58. "The Great Flood of 1936," October 18, 2006, accessed November 22, 2008, http://www.wgby.org/localprograms/flood.

59. Renowned filmmaker Pare Lorentz immortalized the Flood of 1937 in his 1938 WPA film *The River*. It is interesting to note that Lorentz's film actually deals with the 1936 flood and the resulting legislation, but since he was filming in the midst of the Flood of 1937 (and had significant budget constraints), he simply shot footage of the 1937 flood and used it in the film instead.

60. American Red Cross, *The Ohio-Mississippi Valley Flood Disaster of 1937 Report of Operations*, (Washington, DC: American Red Cross, 1937), 10–11.

61. Quoted in "A Business Survey of the Flood," *Barron's*, February 1, 1937, 17.

62. "Flood of '97: Infamous Floods," *Cincinnati Enquirer*.

63. "Catastrophe: Yellow Waters," *Time*, February 8, 1937, accessed February 11, 2010, http://www.time.com/time/magazine/article/0,9171,883569,00.html.

64. American Red Cross, *The Ohio-Mississippi Valley Flood Disaster of 1937*, 17.

65. Ibid., 78.

66. E. E. McCleish to Lawrence Morris and Mrs. Charles Tidd Cole, February 17, 1937, NARA, E839, Box 10, "Flood Area Truck Tour—1937," 1.

67. "Flood Fund at $20,375,000," *New York Times*, February 13, 1937, 28.

68. American Red Cross, *The Ohio-Mississippi Valley Flood Disaster of 1937*, 121.
69. Moren, *The Federal Theatre Project of the Works Progress Administration and the CCC*, 7–8.
70. Ibid., 11–2.
71. Herbert S. Price to Hallie Flanagan, February 5, 1937, NARA, E839, Box 10, "Flood Area Truck Tour—1937," 1.
72. Ibid., 1.
73. Ellen S. Woodward to Hallie Flanagan, February 5, 1937, NARA, E839, Box 10, "Flood Area Truck Tour—1937," 1; McF (probably Mary McFarland) to WPF (probably William P. Farnsworth), February 6, 1937, NARA, E839, Box 10, "Flood Area Truck Tour—1937."
74. "Proposed Intimate Revue," NARA, E938, Box 10, "Flood Area Truck Tour—1937," 2.
75. Moren, *The Federal Theatre Project of the Works Progress Administration and the CCC*, 12.
76. E. E. McCleish to Lawrence Morris and Mrs. Charles Tidd Cole, February 17, 1937, NARA, E839, Box 10, "Flood Area Truck Tour—1937," 2.
77. "Entertaining Flood Sufferers: Federal Theatre Troupes Bring Cheer to Thousands of Homeless," *Federal Theatre* 2, no. 4 (1937): 13.
78. Herbert Price, "Federal Theatre Mobile Variety Unit: Players Entertain Flood Refugees," NARA, E952, Box 523, "Price File—Flood Area Material," 2; "Entertaining Flood Sufferers: Federal Theatre Troupes Bring Cheer to Thousands of Homeless," 13.
79. Valerie Grim, "African American Rural Culture, 1900–1950," *Rural South, 1900–1950,* ed. R. Douglas Hurt, (Columbia: University of Missouri Press, 2003), 108–111.
80. Herbert Price, "Federal Theatre Mobile Variety Unit: Players Entertain Flood Refugees," NARA, E952, Box 523, "Price File—Flood Area Material," 2.
81. Ibid., 9.
82. Moren, *The Federal Theatre Project of the Works Progress Administration and the CCC*, 12.
83. Though there are many songs called "Goin' Home," it is likely that Price is referring to a spiritual based on the second movement of Antonin Dvořák's *Symphony No. 9.* Frequently requested at funerals, some rank it second only to "Amazing Grace" as a hymn for solemn occasions.
84. Herbert Price, "Federal Theatre Mobile Variety Unit: Players Entertain Flood Refugees," NARA, E952, Box 523, "Price File—Flood Area Material," 2–6.
85. Armita Schaumburg to Herbert S. Price, March 1, 1937, NARA, E952, Box 523, "Price File—Flood Area Material," 1.
86. Ruth Ray to Hallie Flanagan, March 8, 1937, NARA, E952, Box 523, "Price File—Flood Area Material," 1.
87. E. E. McCleish to Lawrence Morris and Mrs. Charles Tidd Cole, February 17, 1937, NARA, E839, Box 10, "Flood Area Truck Tour—1937," 3.

88. One important exception to the generalization of scholars skipping over the activities of the CCC Division is Barry Witham's *The Federal Theatre Project: A Case Study*, in which he explores the FTP's tours for the CCC in the state of Washington.

EPILOGUE: AN AMERICAN AUDIENCE FOR THE "PEOPLE'S THEATRE"

1. Hallie Flanagan, "Testimony before the House Committee on Un-American Activities, 1938," quoted in Eric Bentley, ed., *Thirty Years of Treason. Excerpts from Hearings before the House Committee on Un-American Activities, 1938–1968,* (New York: The Viking Press, 1971), 24.
2. Barry B. Witham, "Backstage at *The Cradle Will Rock,*" *Theatre History Studies* 12 (1992): 213–220; *"The Cradle Will Rock,"* Internet Movie Database, accessed September 21, 2010, http://www.imdb.com/title/tt0150216.
3. Mildred Seydell, *"Altars of Steel* Aids Communism with Tax Money," *Atlanta Georgian,* April 4, 1937, 4D.
4. Flanagan, *Arena,* 368–73; Bentley, *Hallie Flanagan: A Life in the American Theatre,* 351–2.
5. Flanagan, *Arena,* 23, 435.
6. Flanagan, *Arena,* 267-9; Alan Kreizenbeck, "The Radio Division of the Federal Theatre Project," *New England Theatre Journal* 2, no. 1 (1991): 35.

Bibliography ❧

PRIMARY SOURCES:

Archival Collections:

Dana, Henry Wadsworth Longfellow Collection. Harvard Theatre Collection. Houghton Library. Harvard College Library. Harvard University. Cambridge, MA.

Federal Theatre Project Collection. Music Division. Library of Congress (LOC). Washington, DC.

Federal Theatre Project Collection. Special Collections & Archives. George Mason University Libraries (GMU). George Mason University. Fairfax, VA.

Federal Theatre Project. Works Projects Administration. Record Group 69. National Archives and Records Administration (NARA). College Park, MD.

Flanagan, Hallie. Papers. T-Mss 1964-002. Billy Rose Theatre Division. New York Public Library for the Performing Arts. New York, NY.

Johnson, Guy Benton. #3826. Southern Historical Collection. The Wilson Library. University of North Carolina at Chapel Hill. Chapel Hill, NC.

National American Suffrage Association Collection, Rare Book and Special Collections Division. Library of Congress. Washington, D.C.

Oral history interview with Margery Hoffman Smith. April 10, 1964. Archives of American Art. Smithsonian Institution. Washington, DC.

Women's Rights Collection 1870–1960. Schlesinger Library. Radcliffe Institute. Cambridge, MA.

Works Progress Administration Clippings Files. Harvard Theatre Collection. Houghton Library. Harvard College Library. Harvard University. Cambridge, MA.

Works Progress Administration. Oral Histories Collection. Special Collections and Archives. George Mason University. Fairfax, VA.

Newspapers & Periodicals:

Atlanta Constitution. 1935–1939.
Atlanta Georgian. 1935–1939.

Atlanta Journal. 1935–1939.

Back Bay Leader. 1936–1939. (Boston Newspaper)

Beacon News. 1935–1939. (Chicago Newspaper)

Birmingham Age-Herald. 1935–1939.

Birmingham News. 1935–1939.

Birmingham Post. 1935–1937.

Birmingham Public Library. Birmingham Federal Theatre. 1936. Clipping File.

Boston Chronicle. 1939.

Boston Globe. 1921–1939.

Boston Herald. 1921–1938.

Bulletin of the American Iron and Steel Institute. 1909.

Chicago Daily News. 1938.

Chicago Daily Tribune. 1928–1939.

Chicago Defender. 1935–1939.

Christian Science Monitor. 1939.

Federal Theatre. 1936–1937.

Jewish Advocate. 1935–1939. (Boston Newspaper)

Journal of Labor. 1935–1939. (Atlanta Newspaper)

Labor Newdealer. 1938. (Portland, Oregon Newspaper)

Marietta Journal. 1936–1937. (Marietta, Georgia Newspaper)

Mid-Town Journal. 1936. (Boston Newspaper)

New Republic. 1935–1939.

New York Times. 1937–1939.

Oregonian. 1935–1939. (also called *Morning Oregonian* from 1935-1937)

Oregon Journal. 1935–1939.

Philadelphia Inquirer. 1937.

Proceedings of the City Council of Boston. April 13, 1931.

Post-Gazette. 1935–1939. (Boston Newspaper)

Reader's Digest. 1937.

Rome News-Tribune. 1936–1937. (Rome, Georgia Newspaper)

Salem News. 1935–1939. (Salem, Massachusetts Newspaper)

Sentinel. 1935–1939. (Chicago Newspaper)

South Boston Tribune. 1935–1939.

Standard. 1935–1939. (Boston Newspaper)

Sunday American. 1935–1939. (Atlanta Newspaper)

Time. 1935–1939.

Variety. 1935–1939.

West Chicago Press. 1935–1939. (Chicago Newspaper).

SECONDARY SOURCES:

Abbott, Philip. *Franklin D. Roosevelt and the American Political Tradition.* Amherst: University of Massachusetts Press, 1990.

————. *State and Local Governments.* New York: McGraw-Hill, 1967.

Alabama: A Guide to the Deep South. Compiled by workers of the Writers' Program of the Work Projects Administration in the State of Alabama. American Guide Series. New York: Richard R. Smith, 1941.

Allen, Frederick Lewis. *Since Yesterday: The 1930s in America.* New York: Harper and Row, 1939.

Allswang, John M. *A House for all Peoples: Ethnic Politics in Chicago 1890–1936.* Lexington: University Press of Kentucky, 1971.

————. *The New Deal and American Politics: A Study in Political Change.* New York: John Wiley & Sons, 1978.

Althusser, Louis. *Lenin and Philosophy and Other Essays.* Translated by Ben Brewster. New York: Monthly Review Press, 1971.

American Red Cross. *The Ohio-Mississippi Valley Flood Disaster of 1937 Report of Operations.* Washington, DC: American Red Cross, 1937.

Anderson, Maxwell. *Valley Forge, Representative Modern American Plays.* Glenview, IL: Scott, Foresman and Company, 1952. In Twentieth Century North American Drama [Internet], Alexander Street Press, http://solomon.nadr.alexanderstreet.com/. Accessed September 15, 2007.

Armes, Ethel. *The Story of Coal and Iron in Alabama.* Birmingham, AL: Chamber of Commerce, 1910.

Beito, David T. *Taxpayers in Revolt: Tax Resistance during the Great Depression.* Chapel Hill: University of North Carolina Press, 1989.

Bentley, Eric, ed. *Thirty Years of Treason. Excerpts from Hearings before the House Committee on Un-American Activities, 1938–1968.* New York: Viking Press, 1971.

Bentley, Joanne. *Hallie Flanagan: A Life in the American Theatre.* New York: Alfred A. Knopf, 1988.

Bigsby, C. W. E. *1900–1940.* Vol. II of *A Critical Introduction to Twentieth Century American Drama.* Cambridge: Cambridge University Press, 1982.

Biles, Roger. *Big City Boss in Depression and War: Mayor Edward J. Kelly of Chicago.* DeKalb: Northern Illinois University Press, 1984.

————. "Edward J. Kelly: New Deal Machine Builder." In *The Mayors: The Chicago Political Tradition.* Rev. ed. Edited by Paul M. Green and Melvin G. Holli (Carbondale: Southern Illinois University Press, 1995).

Blackwell, Alice Stone. *Lucy Stone, Pioneer of Woman's Rights.* Boston: Little, Brown and Company, 1930.

Bourdieu, Pierre. *The Logic of Practice.* Translated by Richard Nice. Stanford, CA: Stanford University Press, 1990.

Boyer, Paul S. *Purity in Print: The Vice-Society Movement and Book Censorship in America.* New York: Charles Scribner and Sons, 1968.

Brandt, Allan M. *No Magic Bullet: Social History of Venereal Disease in the United States since 1880.* New York: Oxford University Press, 1987.

Bucklin, Joseph Bishop. *Theodore Roosevelt and His Time Shown in His Own Letters.* Vol. II. New York: Charles Scribner's Sons, 1920.

The Builders of Timberline Lodge. Workers of the Writer's Program of the Work Progress Administration. Portland: Willamette Printing Company, 1937.

Burner, David, Eugene D. Genovese, and Forrest McDonald. *The American People*. St. James, NY: Revisionary Press, 1980.

Burns, Constance K., and Ronald P. Formisano, eds. *Boston, 1700–1980: The Evolution of Urban Politics*. Westport, CT: Greenwood Press, 1984.

Buttitta, Tony, and Barry Witham. *Uncle Sam Presents: A Memoir of the Federal Theatre, 1935–1939*. Philadelphia: University of Pennsylvania Press, 1982.

Cambridge, John. "Federal Theatre Draws the Fire of Some Defenders of Commercial Drama." *Sunday Worker* (May 29, 1938).

Cantril, Hadley, and Mildred Strunk, eds. *Public Opinion, 1935–1946*. Princeton, NJ: Princeton University Press, 1951.

Cashman, Sean Dennis. *America in the Twenties and Thirties: The Olympian Age of Franklin Delano Roosevelt*. New York: New York University Press, 1989.

"Catastrophe: Yellow Waters." *Time*. February 8, 1937. http://www.time.com/time/magazine/article/0,9171,883569,00.html. Accessed February 11, 2010.

Cohen, Lizabeth. *Making a New Deal: Industrial Workers in Chicago, 1919–1939*. New York: Cambridge University Press, 1990.

Cole, John Y. "Amassing American 'Stuff:' The Library of Congress and the Federal Arts Projects of the 1930s." *The Quarterly Journal of the Library of Congress* 40, no. 4 (Fall 1983): 356–389.

"A Compulsory Test for Syphilis Before Marriage?" *Reader's Digest* 31, No. 187 (November 1937): 129–132.

Craig, E. Quita. *Black Drama of the Federal Theatre Era*. Amherst: University of Massachusetts Press, 1980

Darnton, Robert. *The Great Cat Massacre and Other Episodes in French Cultural History*. New York: Vintage Books, 1984.

Davis, Natalie Zemon. *Society and Culture in Early Modern France: Eight Essays*. Stanford, CA: Stanford University Press, 1965.

Department of Commerce and Labor. Bureau of the Census. *Census of Religious Bodies, 1936*. Association of Religion Data Archives. Washington, DC: Government Printing Office, 1940. http://www.thearda.com/Archive/Files/Downloads/1936CENSCT_DL.asp. Accessed March 12, 2010.

Deutsch, Sarah. *Women and the City: Gender, Space, and Power in Boston, 1870–1940*. New York: Oxford University Press, 2000.

Draper, C.L. "The History of the Atlanta Federal Theatre Project, 1937–1939." MA thesis, University of Tennessee-Knoxville, 1987.

Duffy, Susan. *American Labor on Stage: Dramatic Interpretations of the Steel and Textile Industries in the 1930s*. Westport, CT: Greenwood Press, 1996.

———. *The Political Left in the American Theatre of the 1930s: A Bibliographic Sourcebook*. Metuchen, NJ: Scarecrow Press, Inc., 1992.

Elder, Glen H. *Children of the Great Depression: Social Change in Life Experience*. Chicago: University of Chicago Press, 1974.

Engle, Ron, and Tice L. Miller. *The American Stage; Social and Economic Issues from the Colonial Period to the Present.* New York: Cambridge University Press, 2001.

Ernst, Alice Henson. *Trouping in the Oregon Country: A History of Frontier Theatre.* Portland: Oregon Historical Society, 1961. Reprint, Westport, CT: Greenwood Press, 1974.

Fearnow, Mark. *The American Stage and the Great Depression: A Cultural History of the Grotesque.* Cambridge Studies in American Theatre and Drama. Edited by Don B. Wilmeth. New York: Cambridge University Press, 1997.

The Federal Theatre Project: A Catalog-Calendar of Productions. Compiled by the Staff of the Fenwick Library, George Mason University. With an introduction by Lorraine A. Brown. Bibliographies and Indexes in the Performing Arts, no. 3. Westport, CT: Greenwood Press, 1986.

Feldman, Glenn. *Politics, Society and the Klan in Alabama 1915–1949.* Tuscaloosa: University of Alabama, 1999.

Fishler, Donald W. "Fiber Flax in Oregon." *Economic Botany* 3, no. 4 (Oct.– Dec. 1949): 395–406.

Flanagan, Hallie. *Arena.* New York: Duell, Sloan & Pearce, 1940.

———. "Introduction." In *Federal Theatre Plays.* Edited by Pierre De Rohan (New York: Random House, 1938).

———. "The People's Theatre Grows Stronger," *Federal Theatre* I, no. 6 (May 1936).

———. *Shifting Scenes of the Modern European Theatre.* New York: Coward-McCann, Inc., 1928.

———. "What Was Federal Theatre?" *Survey Graphic* 28 (December 1939). Reprint, Washington, DC: American Council of Public Affairs, 1939.

Fraden, Rena. *Blueprints for a Black Federal Theatre, 1935–1939.* New York: Cambridge University Press, 1994.

Franko, Mark. *The Work of Dance: Labor, Movement, and Identity in the 1930s.* Middleton, CT: Wesleyan University Press, 2002.

French, Warren, ed. *The Thirties: Fiction, Poetry, Drama.* Deland, FL: Everett Edwards, 1969.

Frick, John. "A Changing Theatre: New York and Beyond," *The Cambridge History of American Theatre, Volume II: 1870–1945.* Edited by Don B. Wilmeth and Christopher Bigsby (New York: Cambridge University Press, 1999), 217–8.

Galenson, Walter. *The CIO Challenge to the AFL: A History of the American Labor Movement, 1935–1941.* Cambridge, MA: Harvard University Press, 1960.

General Code of the City of Birmingham Alabama of 1930 (Includes all ordinances of a general and permanent nature except as specified in Sec. 6113). Prepared by the Law Department of the City of Birmingham under direction of W. J. Wynn, City Attorney. By authority of the Commission of the City of Birmingham. Birmingham Printing Company: Birmingham, Alabama, 1930.

Georgia: A Guide to Its Towns and Countryside. Compiled and written by workers of the Writers' Program of the Work Projects Administration in the State of Georgia. American Guide Series. Athens: University of Georgia Press, 1940.

Gill, Glenda E. *White Grease Paint on Black Performers: A Study of the Federal Theatre, 1935–1939.* New York: Peter Lang, 1988.

Goldstein, Malcolm. *The Political Stage: American Drama and Theater of the Great Depression.* New York: Oxford University Press, 1974.

Grafton, John, ed. *Franklin Delano Roosevelt: Great Speeches.* New York: Dover Publications, 1999.

"Great Pox," *Time.* (October 26, 1936) http://www.time.com/time/magazine/article/0,9171,788606-2,00.html. Accessed January 10, 2010.

Green, Paul M., and Melvin G. Holli, eds. *The Mayors: The Chicago Political Tradition.* Revised edition. Carbondale: Southern Illinois University Press, 1995.

Grim, Valerie. "African American Rural Culture, 1900–1950." In *Rural South, 1900–1950.* Edited by R. Douglas Hurt. Columbia: University of Missouri Press, 2003.

Guzda, Henry P. "United Steelworkers of America: 26th Convention." *Monthly Labor Review* 115, no. 12 (1992).

Gysel, Libra Jan Cleveland. "Whisper Out Loud!: *Spirochete*: A Living Newspaper, 1937–1939, produced by the Federal Theatre Project: An Instrument for Public Health Education in the War on Syphilis." Ed.D. thesis, Virginia Polytechnic Institute and State University, 1989.

Halper, Albert. "A Morning with the Doc." In *New Masses: An Anthology of the Rebel Thirties.* Edited by Joseph North. New York: International Publishers, 1969.

Heibrun, James, and Charles M. Gray. *The Economics of Art and Culture,* 2nd ed. New York: Cambridge University Press, 2001.

Hewitt, Barnard. *Theatre U.S.A., 1665–1957.* New York: McGraw-Hill Book Company, 1959.

Himelstein, Morgan. *Drama Was a Weapon.* New Brunswick, NJ: Rutgers University Press, 1963.

Hoffman, Charles Sumner, Jr. "Oregon Low-Lands Suitable for Flax." *Economic Geography* 12, no. 2 (April 1936): 164–6.

Holli, Melvin G. *The American Mayor: The Best & The Worst Big-City Leaders.* University Park: University of Pennsylvania Press, 1999.

Houchin, John. *Censorship of the American Theatre in the Twentieth Century.* Cambridge Studies in American Theatre and Drama. Edited by Don B. Wilmeth. Cambridge, MA: Cambridge University Press, 2003.

House Committee on Patents. *Department of Science, Art and Literature: Hearings Before the Committee on Patents.* Transcript, 75th Congress, 3rd sess., 1938. Washington, DC: Government Printing Office, 1938, 93.

Hunt, Lynn, ed. *The New Cultural History.* With an introduction by Lynn Hunt. Studies on the History of Society and Culture. Edited by Victoria E. Bonnell and Lynn Hunt. Los Angeles: University of California Press, 1989.

Hurt, Melissa. "Oppressed, Stereotyped, and Silenced: Atlanta's Black History with the Federal Theatre Project." Constructions of Race in Southern Theatre: From Federalism to the Federal Theatre Project. *Theatre Symposium* 11 (2003): 74–80.

Hurt, R. Douglas. *The Dust Bowl: An Agricultural and Social History.* Chicago: Nelson-Hall, Inc., 1984.

Hyman, Colette A. *Staging Strikes: Workers' Theatre and the American Labor Movement.* Critical Perspectives on the Past. Edited by Susan Porter Benson, Stephen Brier, and Roy Rosenzweig. Philadelphia, PA: Temple University Press, 1997.

Illinois: A Descriptive and Historical Guide. Compiled and written by workers of the Federal Writers' Project of the Work Projects Administration for the State of Illinois. With a foreword by John T. Frederick. American Guide Series. Chicago, IL: A. C. McClurg & Co., 1939.

Isaacs, Edith J. R. "National Theatre 1940: 'A Record and a Prophecy.'" *Theatre Arts* 24, no.1 (January 1940): 55–63.

Jarrett, Henry. *Perspectives on Conservation: Essays on America's Natural Resources.* Baltimore: Johns Hopkins University Press, 1958.

Jerz, Dennis G. *Technology in American Drama, 1920–1950: Soul and Society in the Age of the Machine.* Westport, CT: Greenwood Press, 2003.

Johnson, Curt, and R. Craig Sautter. "Wicked City Chicago: From Kenna to Capone." *December Magazine* (special issue) 37, no. 1 (1994).

Kelley, Robin D. G. *Hammer and Hoe: Alabama Communists during the Great Depression.* Chapel Hill: University of North Carolina Press. 1990.

Kennedy, David M. *Freedom from Fear: The American People in Depression and War, 1929–1945.* New York: Oxford University Press, 1999.

Kerr, Andrea Moore. *Lucy Stone: Speaking out for Equality.* New Brunswick, NJ: Rutgers University Press, 1992.

Koch, John Charles. "The Federal Theatre Project: Region IV— A Structural and Historical Analysis of How It Functioned and What It Accomplished." PhD diss., University of Nebraska, Lincoln, 1981.

Kreizenbeck, Alan. "The Radio Division of the Federal Theatre Project." *New England Theatre Journal* 2, no. 1 (1991): 27–35.

Kruger, Loren. *The National Stage: Theatre and Cultural Legitimation in England, France, and America.* Chicago: University of Chicago Press, 1992.

Kusmer, Kenneth L. *Down and Out, on the Road: The Homeless in American History.* New York: Oxford University Press, 2003.

Kutler, Stanley I., ed. *American Retrospectives: Historians on Historians.* Baltimore, MD: Johns Hopkins University Press, 1995.

Levine, Lawrence W. *Highbrow Lowbrow: The Emergence of Cultural Hierarchy in America.* Cambridge, MA: Harvard University Press, 1988.

Lindberg, Richard C. *To Serve and Collect: Chicago Politics and Police Corruption from the Lager Beer Riot to the Summerdale Scandal.* New York: Praeger Publishers, 1991.

Lora, Ronald, and William Henry Longton, eds. *The Conservative Press in Twentieth-Century America*. Westport, CT: Greenwood Press, 1999.

Maher, Neil M. "A New Deal Body Politic: Landscape, Labor, and the Civilian Conservation Corps." *Environmental History* 7, no. 3 (July 2002): 435–61.

Marcus, Maeva. *Truman and the Steel Seizure Case: The Limits of Presidential Power*. Durham, NC: Duke University Press, 1994.

Massachusetts: A Guide to Its Places and People. The Federal Writers' Project of the Works Progress Administration for Massachusetts. American Guide Series. Boston: Houghton Mifflin, 1937.

Mathews, Jane de Hart. *The Federal Theatre, 1935–1939: Plays, Relief, and Politics*. Princeton, NJ: Princeton University Press, 1967.

McDermott, Douglas. "The Living Newspaper as a Dramatic Form." PhD diss., University of Iowa, 1963.

McDonald, William F. *Federal Relief Administration and the Arts*. Columbus: Ohio State University Press, 1969.

McKenzie, Richard D. *The New Deal for Artists*. Princeton, NJ: Princeton University Press, 1973.

McKiven, Henry M., Jr. *Iron and Steel: Class, Race and Community in Birmingham, Alabama, 1875–1920*. Chapel Hill: University of North Carolina Press, 1995.

Meredith, Charles H. "America Sings." *Federal Theatre* 1, no. 6 (1936): 12.

Miller, John C. *Alexander Hamilton: Portrait in Paradox*. New York: Harper & Brothers, 1959.

Mitchell, Broadus. *Depression Decade: From New Era through New Deal, 1929–1941*. Vol. 9 of The Economic History of the United States. New York: Rinehart & Company, Inc., 1958.

Nannes, Caspar H. *Politics in the American Drama*. Washington, DC: Catholic University Press, 1960.

North, Joseph, ed., *New Masses: An Anthology of the Rebel Thirties*. New York: International Publishers, 1969.

O'Connor, Francis V. *Federal Support for the Visual Arts: The New Deal and Now*. Greenwich, CT: New York Graphic Society, 1973.

O'Connor, John. "*Spirochete and the War on Syphilis*." *The Drama Review* 21, no.1 (March 1977): 92–98.

———. "The Federal Theatre Project's Search for an Audience." In *Theatre for Working-Class Audiences in the United States, 1830–1980*. Edited by Bruce A. McConachie and Daniel Friedman. Westport, CT: Greenwood Press, 1985.

O'Connor, John, and Lorraine Brown, ed. *Free, Adult, Uncensored: The Living History of the Federal Theatre Project*. With a foreword by John Houseman. Washington, DC: New Republic Books, 1978.

O'Connor, Thomas H. *Boston: A to Z*. Cambridge, MA: Harvard University Press, 2000.

Oregon: End of the Trail. Workers of the Writers' Program of the Works Projects Administration. Reprint. Portland: Binfords & Mort, 1940.

Osborne, Elizabeth A. "Yankee Consternation in the Deep South: Worshipping at the *Altars of Steel*." *Theatre Symposium: Tours of the South* 13 (2005): 51–67.

———. "A Nation in Need: Revelations and Disaster Relief in the Federal Theatre Project." *Journal of American Drama and Theatre* 20, no. 2 (Spring 2008): 49–64.

———. "Disappearing Frontiers and the National Stage: Placing the Portland Federal Theatre Project." *Theatre History Studies* 29 (2009): 103–21.

———. "Storytelling, Chiggers, and the Bible Belt: The Georgia Experiment as the Public Face of the Federal Theatre Project." *Theatre History Studies* 31 (2011): [forthcoming].

Pacyga, Dominic A. "Chicago's Ethnic Neighborhoods: The Myth of Stability and the Reality of Chicago." In *Ethnic Chicago: A Multicultural Portrait*, 4th ed., Edited by Melvin G. Holli and Peter d'A. Jones. Grand Rapids, MI: William B. Eerdmans Publishing Co., 1995.

Paige, John C. *The Civilian Conservation Corps and the National Park Service, 1933–1942: An Administrative History.* Washington [?]: National Park Service, Department of the Interior, 1985. http://www.nps.gov/history/history/online_books/ccc/ccc5.htm. Accessed May 8, 2010.

Parran, Thomas. "Public Health Control of Syphilis." *Annals of Internal Medicine* 10 (July 1940): 65.

Pierce, Neal R. *The Deep South States of America: People, Politics, and Power in the Seven Deep South States.* New York: Norton, 1974.

"Pinocchio Dies in New York as Federal Theatre Drops Curtain." *Life* (17 July 1930): 20.

Poggi, Jack. *Theatre in America: The Impact of Economic Forces: 1870–1967.* Ithaca, NY: Cornell University Press, 1968.

Poirier, Suzanne. *Chicago's War on Syphilis, 1937–1940: The Times, the 'Trib', and the Clap Doctor, with an epilogue on issues and attitudes in the time of AIDS.* Urbana: University of Illinois Press, 1995.

Poole, John Russell. "The Federal Theatre Project in Georgia and Alabama: An Historical Analysis of Government Theatre in the Deep South." PhD diss., University of Georgia, Athens, 1995.

Porter, Susan L., ed. *Women of the Commonwealth: Work, Family, and Social Change in Nineteenth-Century Massachusetts.* Amherst: University of Massachusetts Press, 1996.

Postlewait, Thomas. "The Criteria for Evidence: Anecdotes in Shakespearean Biography, 1709–2000." In *Theorizing Practice, Redefining Theatre History.* Edited by W. B. Worthen and Peter Holland. New York: Palgrave Macmillan, 2003.

Quinn, Susan. *Furious Improvisation: How the WPA and a Cast of Thousands Made High Art out of Desperate Times.* New York: Walker Publishing, 2008.

Rabkin, Gerald. *Drama and Commitment.* Bloomington: Indiana University Press, 1964.

Rikard, Marlene Hunt. "An Experiment in Welfare Capitalism: The Health Care Services of the Tennessee, Coal, Iron and Railroad Company." PhD diss., University of Alabama, 1983.

Robbins, Tim. *The Cradle Will Rock: The Movie and The Moment.* With a foreword by Paul Newman. New York: Newmarket Press, 2000.

Rogers, William Warren, Robert David Ward, Leah Rawls Atkins, and Wayne Flint. *Alabama: The History of a Deep South State.* Tuscaloosa: University of Alabama Press, 1994.

Roosevelt, Theodore. "T. R. Roosevelt to Attorney General Bonaparte on 4 November 1907." *Bulletin of the American Iron and Steel Institute* 43, no. 2 (February 1909): 1.

Rosenzweig, Roy, and Barbara Melosh. "Government and the Arts: Voices from the New Deal Era." *The Journal of American History* 77, no. 2 (September 1990): 596–608.

Ross, Ronald. "The Role of Blacks in the Federal Theatre: 1935–1939." *Journal of Negro History* 59, no. 1 (January 1974): 38–50.

Schilling, Lester Lorenzo, Jr. "The History of the Theatre in Portland Oregon." PhD diss., University of Wisconsin, 1961.

Schmitt, Patrick. "The Chicago Federal Theatre Project: 1935–1939." MA thesis, University of Illinois at Chicago Circle, 1978.

Schottenhamel, George. "How Big Bill Thompson Won Control of Chicago," *Journal of Illinois State Historical Society* 45, 1 (Spring 1952): 46.

Schwartz, Bonnie Nelson, and the Educational Film Center. *Voices from the Federal Theatre.* With a foreword by Robert Brustein. Madison, WI: University of Wisconsin Press, 2003.

Scharine, Richard G. *From Class to Caste in American Drama: Political and Social Themes since the 1930s.* Westport, CT: Greenwood Press, 1991.

Seman, Philip L. *Community Culture in an Era of Depression.* Chicago: Jewish People's Institute, 1932.

Smith, Anthony D. *National Identity.* Las Vegas: University of Nevada Press, 1991.

Smith, Guy-Harold. *Conservation of Natural Resources.* New York: John Wiley & Sons, 1950.

"*Spirochete,*" *Time.* (May 9, 1938) http://time-proxy.yaga.com/time/archive/printout/0,23657,759611,00.html. Accessed June 12, 2010.

Sporn, Paul. *Against Itself: The Federal Theater and Writers' Projects in the Midwest.* Detroit, MI: Wayne State University, 1995.

Stack, John F. *International Conflict in an American City: Boston's Irish, Italians and Jews, 1935–1944.* Contributions in Political Science, no. 26. Westport, CT: Greenwood Press, 1970.

Stein, Judith. *Running Steel, Running America: Race, Economic Policy and the Decline of Liberalism.* Chapel Hill: University of North Carolina Press, 1998.

Stuhler, Barbara. *For the Public Record: A Documentary History of the League of Women Voters.* Westport, CT: Greenwood Press, 2000.

Sundgaard, Arnold. *Spirochete.* In *Federal Theatre Plays.* Edited by Pierre de Rohan. New York: Random House, 1938.

———. "Susan Glaspell and the Federal Theatre Revisited." *Journal of American Drama and Theatre* 9 (Winter 1997): 1–10.

Susman, Warren I. *Culture as History: The Transformation of American Society in the Twentieth Century.* Washington, DC: Smithsonian Institution Press, 2003.

Swortzell, Lowell, ed. *Six Plays for Young People from the Federal Theatre Project.* New York: Greenwood Press, 1986.

Tager, Jack. *Boston Riots: Three Centuries of Social Violence.* Boston, MA: Northeastern University Press, 2001.

Trout, Charles H. *Boston, The Great Depression, and the New Deal.* New York: Oxford University Press, 1977.

"Unemployed Arts." *Fortune* (May 1937): 112.

U.S. Bureau of the Census. *Fifteenth Census of the United States: 1930, Volume 1, Population, Number and Distribution of Inhabitants.* Washington, DC: Government Printing Office, 1931. http://www.census.gov/prod/www/abs/decennial/1930.html. Accessed March 12, 2010.

Vonderlehr, R. A. "Are We Checking the Great Plague?" *Survey Graphic* (April 1, 1940).

Warren, Kenneth. *Big Steel: The First Century of the United States Steel Corporation, 1901–2001.* Pittsburgh, PA: University of Pittsburgh Press, 2001.

Watkins, T. H. *The Great Depression: America in the 1930s.* New York: Back Bay Books, 1993.

Weir, Jean Burwell. "Timberline Lodge: A WPA Experiment in Architecture and Crafts, Vol. 1." PhD diss., Ann Arbor: University of Michigan, 1977.

White, Marjorie Longenecker. *The Birmingham District: An Industrial History and Guide.* Birmingham, AL: Birmingham Historical Society at the Birmingham Publishing Company, 1981.

Whitman, Willson. *Bread and Circuses.* New York: Oxford University Press, 1937.

Williams, Raymond. *Culture and Society, 1780–1950.* New York: Columbia University Press, 1952.

Wickre, Karen. "An Informal History of Oregon's WPA Federal Theatre Project, 1936–1939." Unpublished document. George Mason University, 1981.

Wilmer, S. E. *Theatre, Society and the Nation: Staging American Identities.* Cambridge Studies in American Theatre and Drama. Edited by Don B. Wilmeth. Cambridge: Cambridge University Press, 2002.

Wilmeth, Don B., and Christopher Bigsby, eds. *1870–1945. Vol. II of Cambridge History of American Theatre.* New York: Cambridge University Press, 1999.

Witham, Barry B. "Backstage at *The Cradle Will Rock*." *Theatre History Studies* 12 (1992): 213–20.

Witham, Barry B. "Censorship in the Federal Theatre." *Theatre History Studies* 17 (1997): 3–15.

———. *The Federal Theatre Project: A Case Study.* Cambridge Studies in American Theatre and Drama. Edited by Don B. Wilmeth. New York: Cambridge University Press, 2003.

Wyatt, Steve. "The Flax Industry of Lane County." *The Lane County Historical Society* 35, no. 2 (Summer 1990): 27–31.

———. "Flax and Linen: An Uncertain Oregon Industry." *Oregon Historical Quarterly* (1994): 150–175.

Index ✥

Bolded page numbers refer to illustrations.